IMAGES
of America

OCEAN CITY
1950–1980

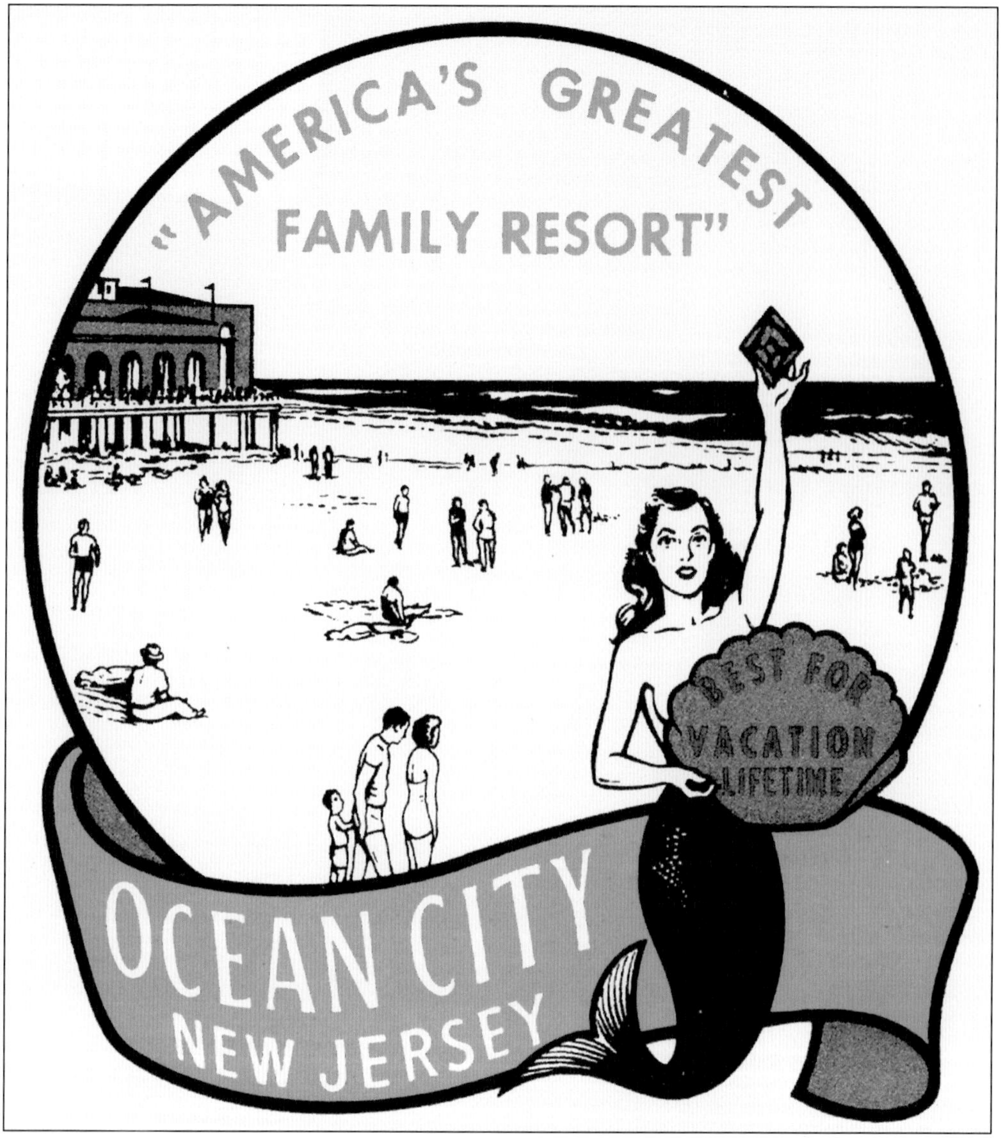

This decal is a souvenir of "America's Greatest Family Resort."

On the cover: The 1967 Ocean City Beach Patrol zone queens pose in front of a lifeguard boat. From left to right are Pat Behrle, Pam Meyer, Stephanie Hyde, and Lynn Hemmenway. Hemmenway was crowned Miss Ocean City Beach Patrol at the annual Lifeguard Ball held on August 25 at the Music Pier. (Courtesy of Grainger Studios.)

IMAGES
of America

OCEAN CITY
1950–1980

Fred Miller

ARCADIA
PUBLISHING

ISBN 978-0-7385-4536-3

Published by Arcadia Publishing
Charleston, South Carolina

Printed in the United States of America

Library of Congress Catalog Card Number: 2006923208

For all general information contact Arcadia Publishing at:
Telephone 843-853-2070
Fax 843-853-0044
E-mail sales@arcadiapublishing.com
For customer service and orders:
Toll-Free 1-888-313-2665

Visit us on the Internet at www.arcadiapublishing.com

This book is dedicated to my family—Millers, Maderas, Okins, Leventhals, Wasnacs, Currens, Coglios, and Sheridans—all of whom agree with me that Ocean City is truly America's greatest family resort.

Contents

Acknowledgments

I wish to thank my wife, Susan, for her patience and help; my sister and brother-in-law, Joan and Allan Okin, for their editing skills; and Stu Sirott for all of his technical help.

I also thank the following people for photographs: Jane Charles, Valerie Davis, Chet and Denny Derr, Ben Dungan, Cathy and Jim Finnegan, John Flood, Bob French, Jay and Michele Gillian, Mike Hamilton, Vince Hink, Sally Huff, George T. Lafferty, Lizanne Kelly LeVine, Gene Lindacher, Dominick Longo, Carol Madera, Doris Marts, Edna Streaker May, Marion McCaughey, Tom McGill, Susan Miller, John Nieveen, Bob Schneider, Hope Shaw, Joan Shaw, Stu Sirott, Mark Soifer, Pete Trofa, and John and Carol Walton.

Lastly, I thank the following organizations for their help, pictures, and information for the book: the Ocean City Historical Museum, the Ocean City Lifesaving Museum, and the *Ocean City Sentinel*.

INTRODUCTION

Ocean City, New Jersey, was founded in 1879 by the Lakes, a family of Methodist ministers, along with two others, the Reverends William H. Burrell and William B. Wood. The ministers wanted to establish a "Christian Seaside Resort," one that would be not only for summer visitors, but also a fully functioning year-round community. They bought up all of the land on what was then called Peck's Beach, an eight-mile-long barrier island off the southern coast of New Jersey. By doing this, they were able to tightly restrict commerce and recreation on Sundays and to ban liquor, gambling, and prostitution by deed restriction. They quickly established a government, a school, and a newspaper and built a rail line and ferry to bring people to the resort.

Ocean City grew into a prosperous community with businesses, an excellent school system, many retail stores, a concert hall for year-round residents, and many hotels, restaurants, and amusements for summer vacationers. For much of that time, the city was governed by three elected commissioners, one of whom was appointed mayor.

The decades between 1950 and 1980 saw many changes in Ocean City as well as in the rest of America. The building of the New Jersey Turnpike, the Garden State Parkway, and the Atlantic City Expressway made it much easier for people to come to Ocean City for a day or a weekend. This led to the decline of the large hotels and the increase of motels, modern duplexes, and condominiums, and eventually led to the end of rail service to the shore.

Women in this country were gaining stature, and these years saw many firsts in Ocean City. The first woman commissioner, Marilyn Moore, was appointed, and the first woman county clerk, Angela Pulvino, an Ocean City resident and native, was elected. The Ocean City Beach Patrol hired its first female lifeguard, Judith Lichtner, and, in the new form of government, Jeanne Clunn was the first woman elected to the council. Margaret Sharp was the first woman chosen when the school board began holding elections.

For the first time, a Miss Ocean City, Laurie Berchtold, represented the state as Miss New Jersey in the Miss America Pageant in Atlantic City. And Ocean City's own Grace Kelly won an Academy Award for *The Country Girl*! The Kellys were longtime homeowners and part-time residents of Ocean City; Grace and her sisters, Lizanne and Margaret, and brother Jack, had grown up spending the summers here. Grace starred in many movies, including *High Noon*, *Rear Window*, and *Dial M for Murder*, before marrying Prince Rainier of Monaco and retiring from Hollywood. She, the prince, and their children continued to consider Ocean City a second home and visited during many summers. Jack Kelly won a bronze medal for rowing in the 1956 Summer Olympics.

Ocean City also produced other well-known people. Preston Foster, who starred in many movies and early television shows, grew up in Ocean City where his father was a police officer.

In addition, Ocean City native Marla Adams starred in television soap operas for many years. Novelist Gay Talese was born and raised in the city and based some of his writing here.

Athletics continued to be a big attraction in Ocean City as, guided by Dixie Howell, the boys' high school basketball team was state champion in both 1955 and 1964. With Fenton Carey coaching, the high school's football teams won multiple championships. The girls' high school basketball team, coached by Patricia Dougherty, was the South Jersey champion in 1979. The Ocean City Beach Patrol won its 11th straight South Jersey titles in ocean and pool meets in 1971.

Two new schools were built, and a state park was established in the south end of the city. A golf course was developed on Bay Avenue. The form of government was changed to an elected mayor and council. Many of the city's most beloved traditions were revived or embellished, including Night in Venice and the Halloween parade, and more were begun, including the Boardwalk Art Show, the Spring Block Party, Martin Z. Mollusk Day, and the Miss Crustacean Beauty Pageant.

Turn the pages and join us in a visual tour of Ocean City during these exciting years.

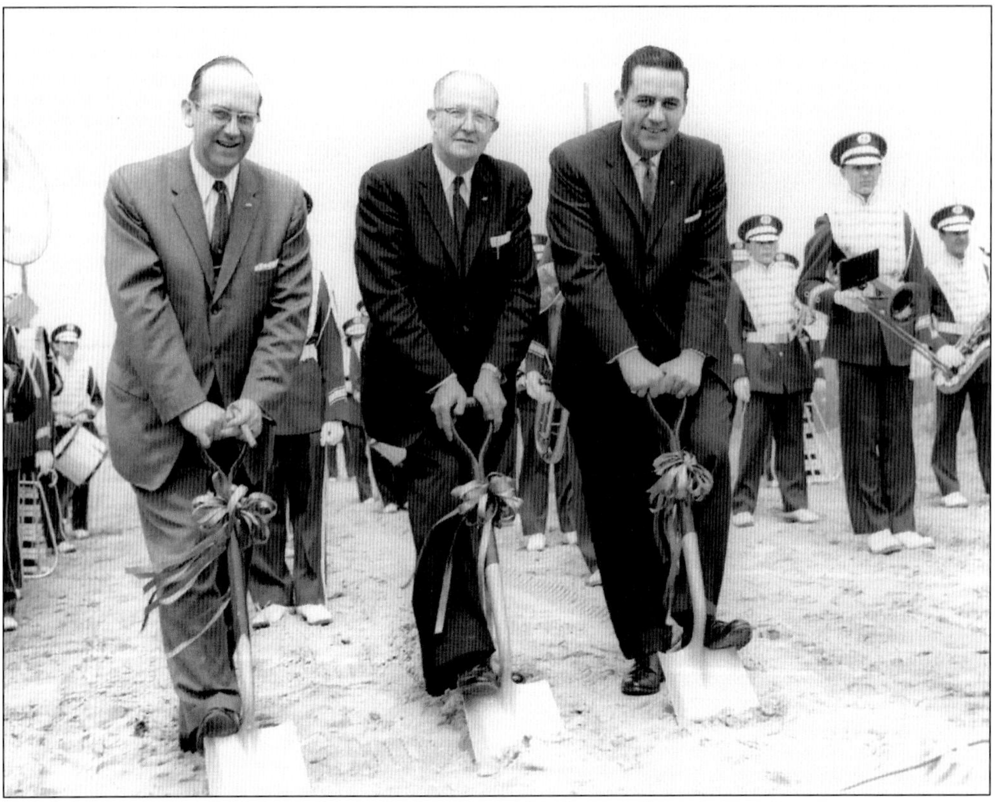

Breaking ground for the municipal sewage plant for the southern part of town was reason to celebrate in 1961, as can be seen in this photograph. The Ocean City High School marching band turned out in full uniform and posed for pictures with, from left to right, Commissioner D. Allen Stretch, Mayor Nathaniel C. Smith, and Commissioner B. Thomas Waldman. A $1.2 million bond was issued to defray the cost, and the plant was expected to spur development on that part of the island.

One

The Fabulous Fifties
1950–1954

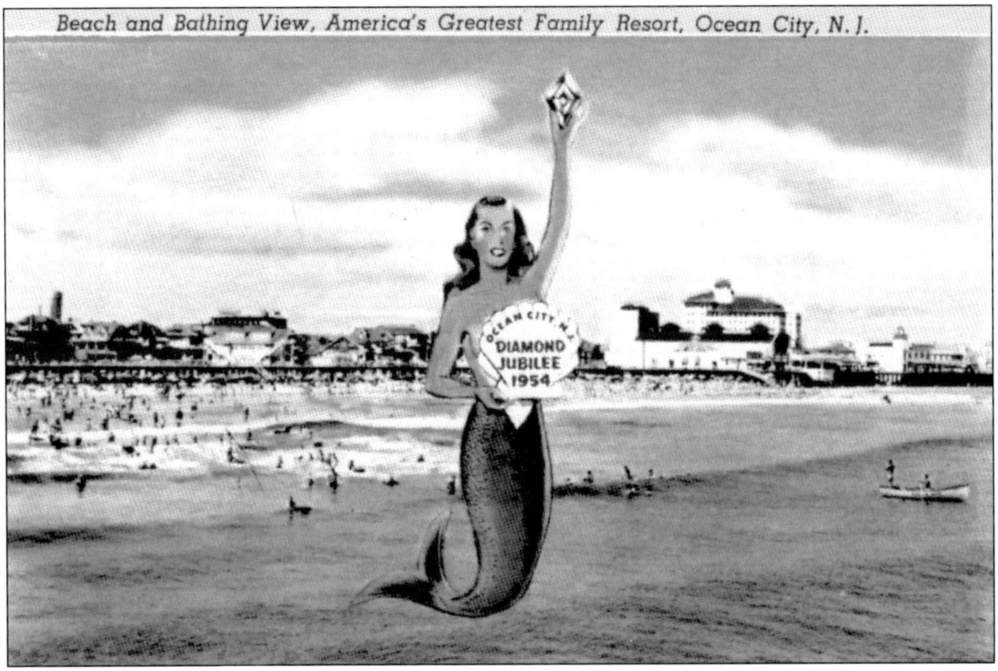

Ocean City celebrated its Diamond Jubilee in 1954 by staging special attractions all year, pointing up its 75 years of progress from sand dunes to "America's Greatest Family Resort." This mermaid, holding aloft a diamond and a seashell with "Ocean City, NJ Diamond Jubilee 1954" printed on it, was one of the many souvenirs produced to commemorate the anniversary.

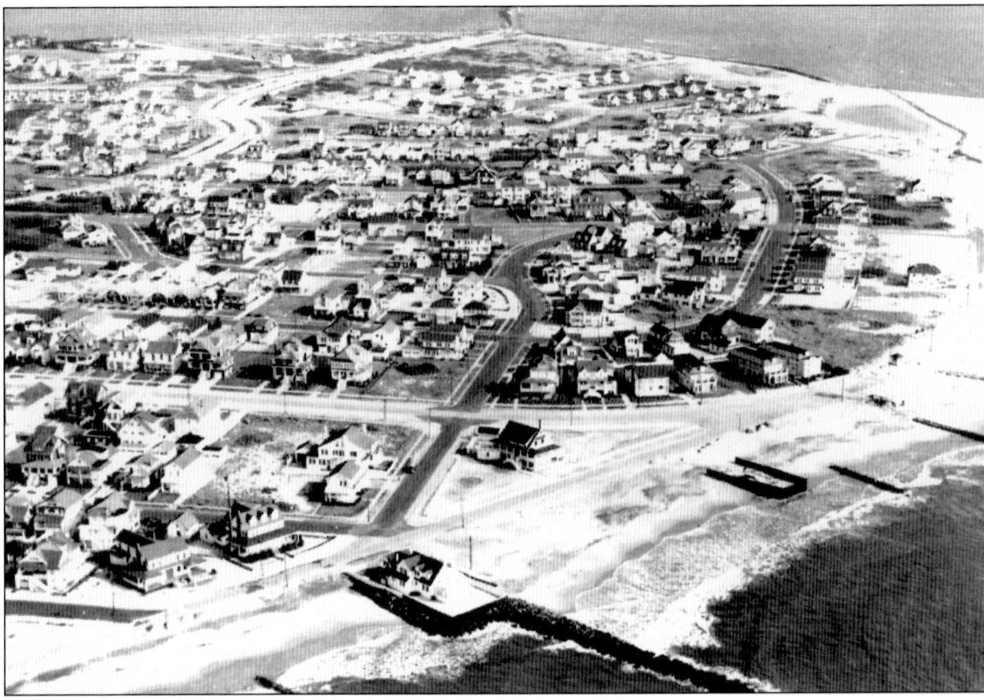

This aerial view of Ocean City's Gardens section, on the north end of the island, was taken in 1950. The area is one of the highest in elevation on the island, but the streets were still laid out in curves to prevent the ocean from rushing through the area in case of flooding.

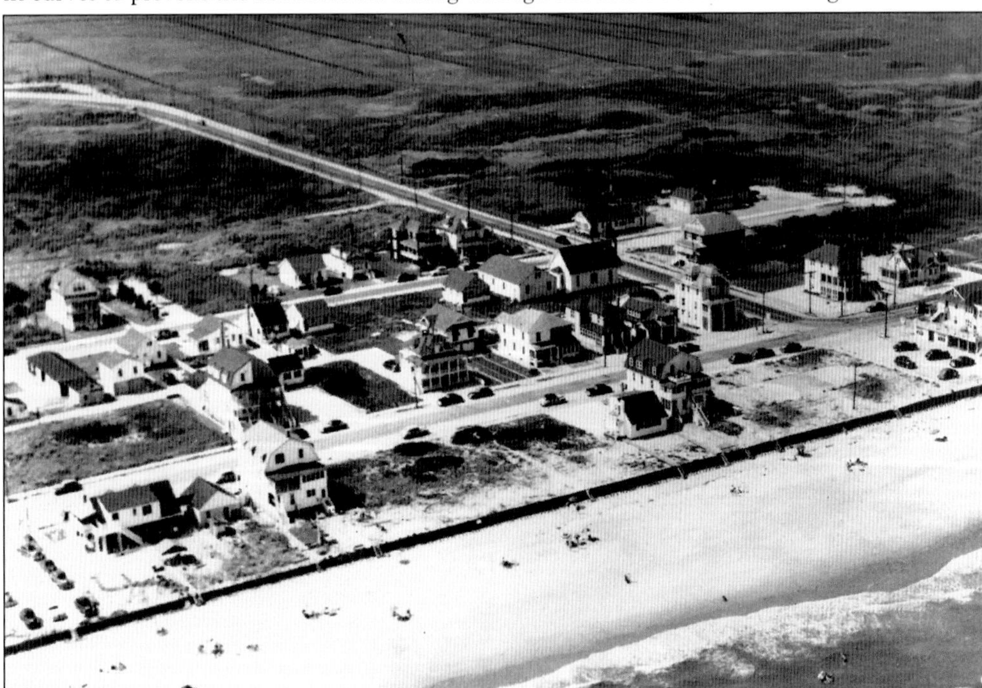

This aerial view of the south end of the island was also taken in 1950. This area was much less developed than the rest of town until the 1970s.

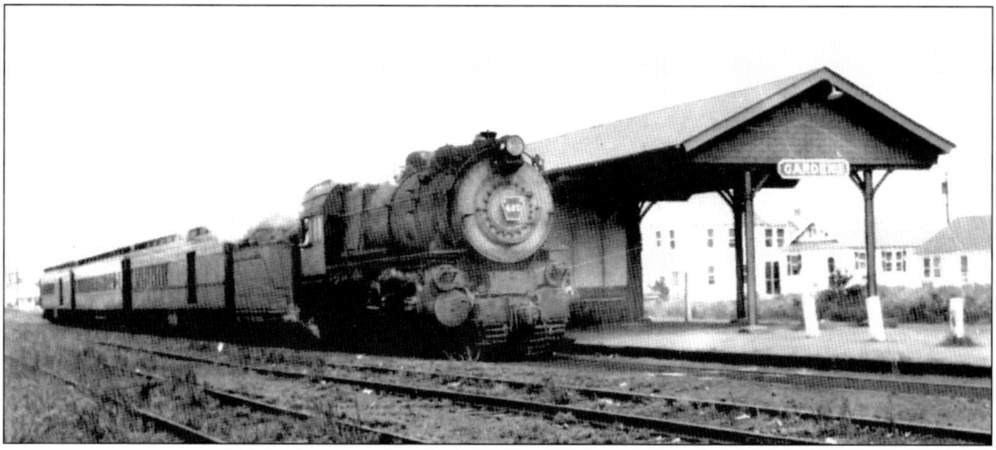

The founding fathers brought the railroads to Ocean City starting in 1884 to encourage tourists to come to town, but by the 1950s, usage was down.

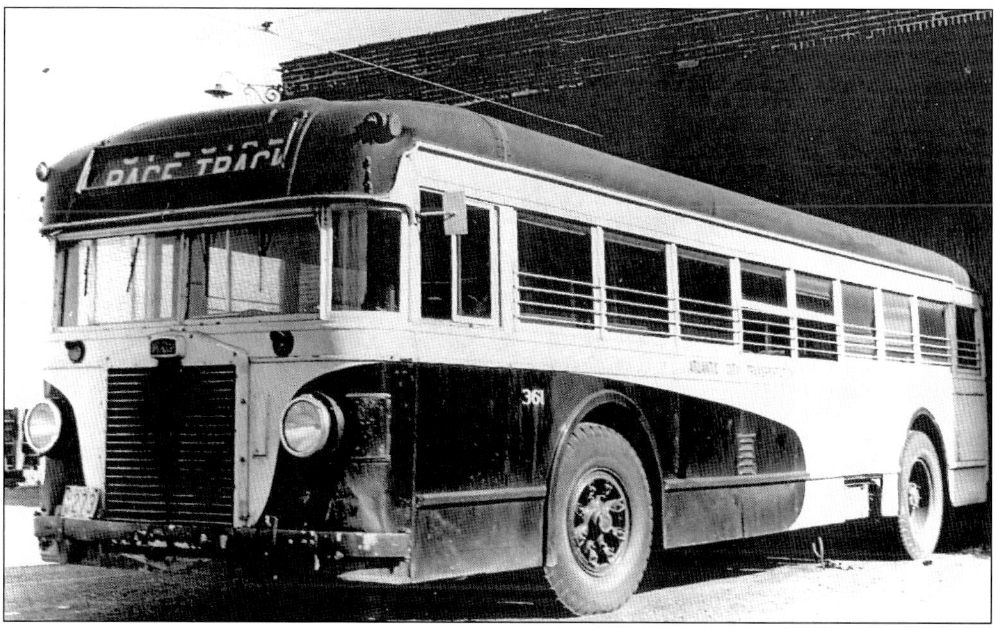

Bus service was plentiful during the 1950s. The Atlantic City Transportation Company offered "Wonderfully refreshing and interesting rides across the great salt meadows and through the pines of the mainland" between Ocean City and the Atlantic City Race Track for only 75¢ round trip, according to their advertisements. They also ran local buses within the city. The Public Service Bus Company ran frequently between Ocean City and Philadelphia each day, as well.

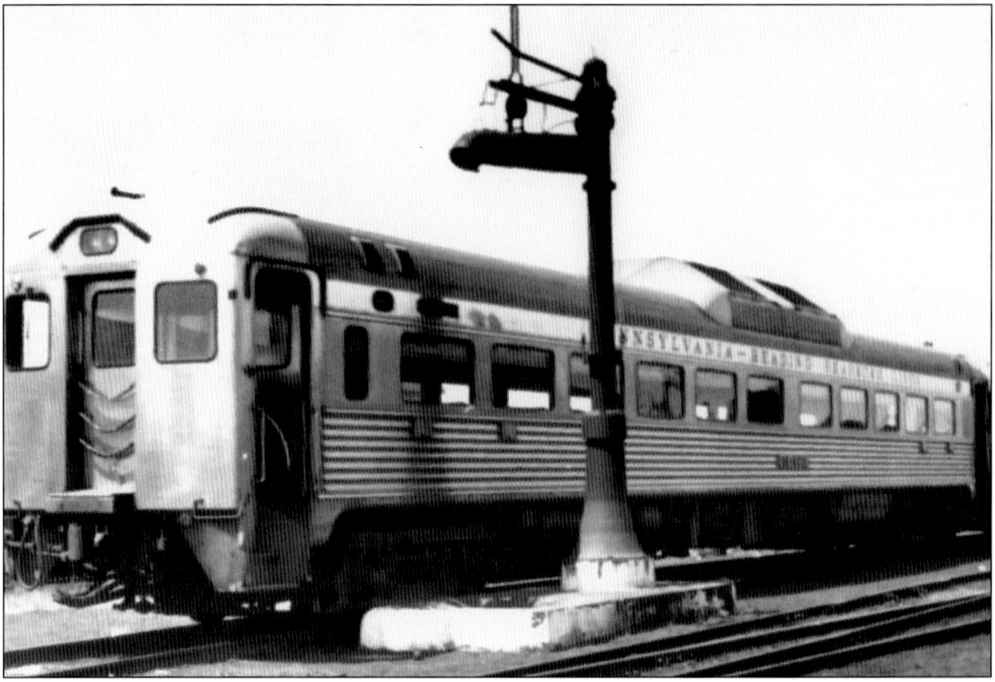

A new kind of railway passenger car began serving Ocean City residents in the fall of 1950. The rail diesel cars were developed by the Budd Company and were known as Budd diesels. The Ocean City Commuters Club, whose privileges included seats in a reserved car, traveled daily between Philadelphia and Ocean City.

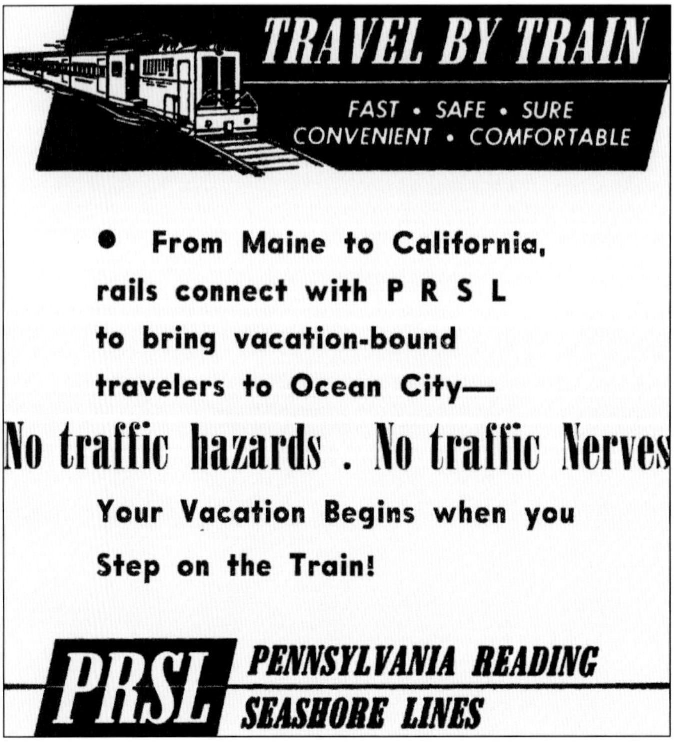

This advertisement says it all!

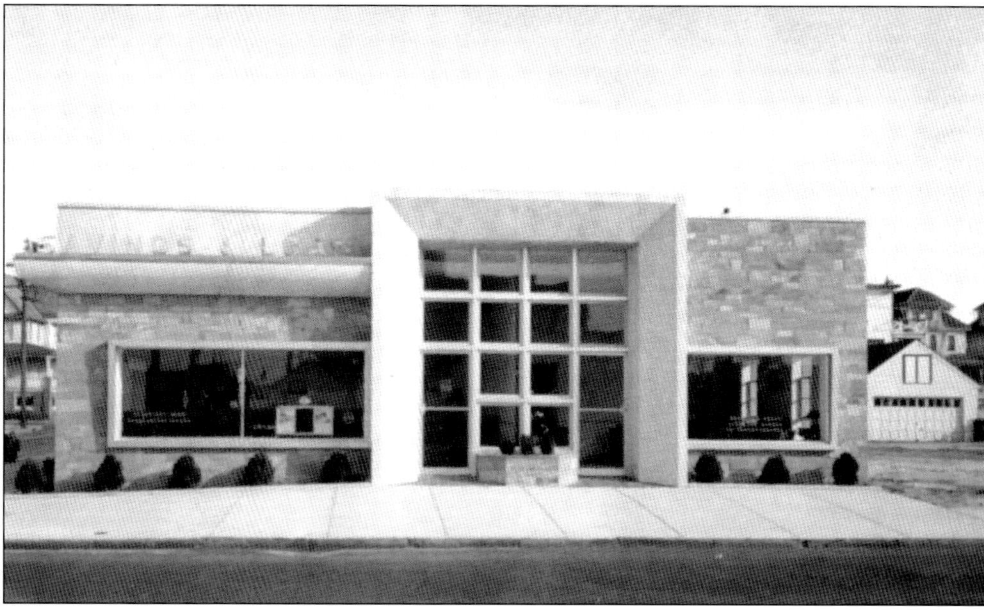

On August 16, 1950, the Ocean City Home Savings and Loan Association invited the public to tour its new building at Tenth Street and Asbury Avenue. The financial institution traced its roots back to 1887.

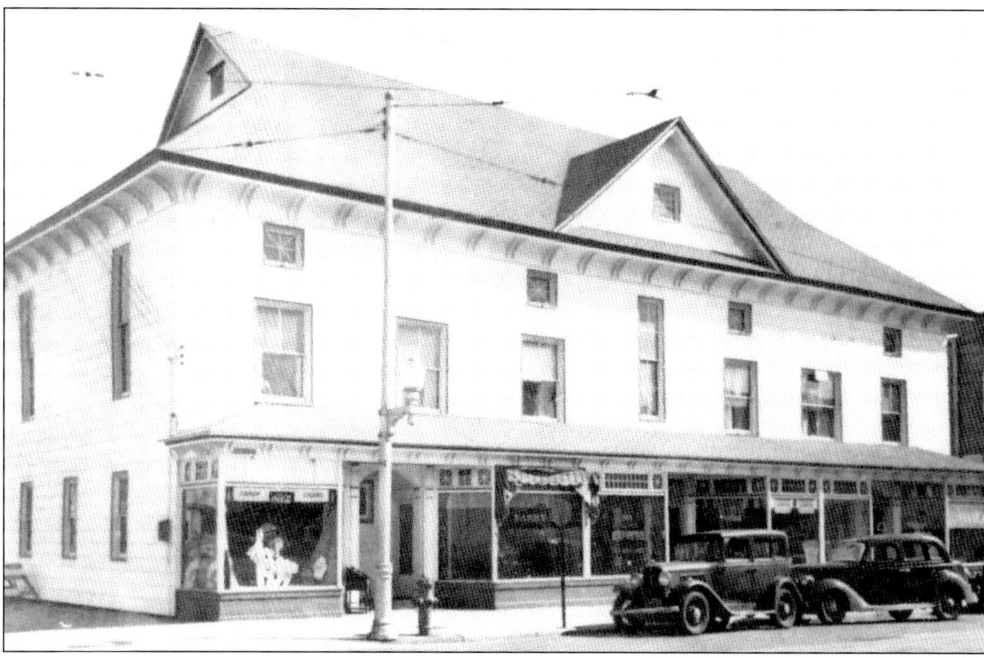

The Hahn Building was built in 1885 on what was assumed would be one of the major business corners, the northeast corner of West Avenue and Eighth Street. It had retail space on the first floor with apartments above. Several different businesses, including a butcher shop, a shoemaker, a bakery, and a candy store, occupied the building until it was torn down in 1965.

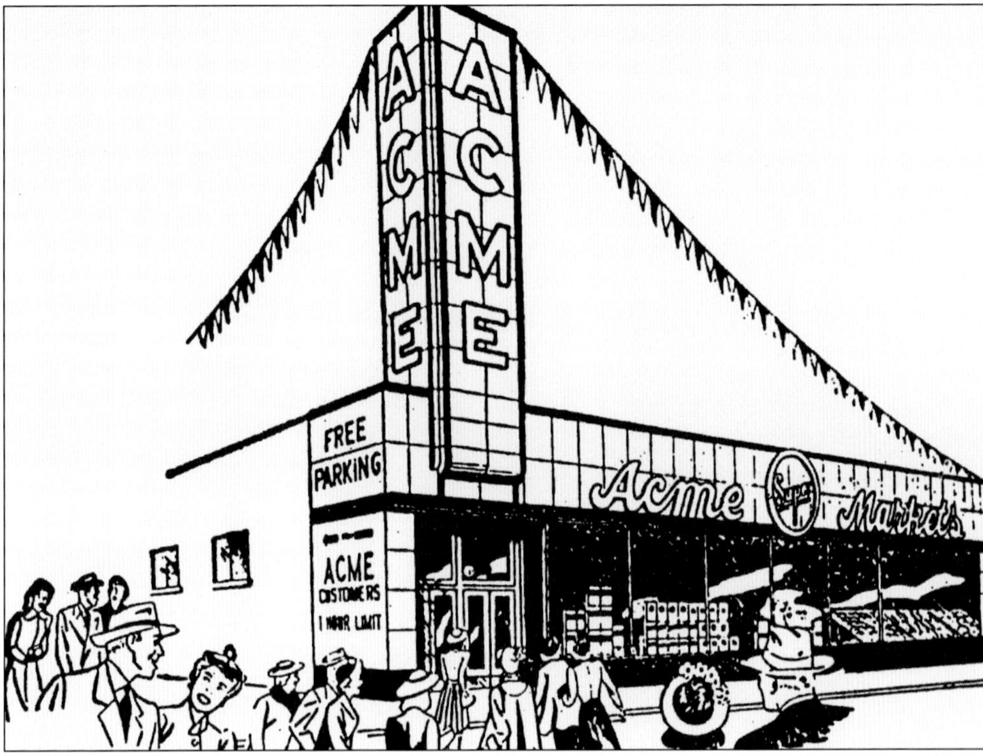

On June 29, 1950, the Acme Super Market opened at the corner of Eighth Street and West Avenue. It advertised the "Finest food market on the Jersey Coast with hundreds of money-saving big values."

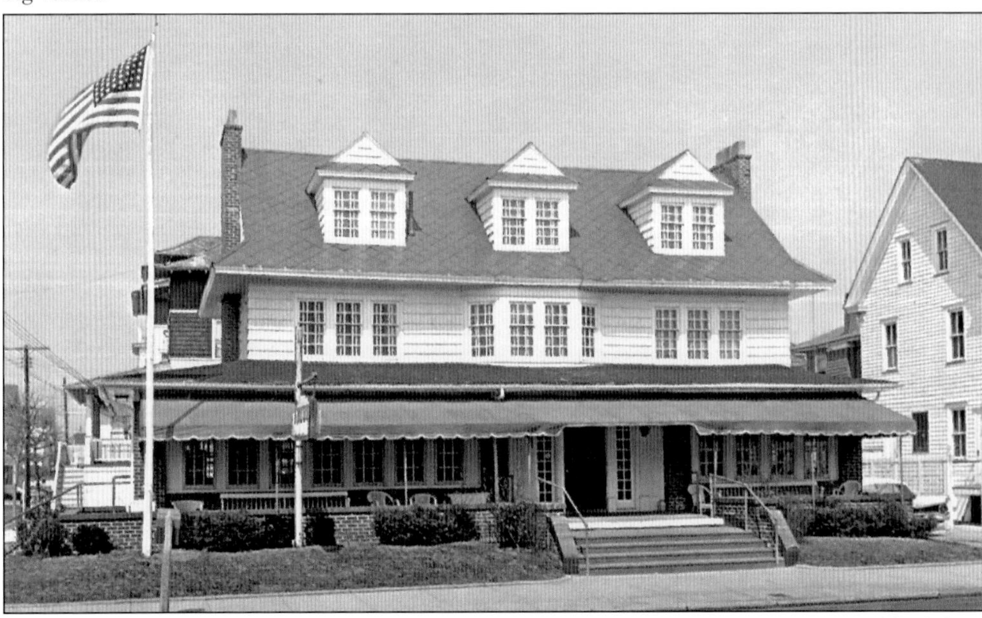

This postcard of the Plymouth Inn, at 710 Atlantic Avenue, praised its amenities: one block from the boardwalk, open all year, offering three meals daily, and catering to weddings, banquets, and club affairs. The Exchange Club, Rotary Club, and Lions Club all met there.

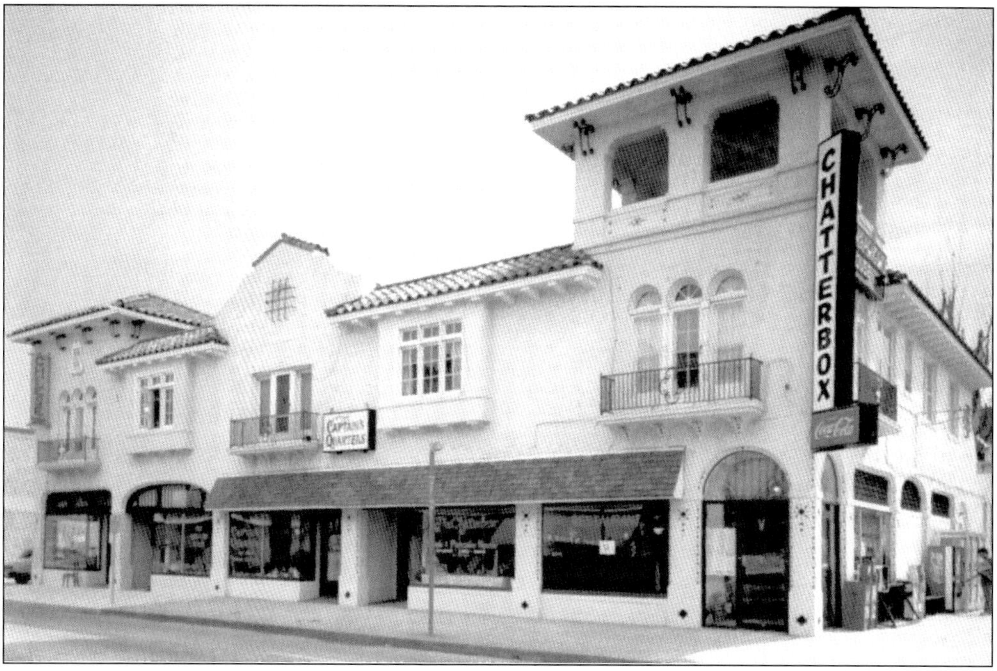

The Chatterbox, on the southeast corner of Ninth Street and Central Avenue, was a popular restaurant "where friends meet to eat." It was popular with high school students. It had good food at reasonable prices and a warm, inviting atmosphere. The owner, Jean Campbell, kept the restaurant open from early morning until late at night.

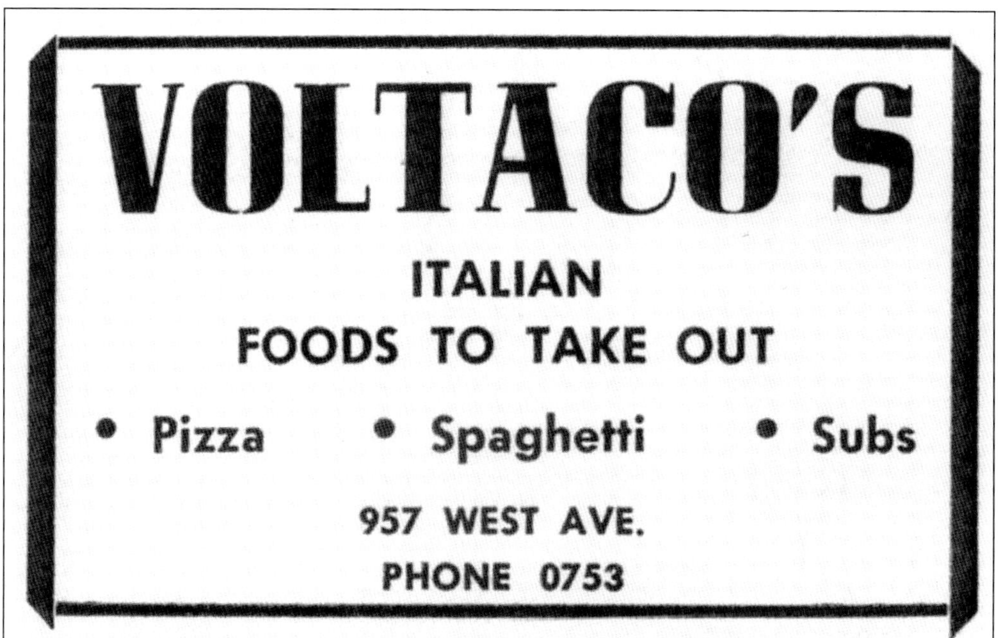

Voltaco's, at 957 West Avenue, served take-out food only. Visitors and residents alike kept the business busy all summer.

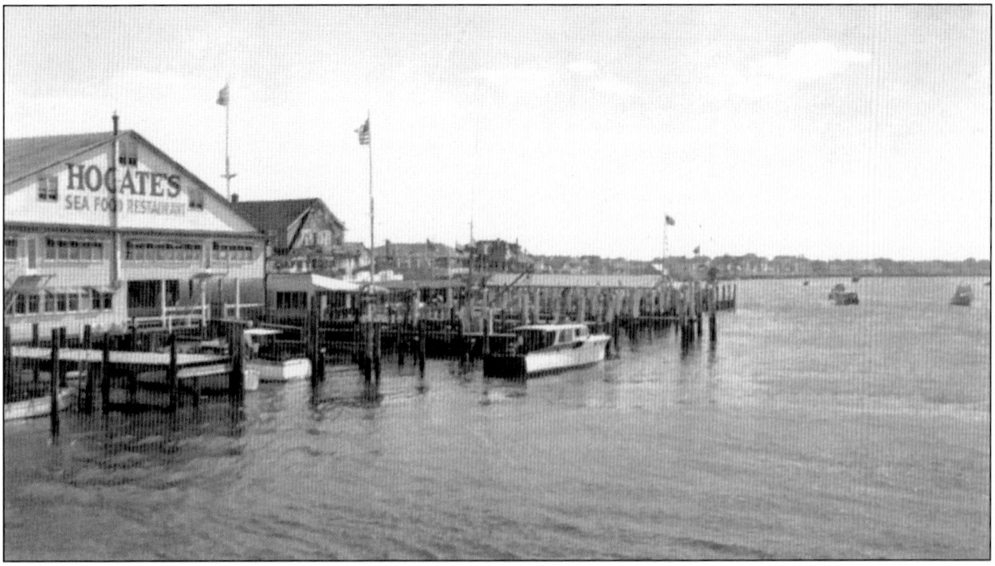

Hogate's seafood restaurant on the bay at Ninth Street advertised its "Marvelous views across Great Egg Harbor Bay." It had good food, too. It was torn down after the summer of 1972.

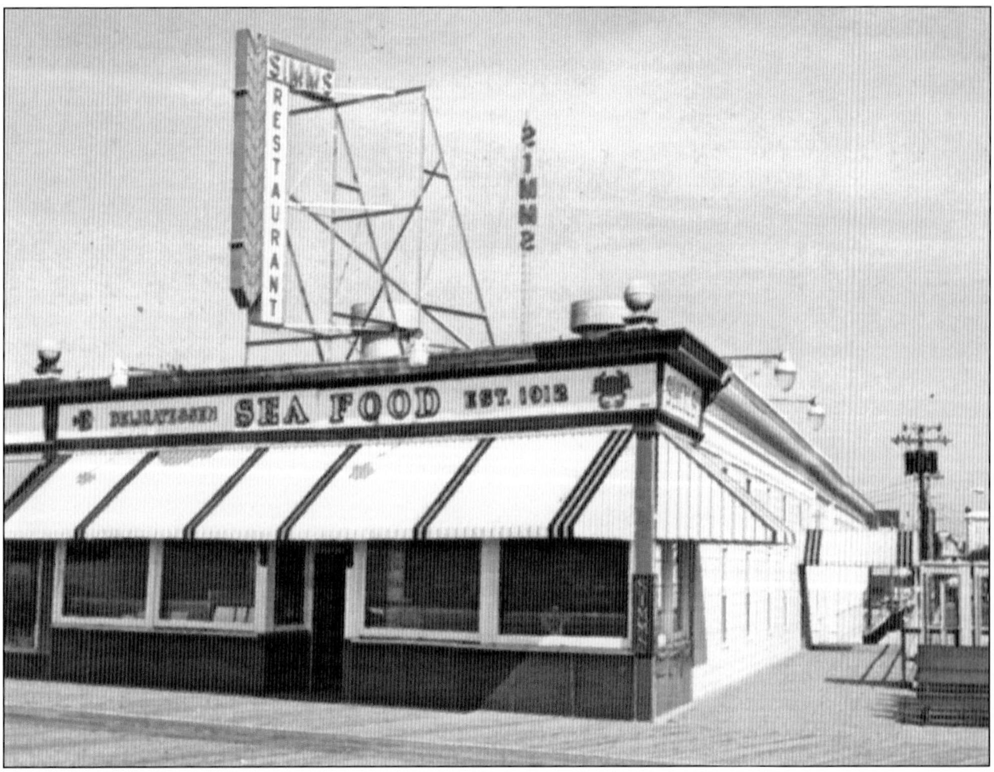

Eleanor and Floyd Simms opened Simms' Restaurant on the boardwalk at Moorlyn Terrace, across from the Music Pier, in 1912. It was a seasonal restaurant with beautiful stained-glass windows, hand painted chandeliers, giant cooling fans, and pine floors. From early morning sticky buns to sumptuous seafood dinners, it catered to 2,000 diners daily at the peak of the season.

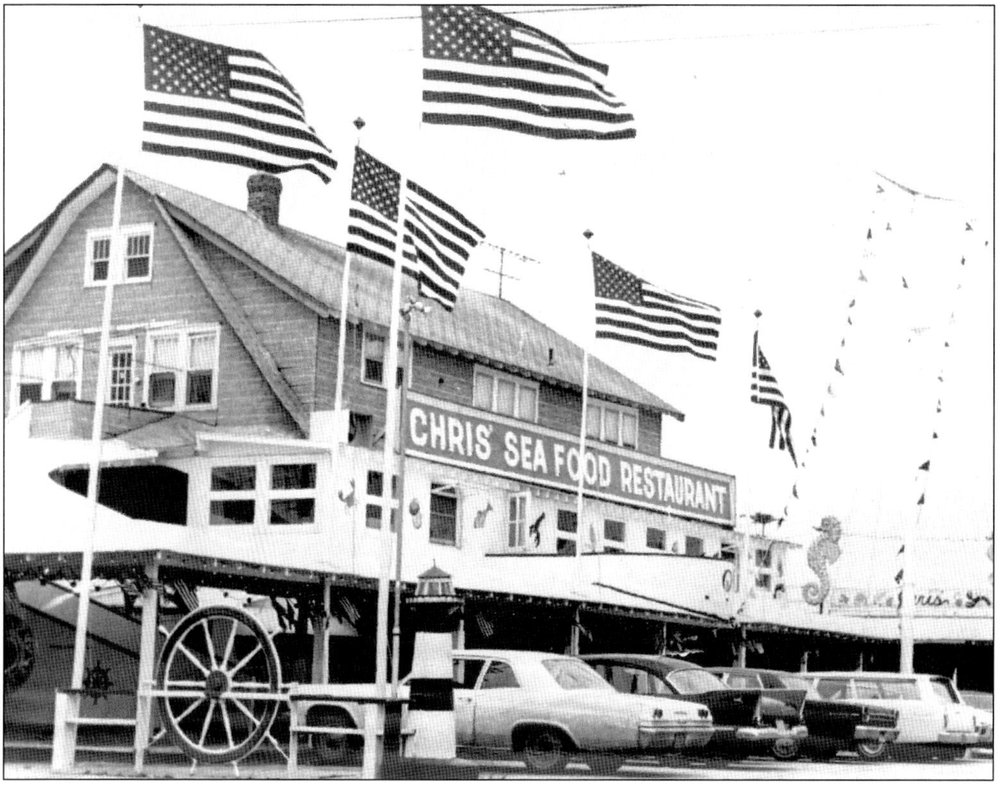

Chris' Seafood Restaurant and Fish Market, at the base of the Ninth Street bridge on the bay, served fish caught daily by its own fleet. The restaurant accommodated 250 diners, and the market packed and shipped fish to all parts of the country. Patrons were invited to watch the boats unload the day's catch at the docks from 4:00 to 5:00 p.m.

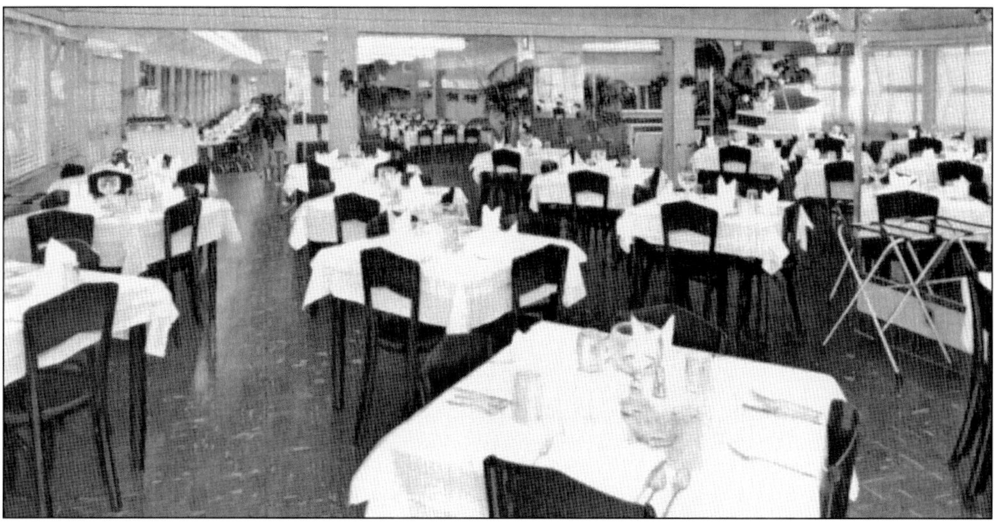

This postcard shows the inside of Chris' Seafood Restaurant. Chris was Chris Montagna. His wife, Dr. Marcia Smith, was a local physician known for her humanitarian work both in Ocean City and during her extensive travels around the world. There is a small monument to her in the park at Sixth Street and Ocean Avenue given by the country of Israel for her work there.

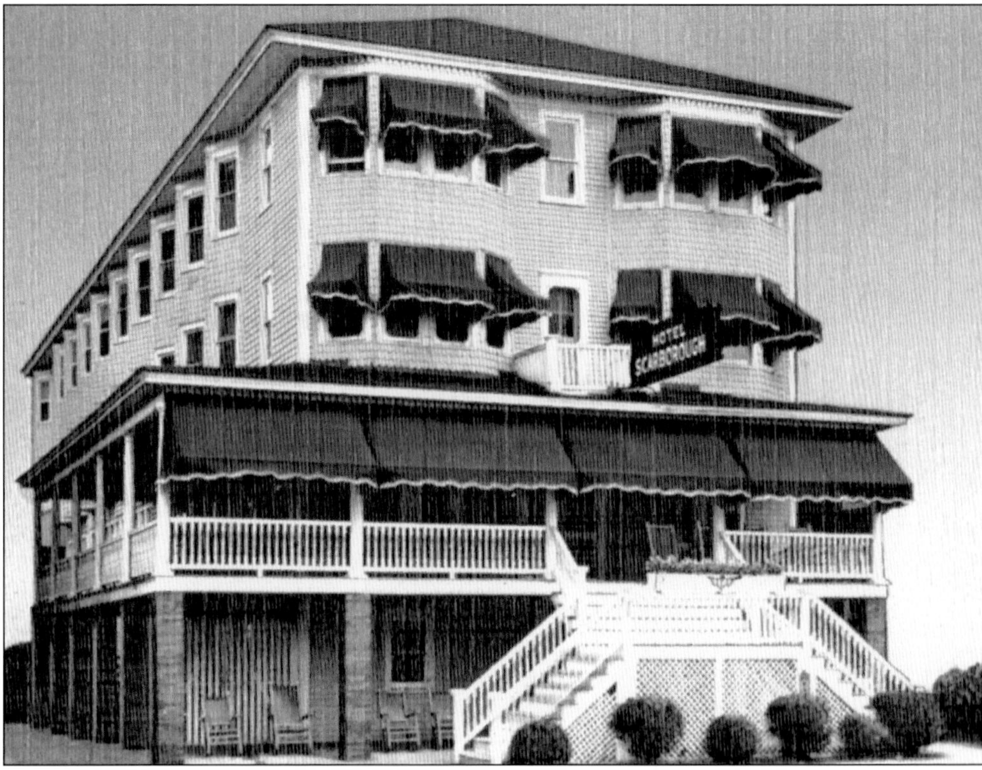

The Hotel Scarborough, 720 Ocean Avenue, had 60 rooms, most with private baths, all with running water. It offered moderate rates, off-street parking, courtesy morning coffee, a terrazzo shuffle court, and a game room.

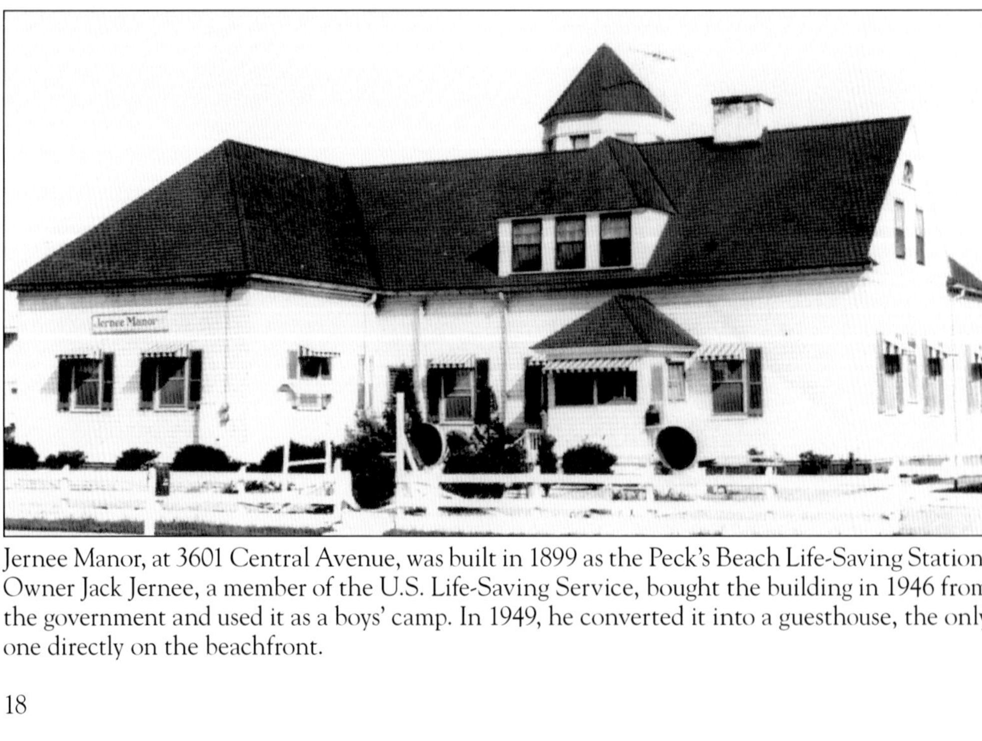

Jernee Manor, at 3601 Central Avenue, was built in 1899 as the Peck's Beach Life-Saving Station. Owner Jack Jernee, a member of the U.S. Life-Saving Service, bought the building in 1946 from the government and used it as a boys' camp. In 1949, he converted it into a guesthouse, the only one directly on the beachfront.

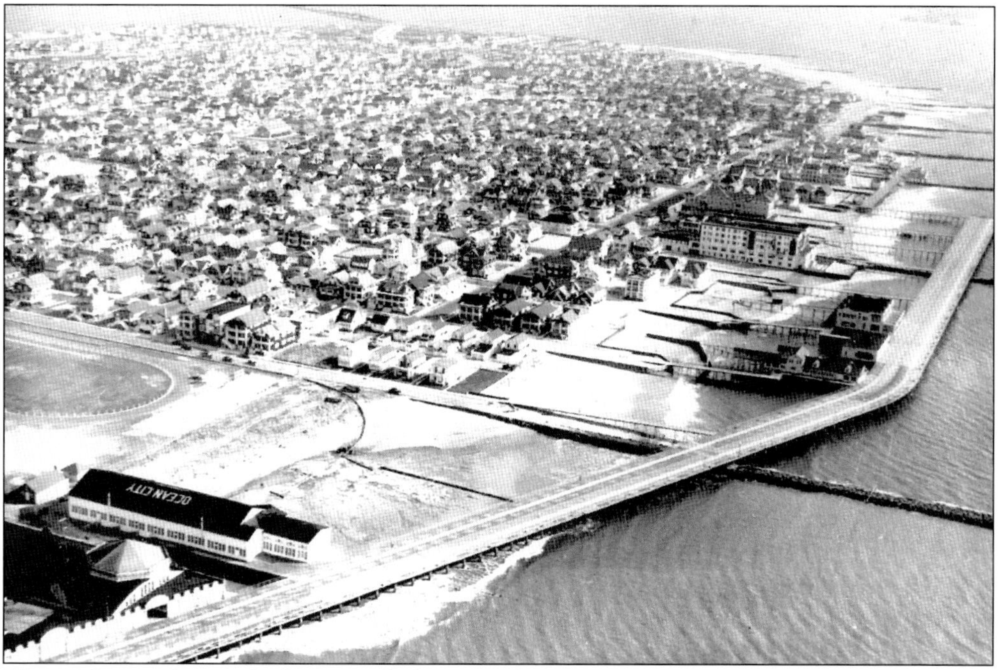

This 1951 aerial view, looking north from Sixth Street and the boardwalk, shows Playland Amusement Center in the lower left corner, Convention Hall (with Ocean City on its roof), boardwalk stores, the Delaware and Breakers hotels, and the boardwalk jutting far into the ocean. By 1980, this scene would be completely altered. Fires had destroyed Playland, Convention Hall, and some of the boardwalk stores, and the boardwalk from Fifth Street to Second Street would be moved closer to the beach.

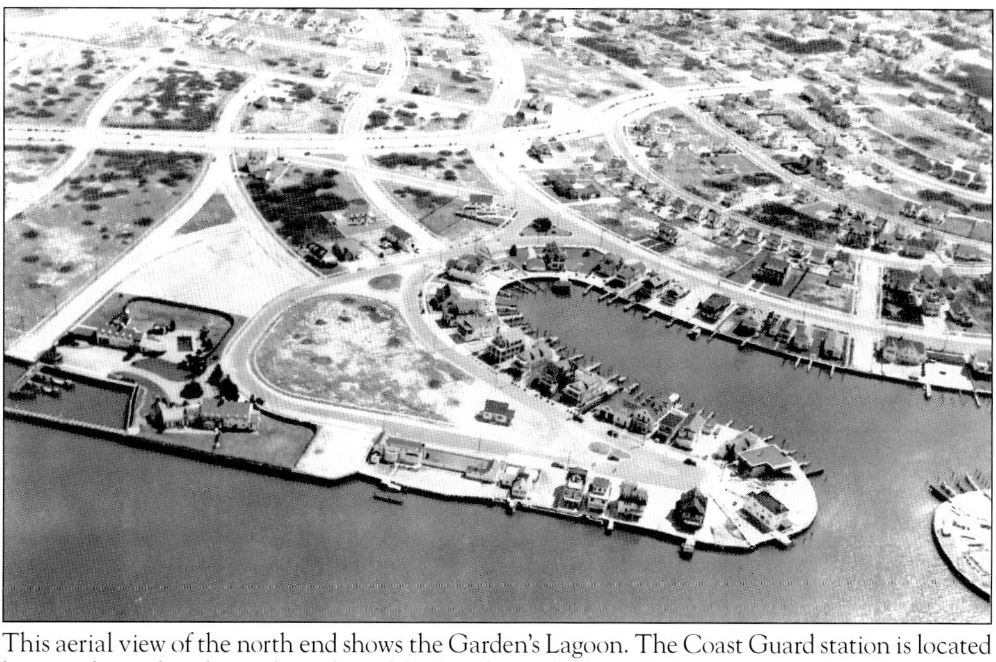

This aerial view of the north end shows the Garden's Lagoon. The Coast Guard station is located here in the midst of a residential neighborhood, not far from the Great Egg Harbor Inlet.

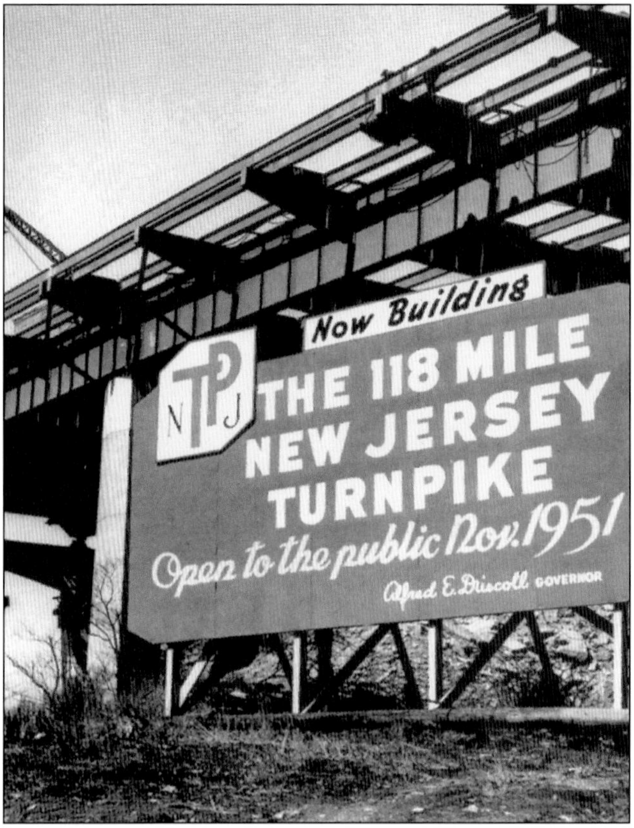

When the New Jersey Turnpike opened in November 1951, it was advertised as "The smart vacationers way to travel!" The turnpike was 118 miles long with no stoplights, no cross traffic, and a speed limit of 60 miles per hour. It was the beginning of the end for trains to the shore communities.

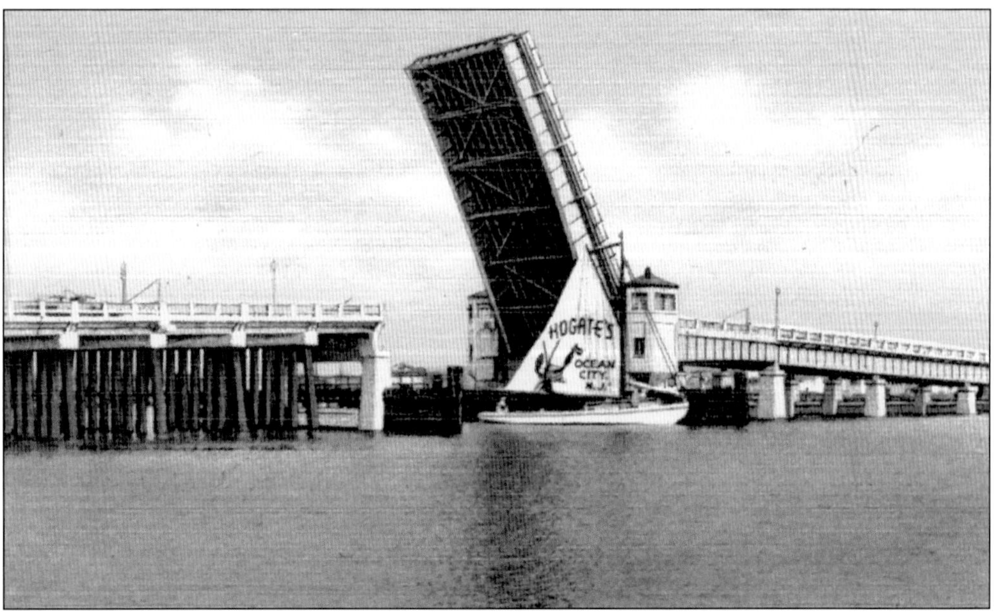

The drawbridge on the Ninth Street Bridge, raised to allow a sailboat to pass through, was an all too familiar sight to visitors on their way home after a day at the beach.

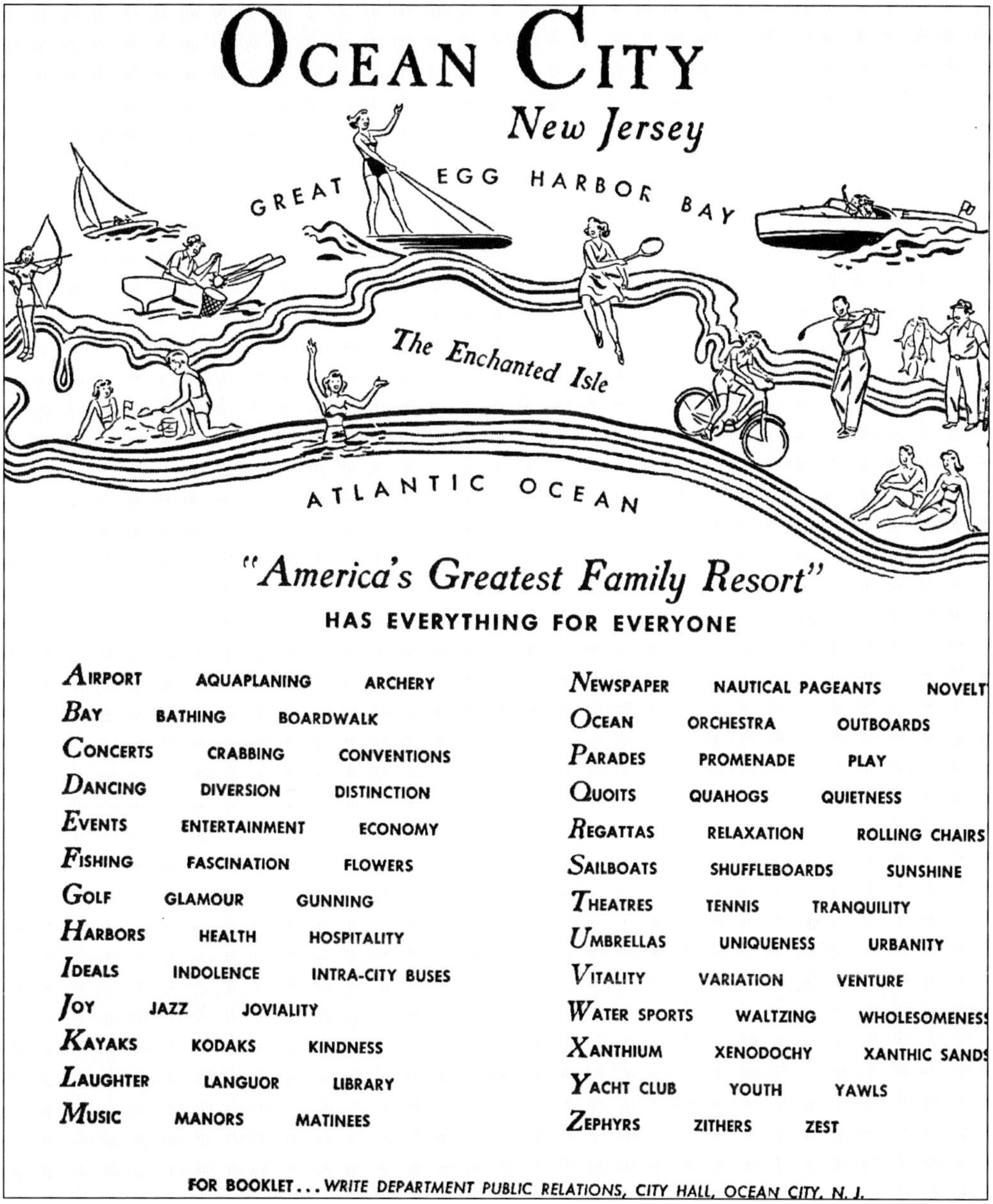

This Ocean City publicity piece was included in the annual *Cape May County Resort Guide* for 1952. Written by the public relations department, it explains how Ocean City had something for everyone, from A to Z.

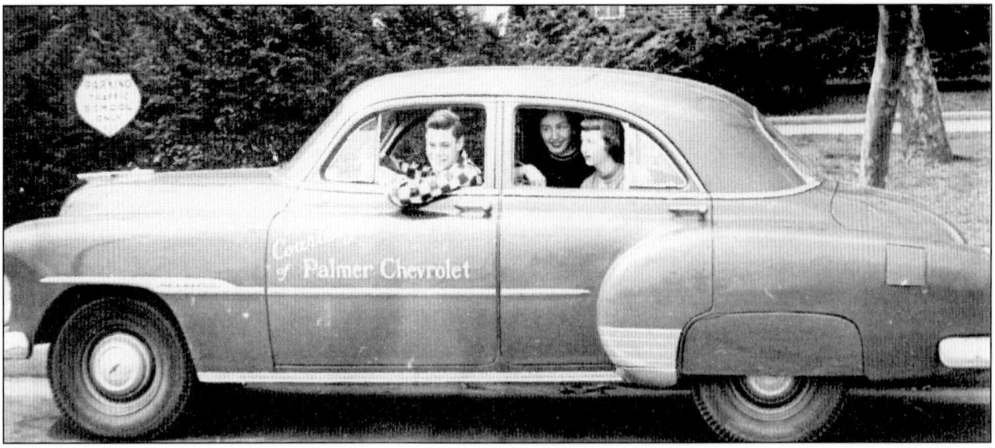

Palmer Chevrolet and Oldsmobile Company, located at 1119 Asbury Avenue, donated a new car each year for the use of the high school's driver training program.

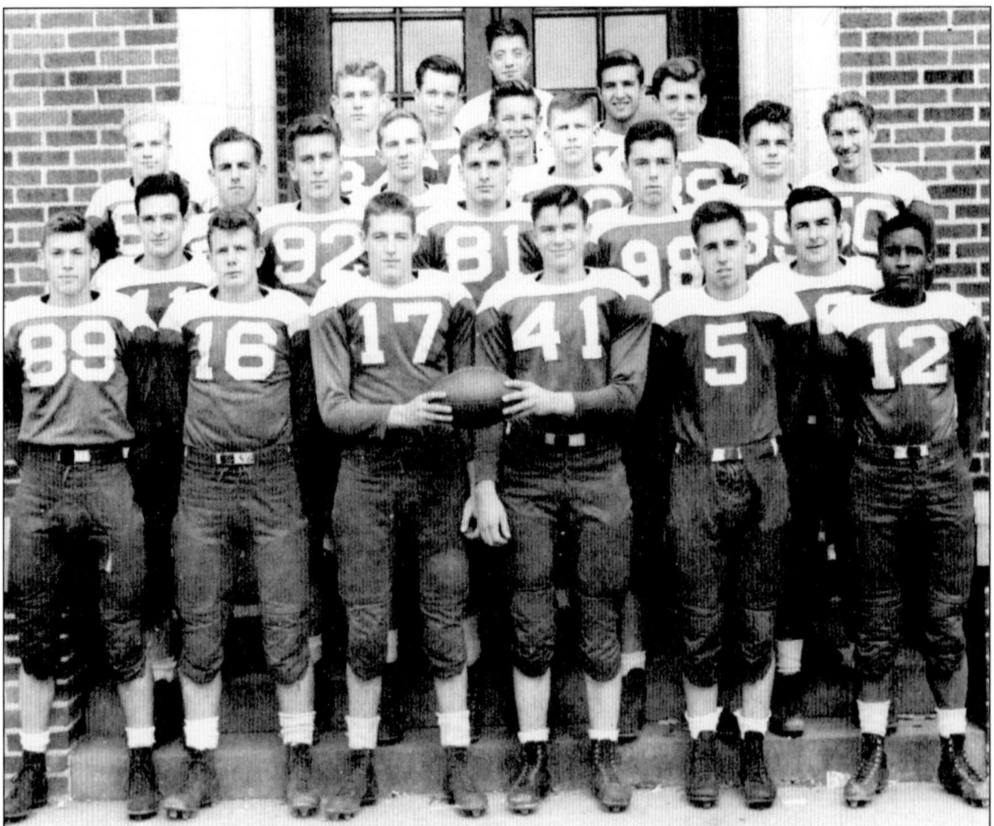

This is the 1952 high school football team, coached by E. Fenton Carey. Their biggest disappointment of the season was the 44-6 loss to archrival Pleasantville on Thanksgiving Day.

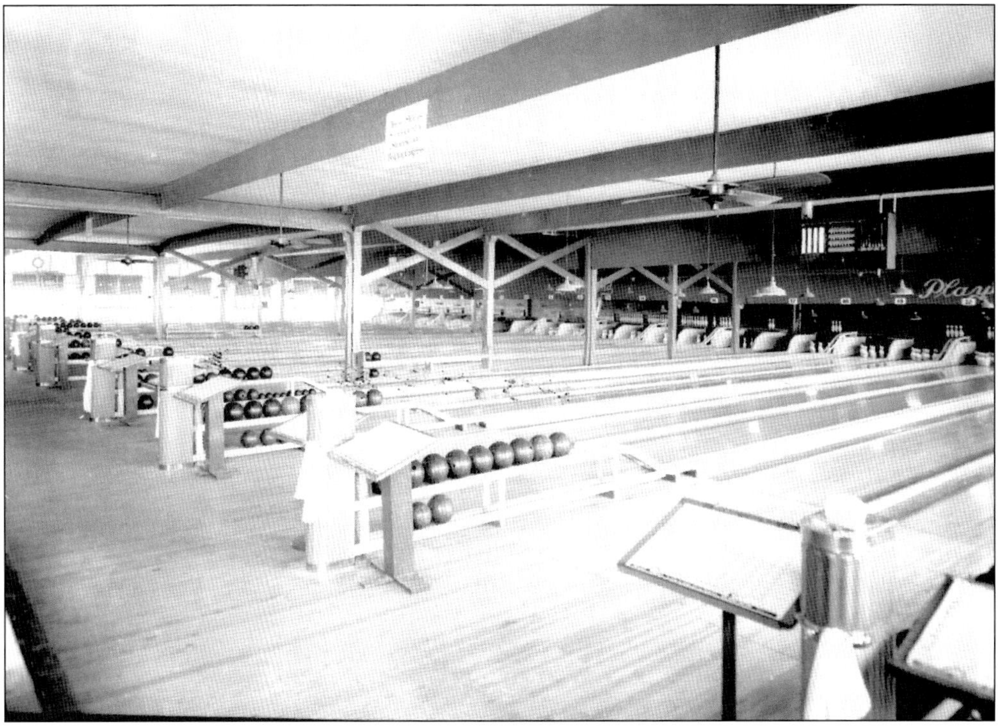

The Playland Amusement Center, located at Sixth Street and the boardwalk and owned by Howard S. Stainton, contained one of the largest bowling establishments in the state, with 34 alleys. It was popular with summer visitors and was where the South Jersey City League played during the winter.

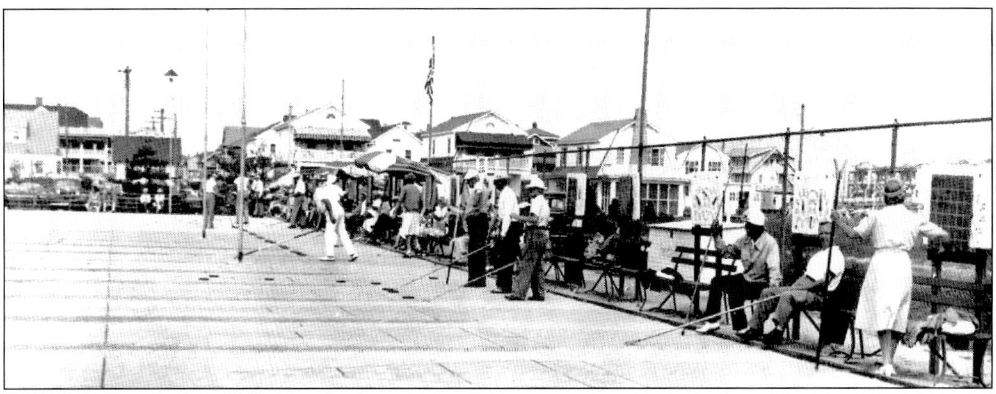

The Ocean City Recreation Department's shuffleboard courts, adjacent to the boardwalk near Fifth Street, were a popular pastime. Play was free, and the courts were open well into the evening.

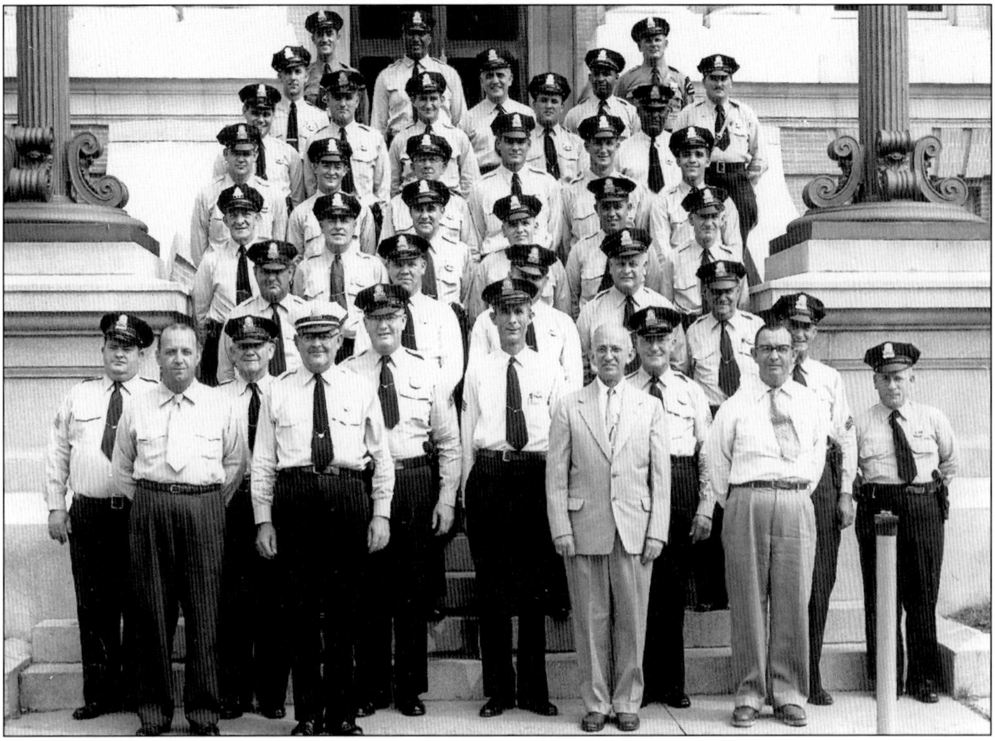

In this 1952 picture of the Ocean City Police Department, Commissioner Laurence P. Lunny is in the suit, center, with police chief William Smith Jr. on his right.

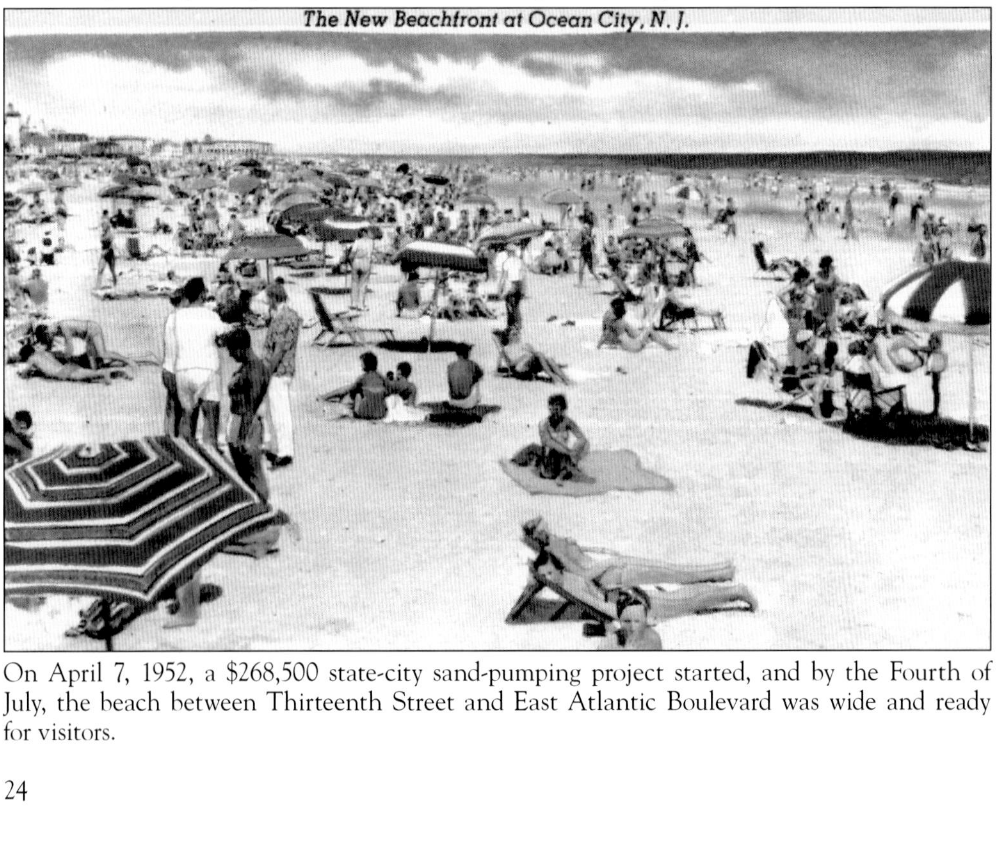

On April 7, 1952, a $268,500 state-city sand-pumping project started, and by the Fourth of July, the beach between Thirteenth Street and East Atlantic Boulevard was wide and ready for visitors.

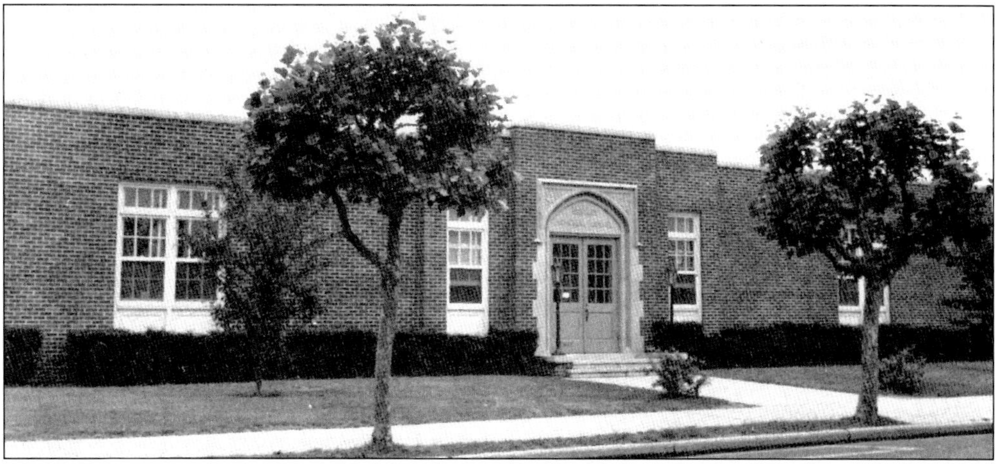

The Headley Memorial Library located on the grounds of the high school, on Ocean Avenue between Fifth and Sixth Streets, was given to the people of Ocean City by former mayor Harry Headley, in memory of his wife, Gertrude Price Headley.

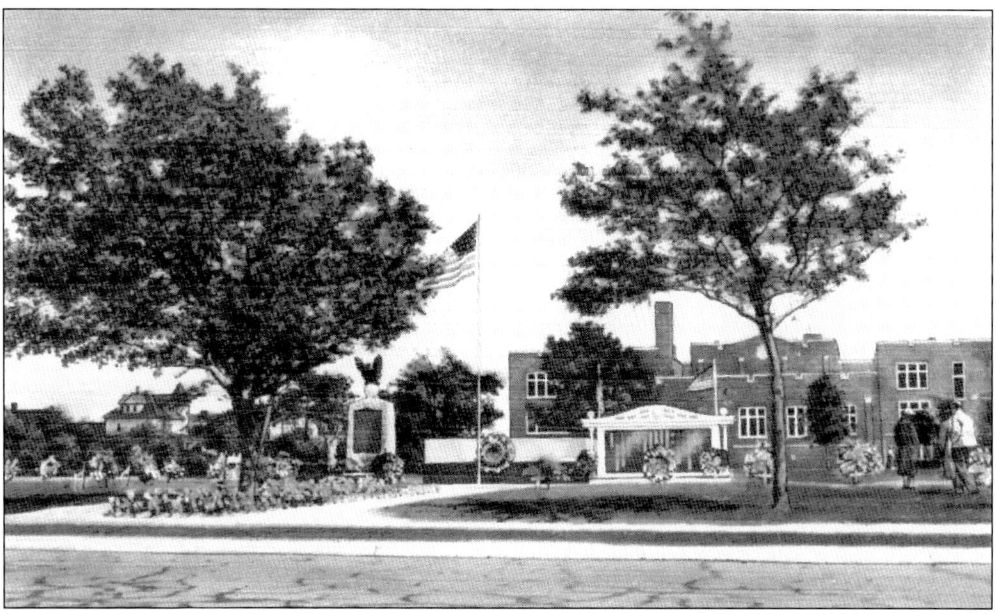

By the time the Korean Armistice was signed in 1953, some 25,000 American soldiers had been killed, including three from Ocean City: Melvin A Schmatz, John Miner, and Kent Stinger. Each year, the city held services at this memorial in the park on Wesley Avenue between Fifth and Sixth Streets.

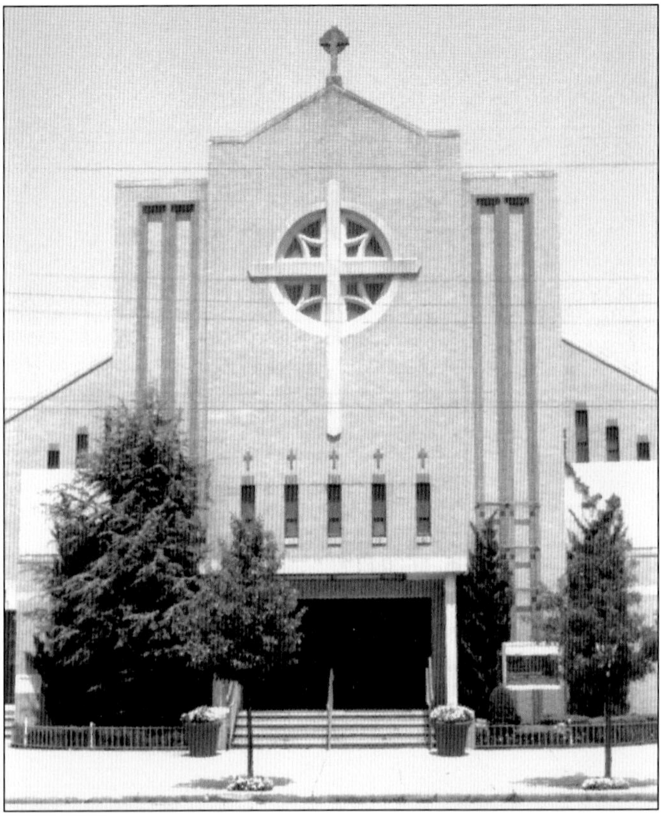

Although founded by Methodist ministers, Ocean City welcomed those of all denominations. In 1953, Our Lady Queen of Martyrs Church was built on the corner of Second Street and Atlantic Avenue. The name of the church was changed to St. Frances Cabrini in 1966.

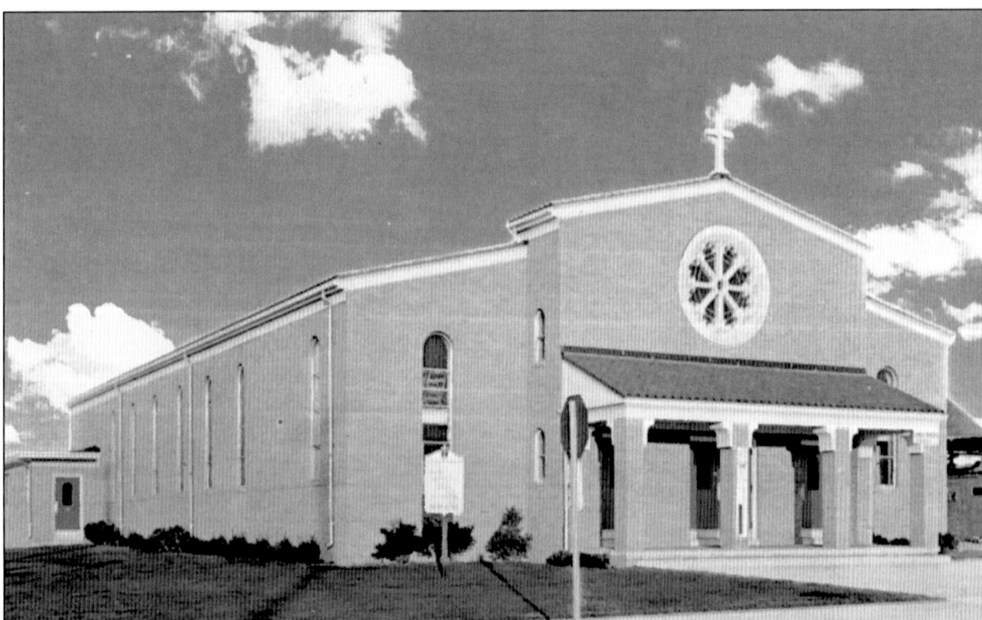

Three Catholic churches were established in Ocean City: St. Frances Cabrini, Our Lady of Good Counsel (dedicated June 19, 1955) at Fortieth Street and Asbury Avenue (above), and St. Augustine's at Thirteenth Street and Wesley Avenue.

The lines were long at the Strand Theatre, located on the boardwalk at Ninth Street, on August 1, 1952. People were anxious to see summer resident Grace Kelly in *High Noon*. Gary Cooper played her leading man.

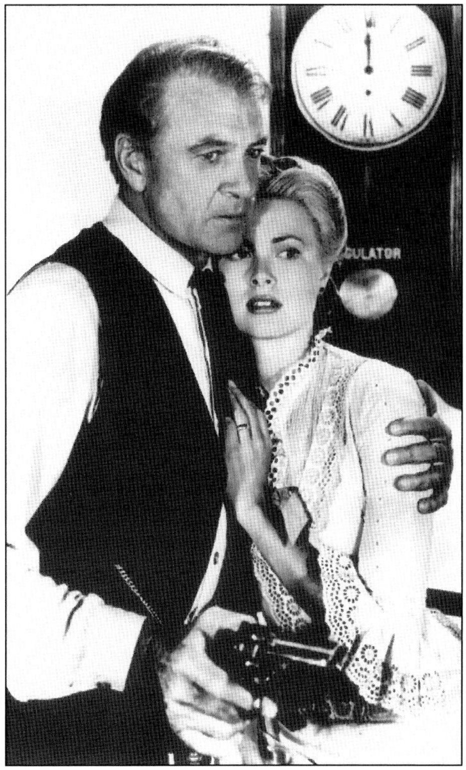

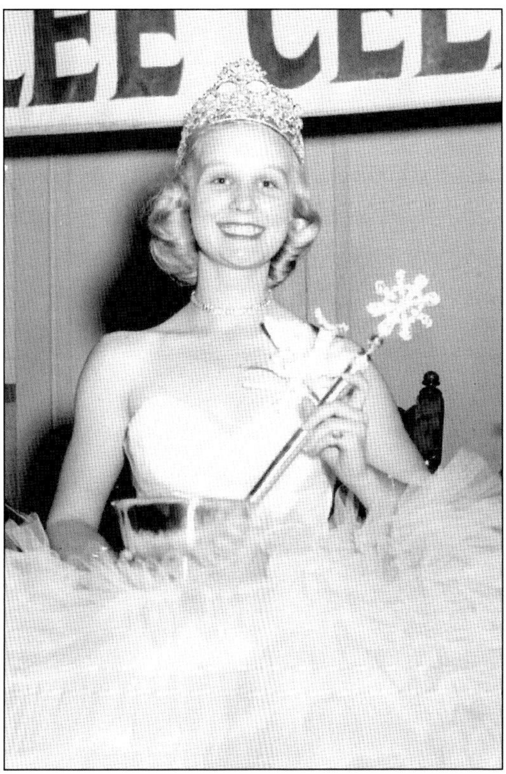

Marla Adams, an Ocean City native and a descendent of the Lake family, the founders of the city, was crowned Queen of the Diamond Jubilee Celebration. She graduated from the American Academy of Dramatic Arts in New York City and performed in Broadway plays and in the movie *Splendor in the Grass*. She also had a leading role in the daytime television soap opera *The Secret Storm*.

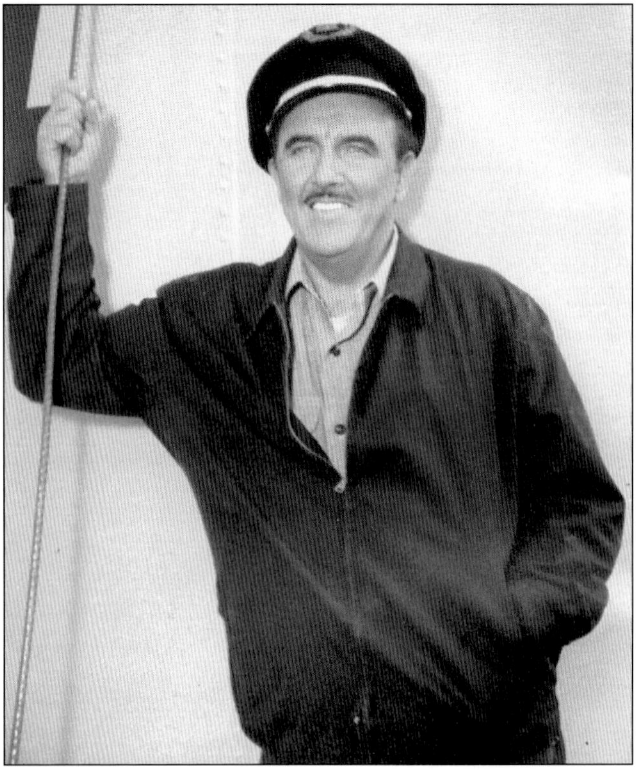

Preston Foster was born and grew up in Ocean City, where his father was one of the earliest paid lifeguards and later an Ocean City police officer. He starred in the television series *Waterfront* as Cap'n John.

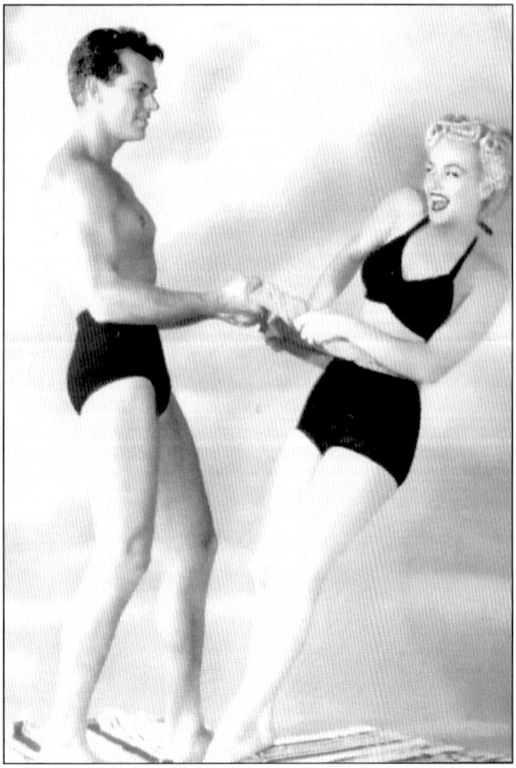

Keith Andes, born John Charles Andes in Ocean City on July 12, 1920, starred in the 1952 film *Clash by Night* with Marilyn Monroe.

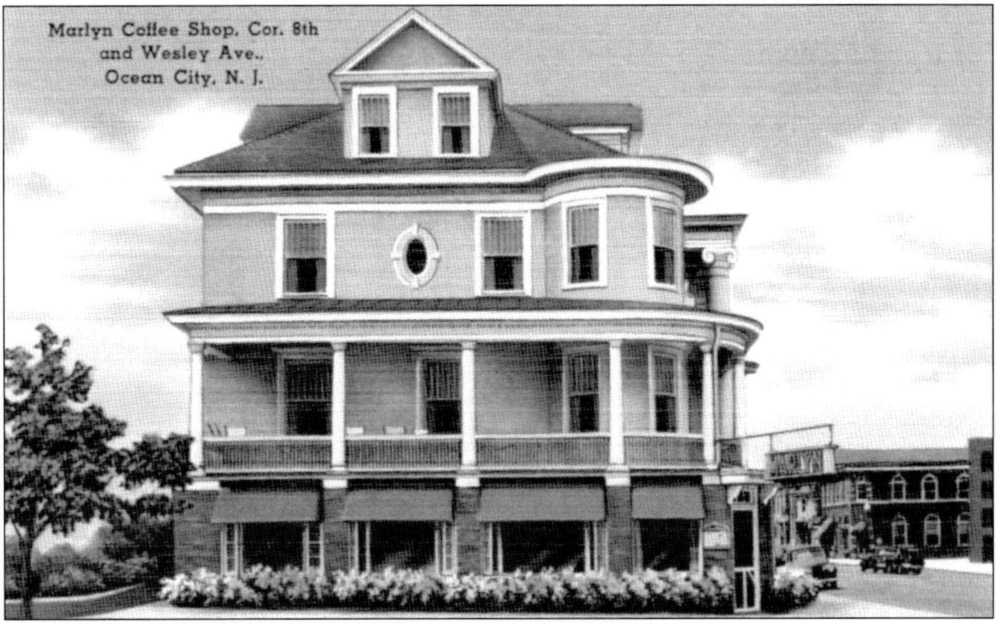

The Marlyn Coffee Shop on the corner of Eighth Street and Wesley Avenue was advertised as "Ocean City's Leading Popular Priced Restaurant. . . . Make Marlyn a Habit, It's a Good One."

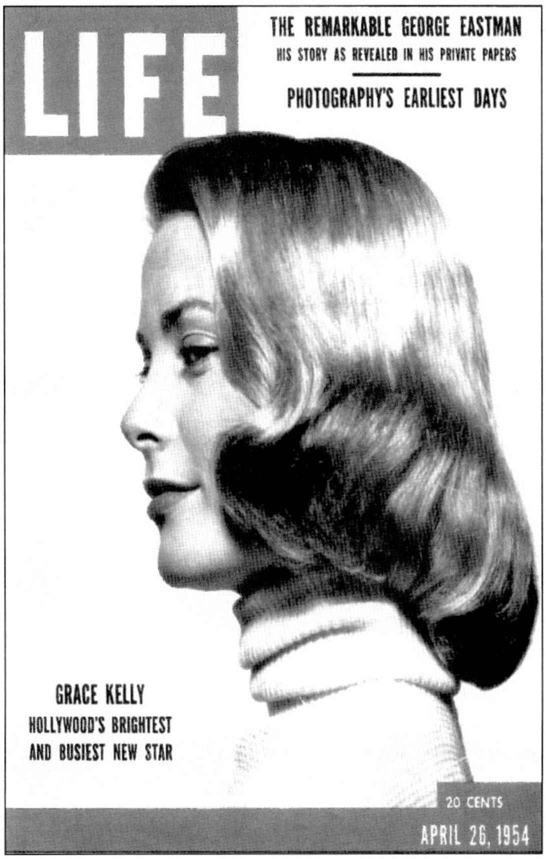

In 1954, when she appeared on the cover of *Life* magazine, Grace Kelly was starring in five movies: *Dial M for Murder, Rear Window, The Country Girl, The Bridges at Toko-Ri,* and *Green Fire*.

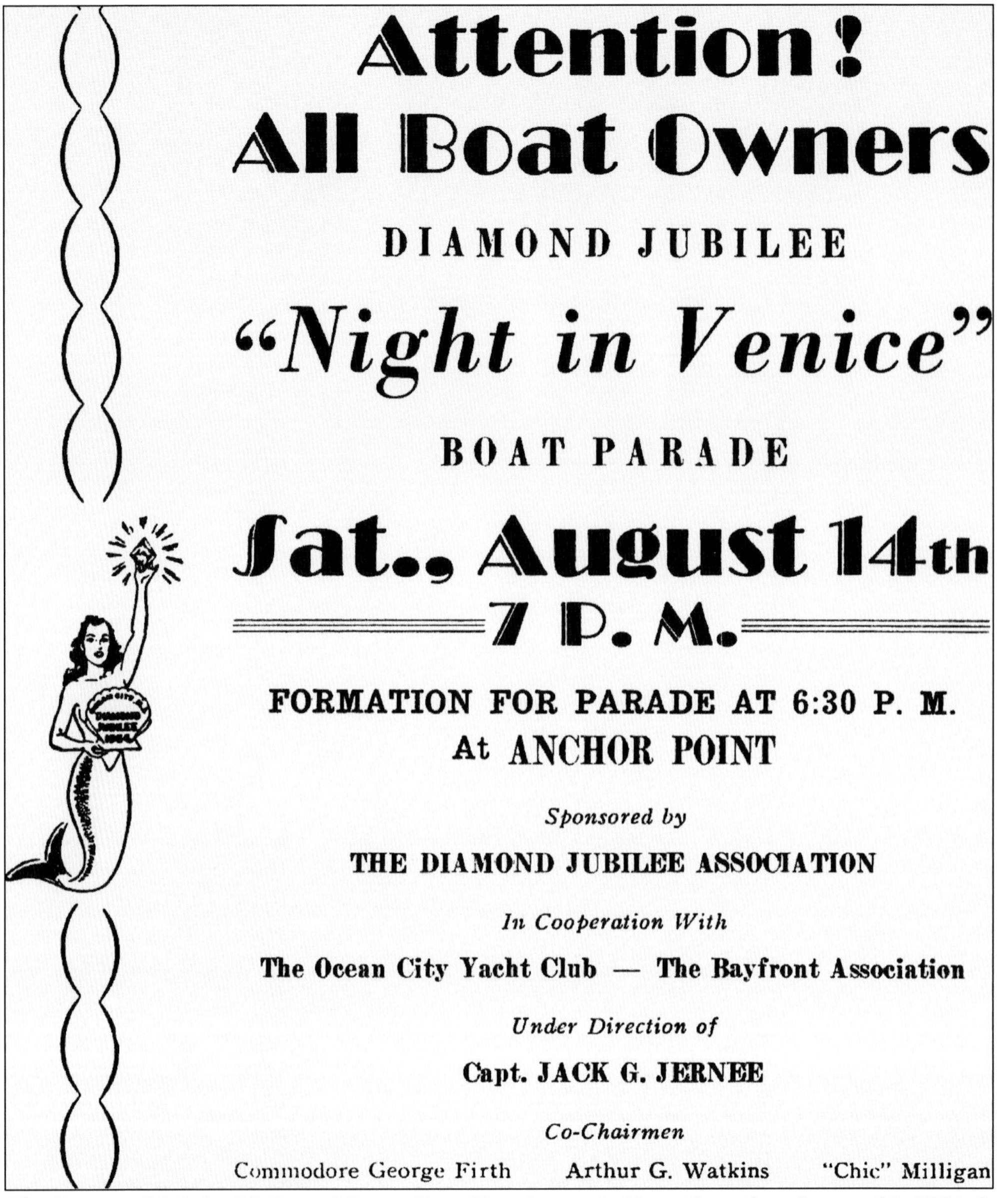

The Diamond Jubilee Night in Venice Boat Parade was held on Saturday, August 14, 1954. It was reported that one of the largest crowds ever assembled along the bay watched 115 decorated boats pass by. Jack G. Jernee, former captain of the Ocean City Beach Patrol and a member of the Jubilee committee, directed the parade.

Two

GRACE KELLY REIGNS
1955–1959

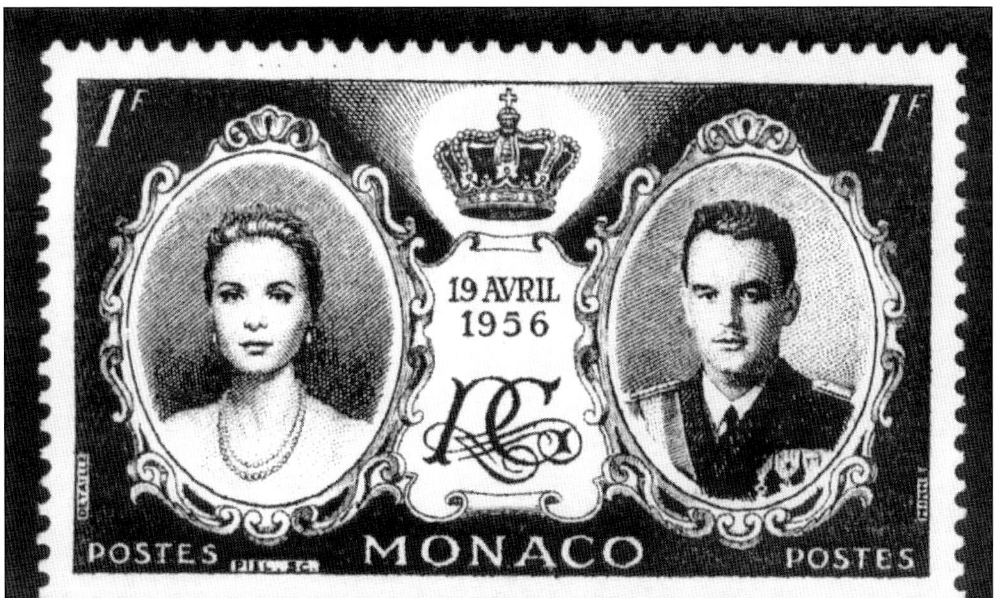

When Ocean City summer resident Grace Kelly married Prince Rainier III on April 19, 1956, Monaco released this stamp in their honor. Princess Grace left Hollywood after 11 films and one Oscar. On July 3, the Strand movie theater, located at Ninth Street and the boardwalk, presented MGM's *The Wedding in Monaco*, the only complete, official coverage of the event.

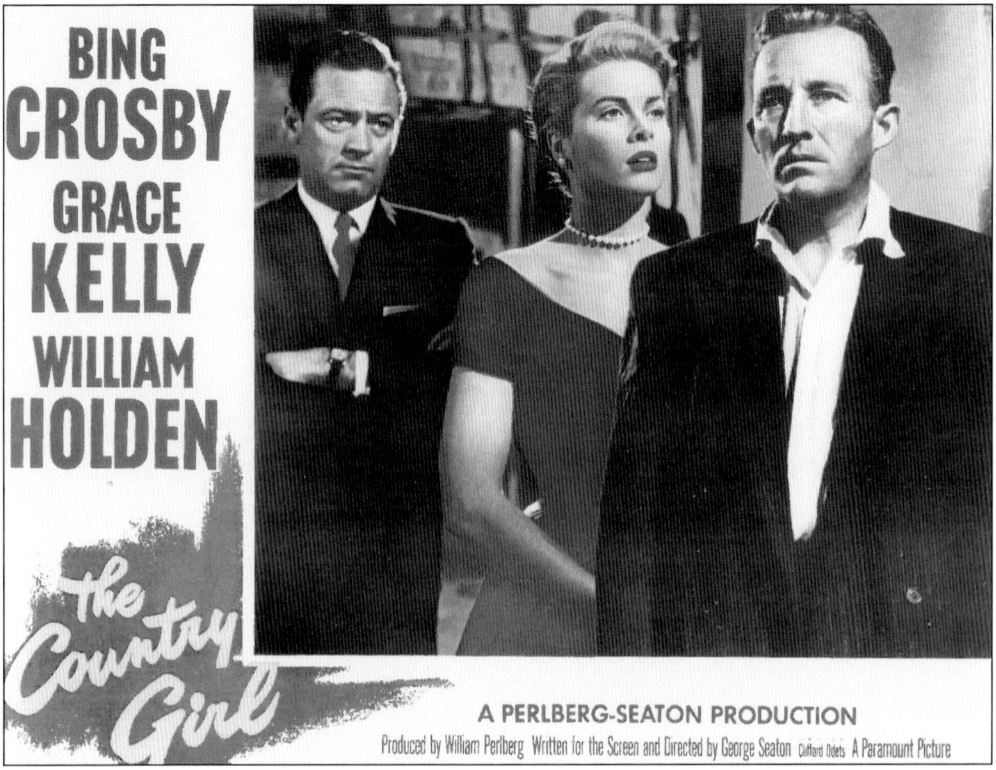

Grace Kelly won the 1954 Academy Award for best actress for her role in *The Country Girl* with Bing Crosby. This poster was displayed in Ocean City's Village Theater.

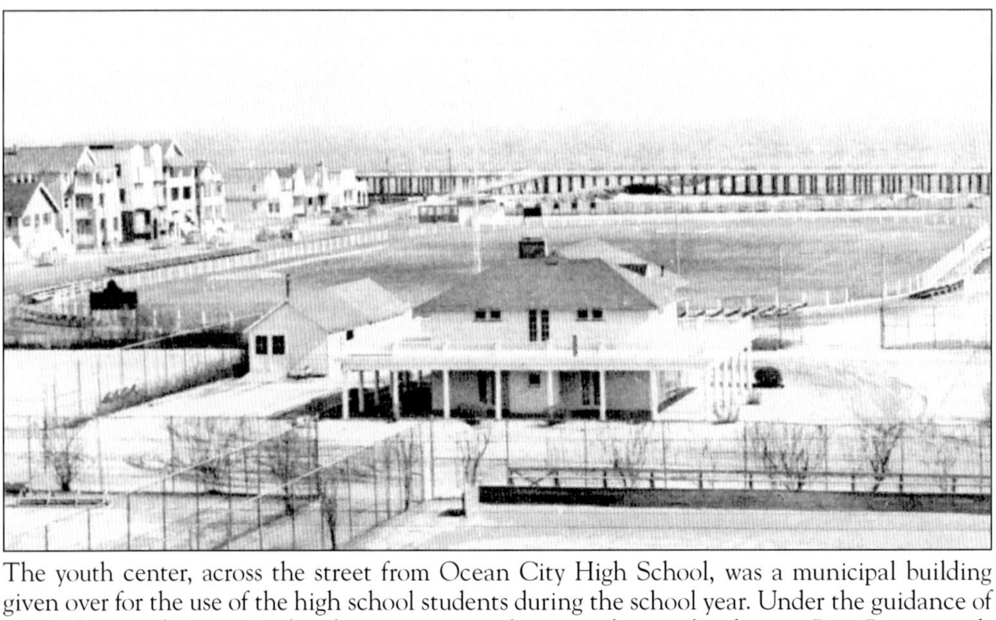

The youth center, across the street from Ocean City High School, was a municipal building given over for the use of the high school students during the school year. Under the guidance of Don Pileggi and George Loder, the teens were welcome to dance, play darts or Ping-Pong, watch television, or just relax.

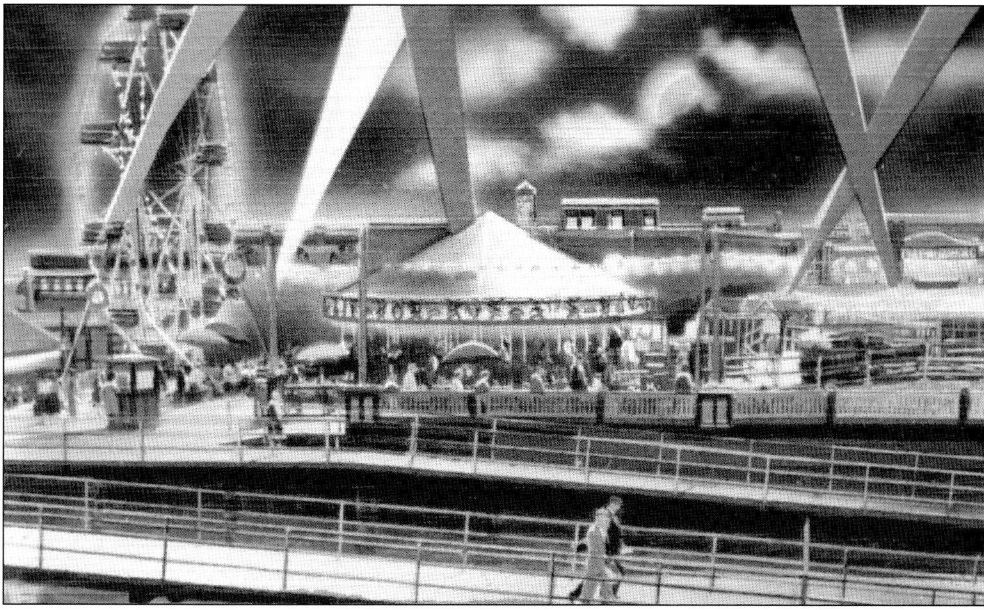

When David Gillian opened Gillian's Fun Deck at Plymouth Place and the boardwalk, he had only one ride, the Ferris wheel. Each year he added more rides until the Fun Deck was one of the most popular tourist attractions.

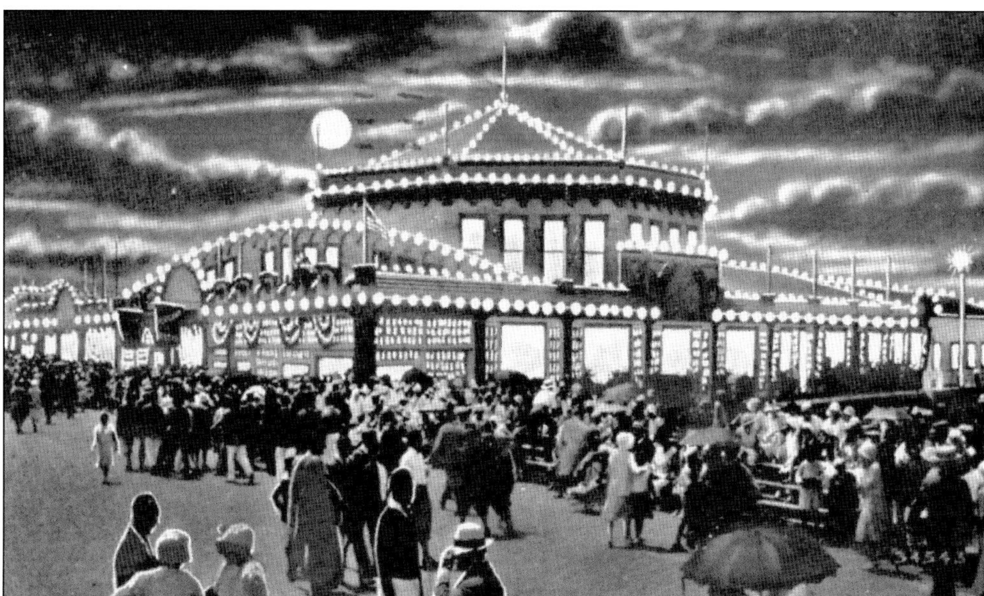

The famous Playland Amusement Center at Sixth Street and the boardwalk was leveled by fire on February 9, 1955. Founded in 1930 by Howard S. Stainton, the year-round recreation building housed a large indoor roller skate rink and a 34-lane bowling alley. It was a great loss to the community.

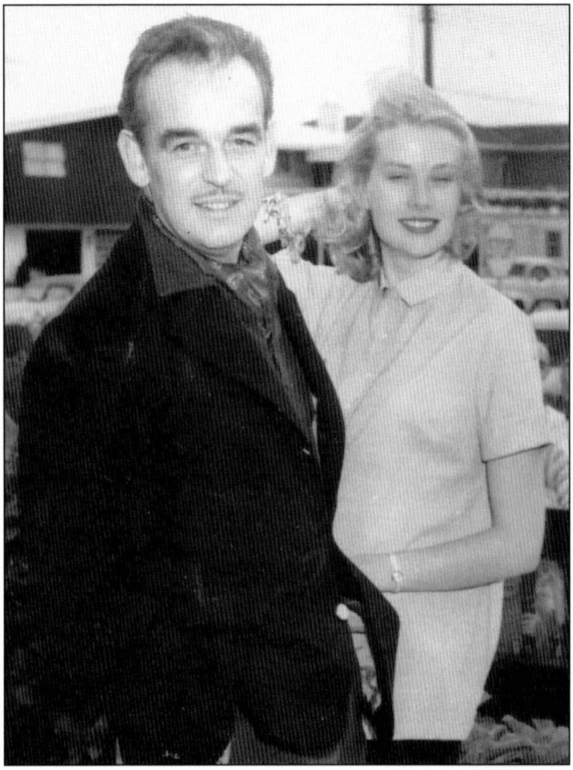

Five months after their wedding, Princess Grace and Prince Rainier visited her parents in Ocean City. This photograph was taken on September 14, 1956, in front of the Kelly home at Twenty-sixth Street by Al Senior.

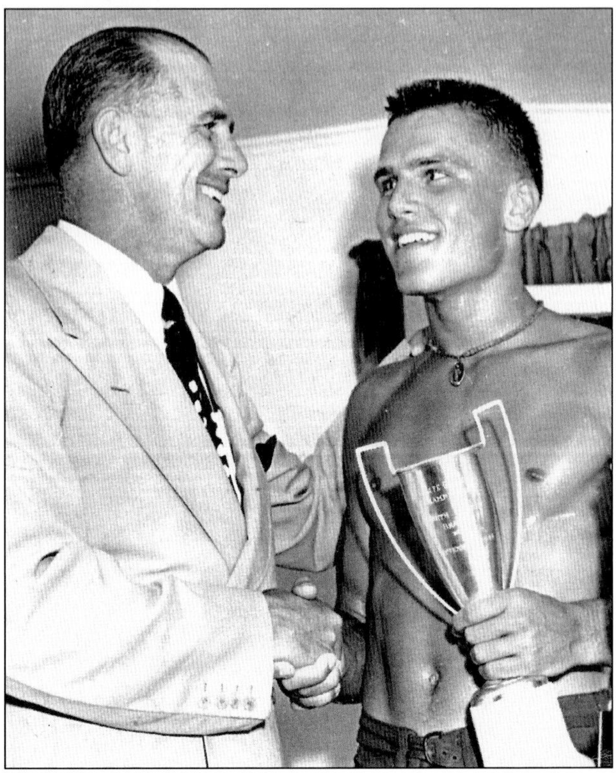

Jack Kelly Jr., Princess Grace's brother, won a bronze medal competing in the single sculls at the 1956 Olympic Games held in Melbourne, Australia. His father had won three gold medals competing in single and double sculls in the 1920 and 1924 Olympic Games.

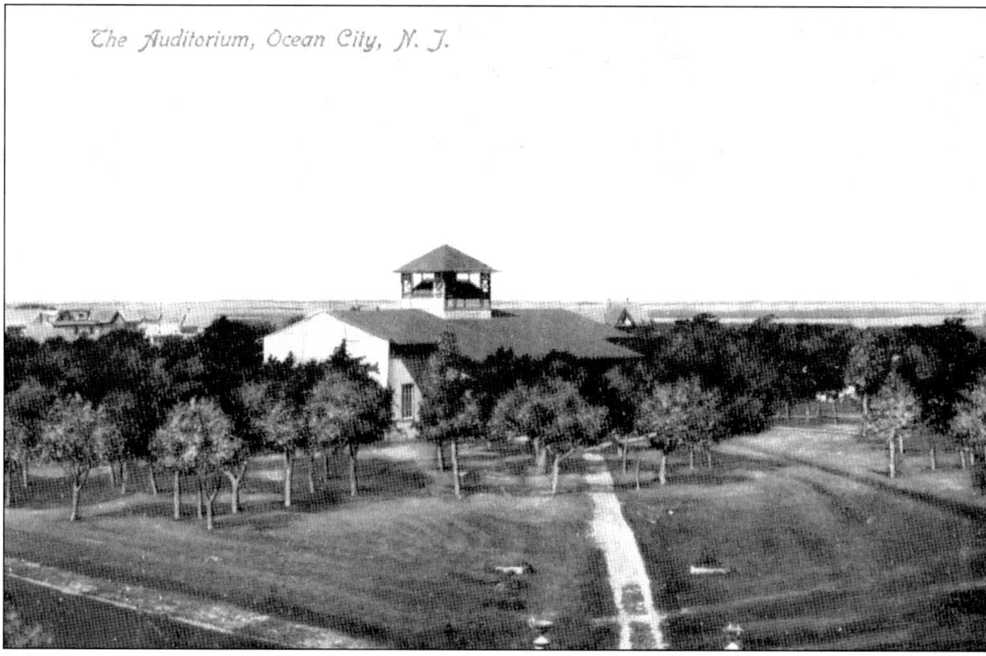

On December 17, 1956, work began to demolish the 75-year-old Tabernacle building on Wesley Avenue between Fifth and Sixth Streets to make way for a new $300,000 structure.

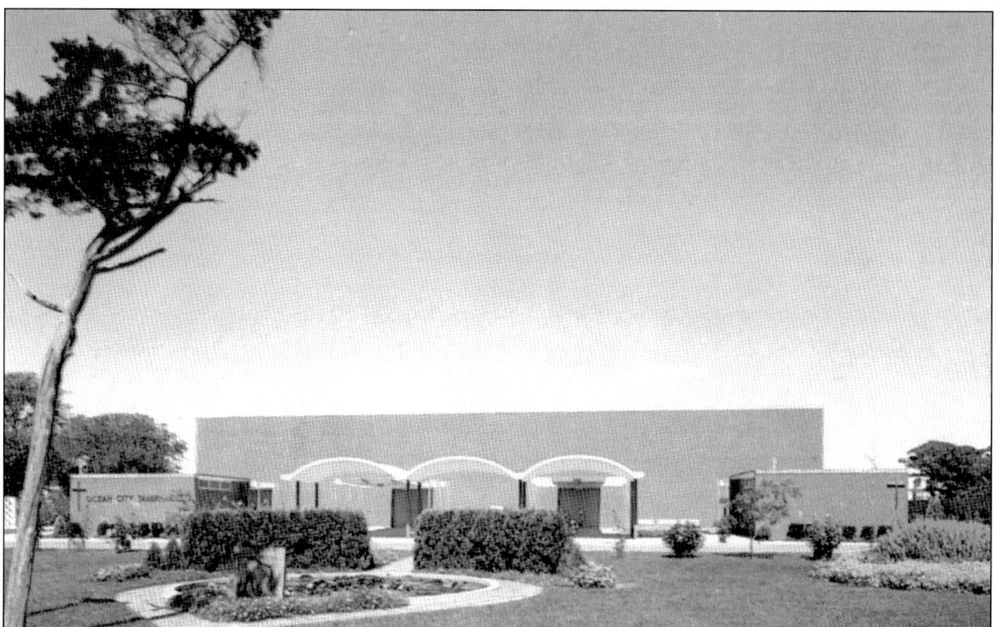

On June 23, 1957, nearly 2,000 people crowded into the new Tabernacle building for its formal dedication by Bishop Fred Pierce Corson, resident bishop of the Philadelphia area of the Methodist church.

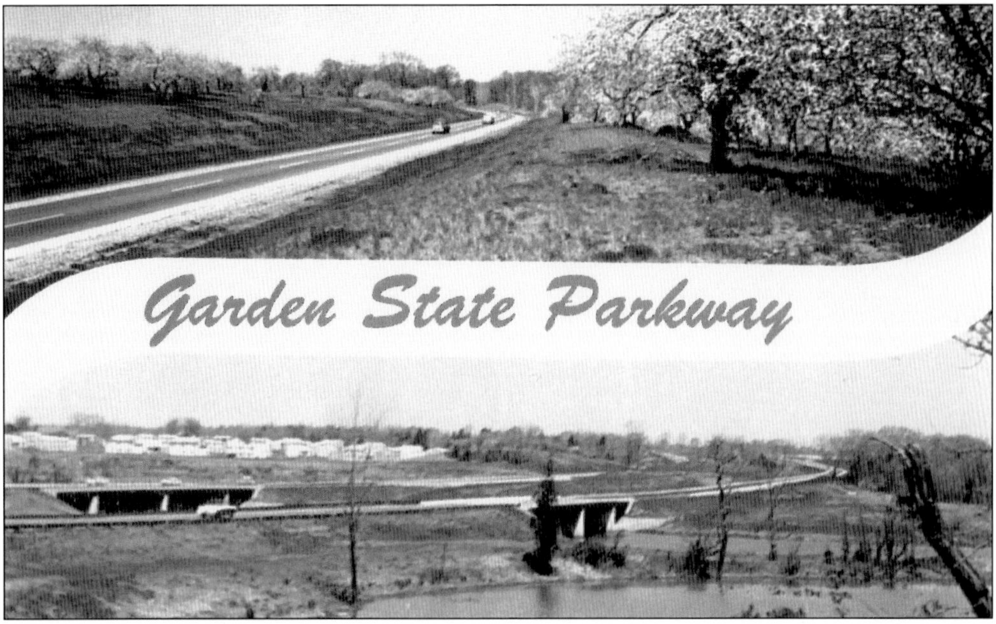

The 173-mile-long Garden State Parkway runs the length of New Jersey from its southernmost tip in Cape May to Montvale in the north where it connects with the New York State Thruway. The parkway was completed on May 26, 1956, when the Great Egg Harbor Bridge opened to traffic. The bridge was one lane in each direction. In 1972, a second bridge was built to carry northbound traffic while the older span carried southbound traffic.

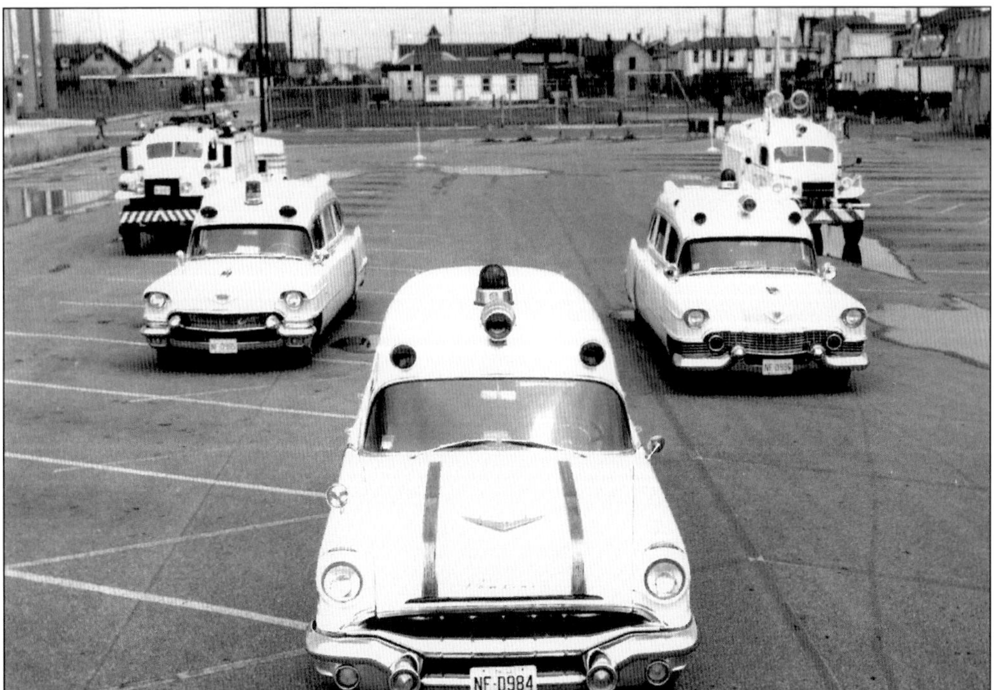

The Cape May County Rescue Squad was founded in 1951 with a used ambulance. By 1956, it had five vehicles ready to respond to a wide variety of emergencies.

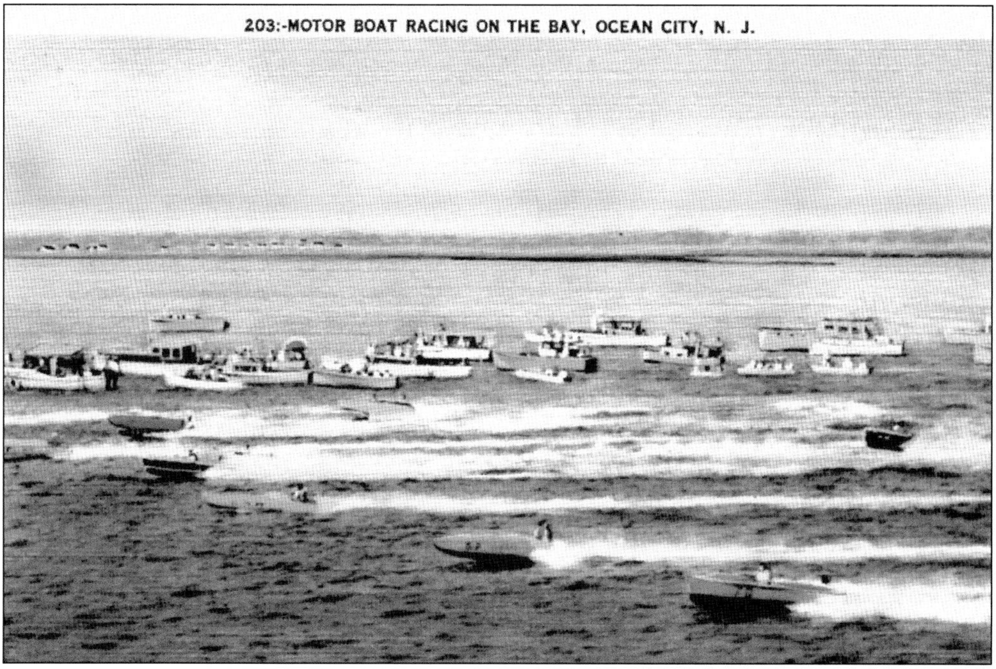

Speedboat racing had been a big part of yacht club life since the Ocean City Yacht Club began sponsoring the races in the late 1930s. The races were staged on Great Egg Harbor Bay off the yacht club at Battersea Road and the bay. The Labor Day regatta was the grand finale for South Jersey speedboat racing each summer.

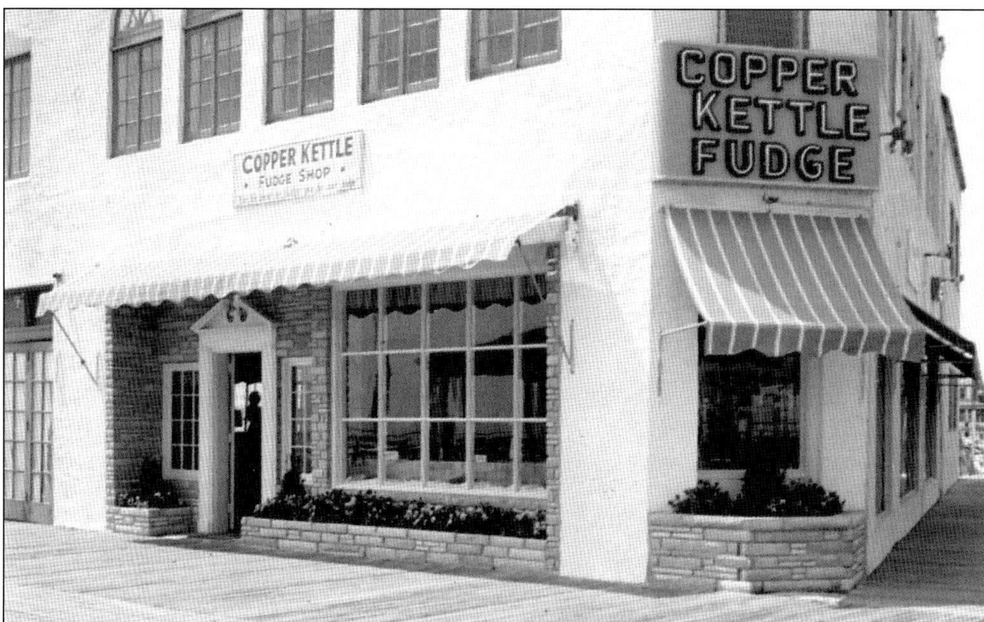

The Copper Kettle Fudge Shop at 1100 Boardwalk, owned and operated by Harry Anglemyer, was one of six confectioners on the boardwalk. The others were Mintzer's Candies at 972–974 Boardwalk; Morrow's Nut House at 944 Boardwalk; Shriver's on the boardwalk at Ninth Street; Steel's Fudge Shop at 828 Boardwalk; and Winner's Candies at 1108 Boardwalk.

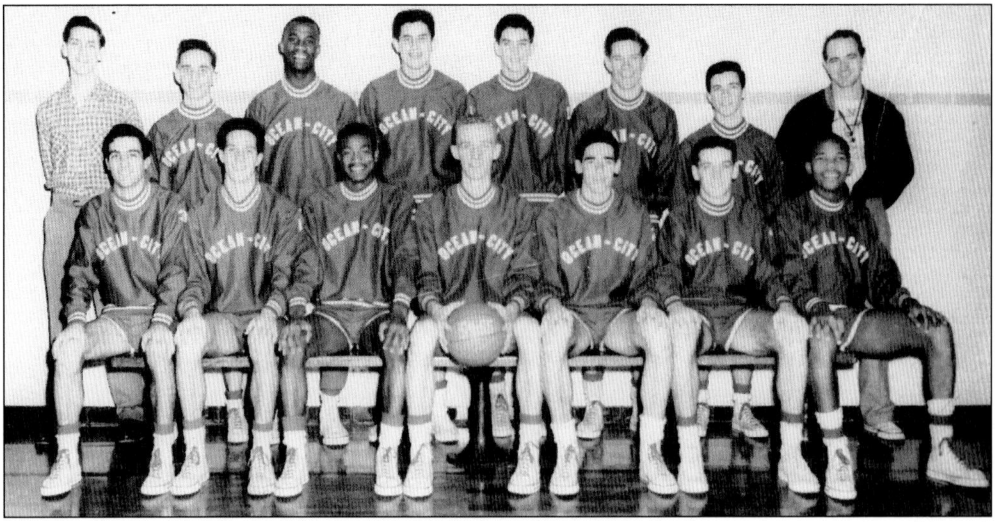

The Ocean City High School basketball team, coached by Fred "Dixie" Howell, defeated North Arlington High School 58-56 to win the Group I state championship on March 19, 1955. From left to right are (first row) Sam Foglio, Harry Hoff, Ted Ford, captain Frank Wickes, Joe Kennedy, Chick McDowell, and Nate Davis; (second row) Jim Jeffries, Phil Huber, Bernie Carter, Wayne Hudson, Tom Adams, George Loder, Mike Verano, and coach Howell.

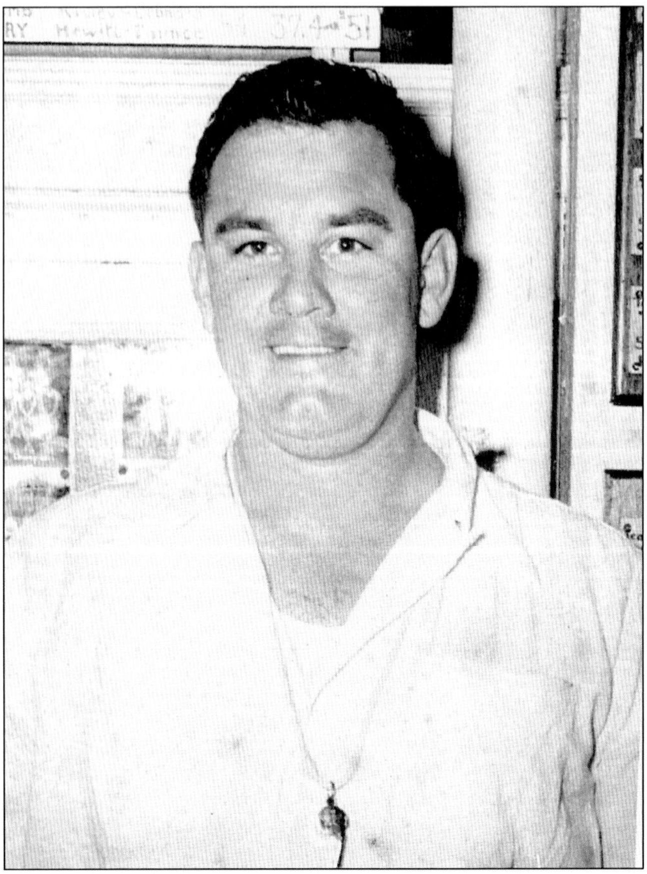

After a long, illustrative career teaching physical education and coaching at Ocean City High School, T. John Carey left teaching to run his family's real estate business. The office of Carey's Real Estate was located at Fifteenth Street and the boardwalk. His students dedicated the 1952 yearbook, *The Caravel*, to him.

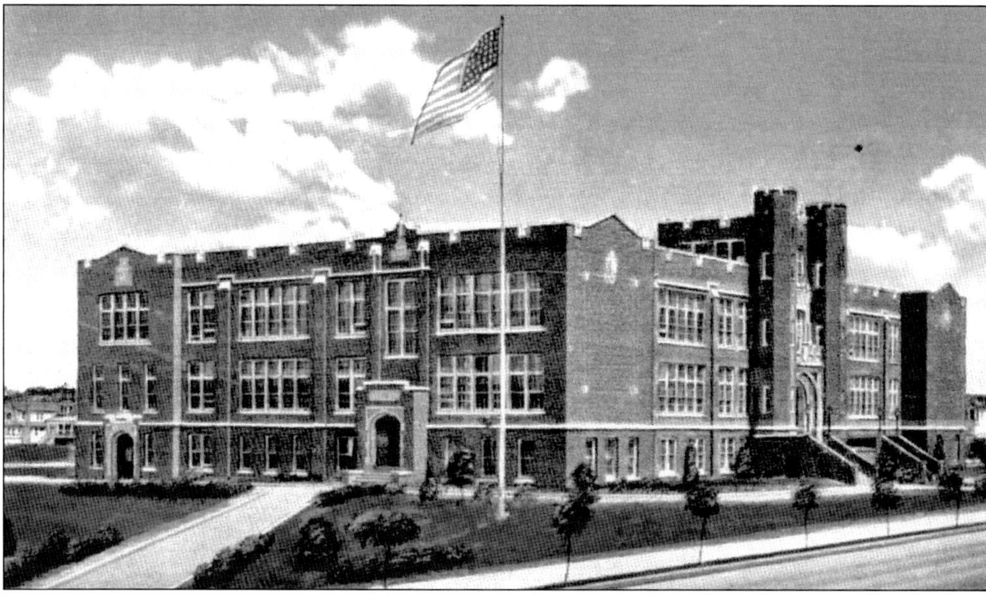

The space age began on October 4, 1957, when the Soviet Union launched *Sputnick I*, the first spacecraft, and forced America to place more emphasis on science and math in the schools. Ocean City responded by giving its high school students a chance to go to school on Saturday. The classes were voluntary and limited to students interested in taking advanced classes in science and math. The instructors were Melvin Thompson of the mathematics department and George Bowman of the science department.

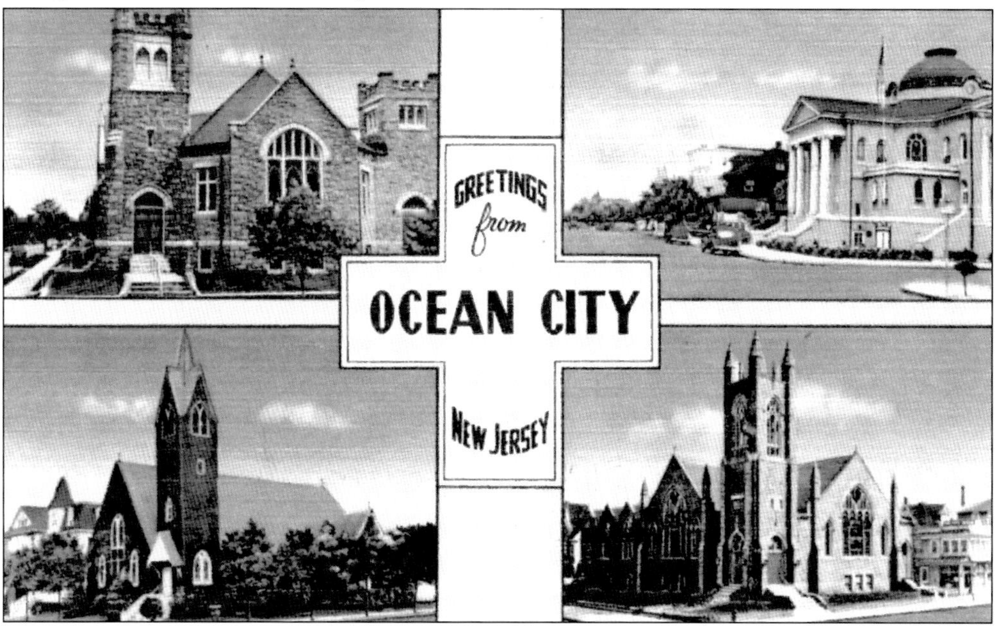

Church and religion continued to be an important part of life in Ocean City, and all denominations were welcome. On the top left is the First Presbyterian Church at Seventh Street and Wesley Avenue, bottom left is Holy Trinity Episcopal Church at Eleventh Street and Central Avenue, top right is the Baptist Church at Tenth Street and Wesley Avenue, and bottom right is the First Methodist Church at Eighth Street and Central Avenue.

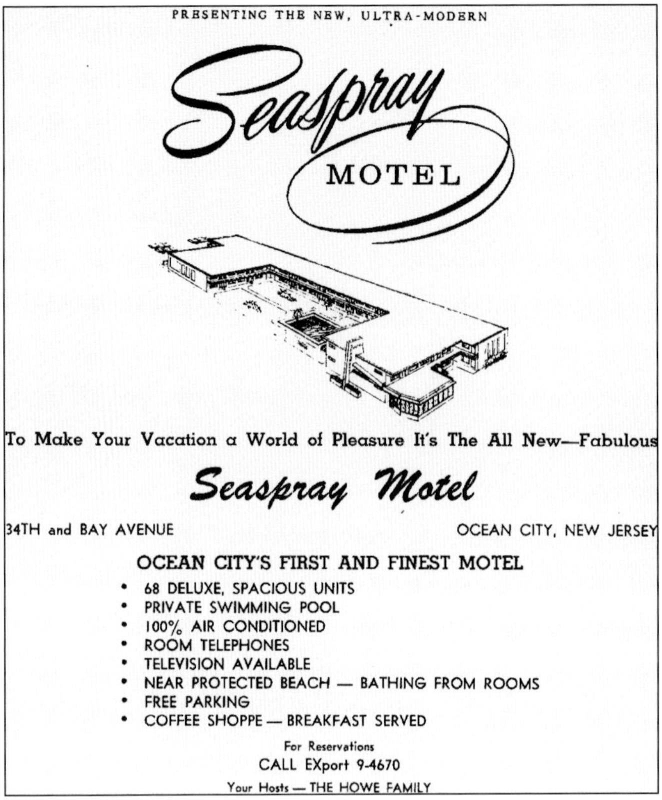

In the spring of 1950, Ocean City's hotel and guesthouse owners were concerned that the modern motels being built in neighboring communities would come to town and give them competition. Through their prodding, the city commissioners and mayor adopted an amendment to the zoning laws forbidding the building of motels. This was effective until May 1956, when a Superior Court ruling stated motels were legally permissible wherever hotels and guesthouses were. The Seaspray Motel, opened July 1, 1958, at Thirty-fourth Street and Bay Avenue, was the first motel built on the island.

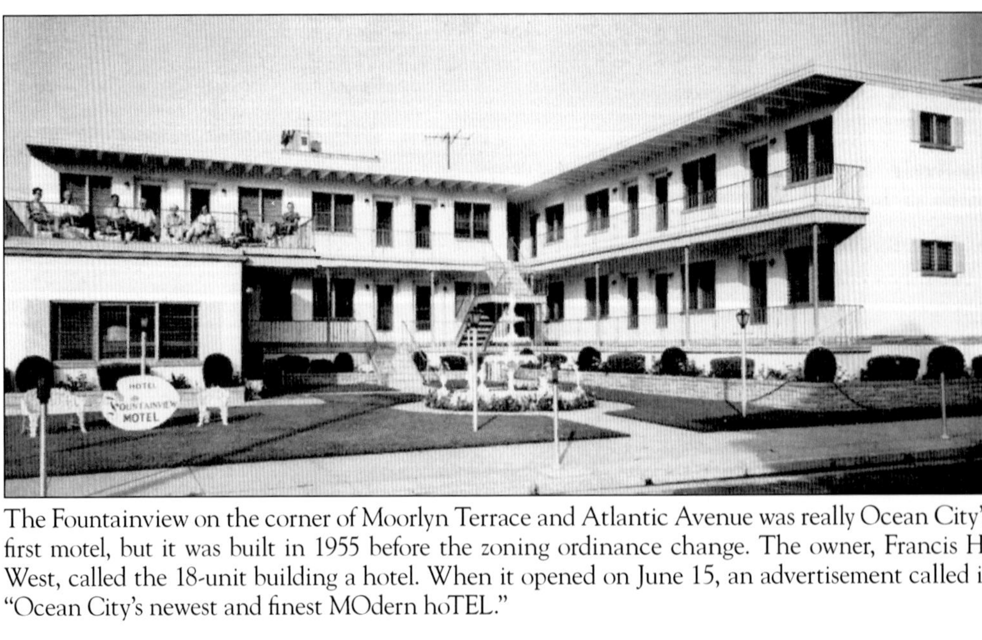

The Fountainview on the corner of Moorlyn Terrace and Atlantic Avenue was really Ocean City's first motel, but it was built in 1955 before the zoning ordinance change. The owner, Francis H. West, called the 18-unit building a hotel. When it opened on June 15, an advertisement called it "Ocean City's newest and finest MOdern hoTEL."

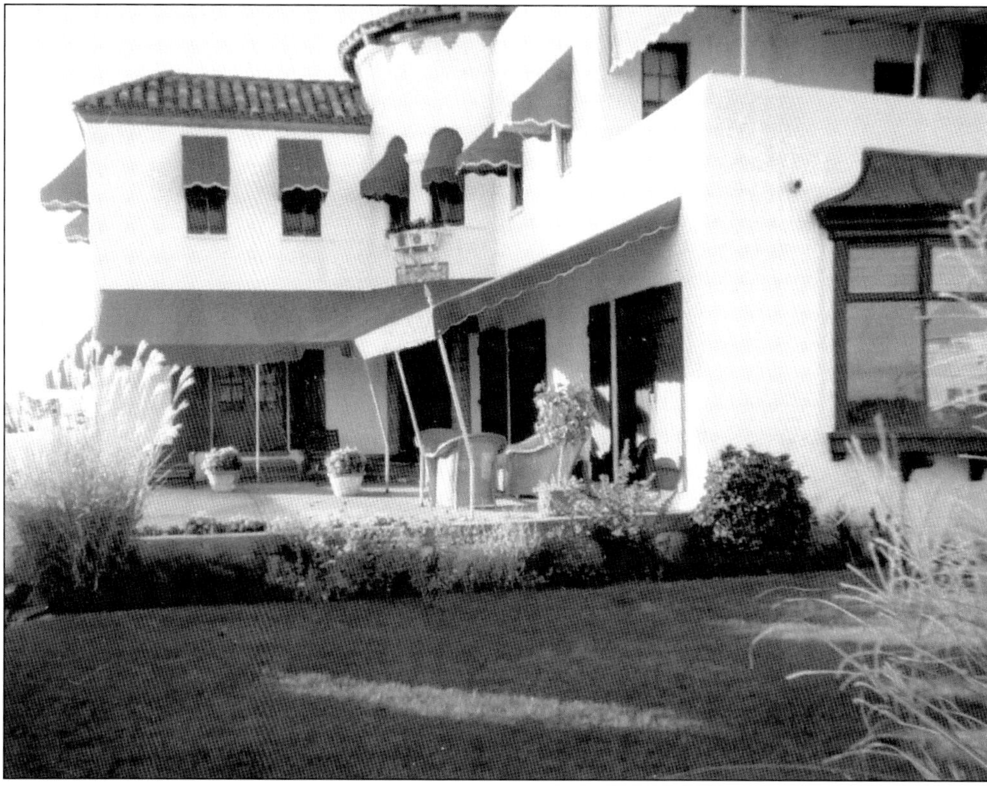

In 1931, when Grace Kelly's parents, Margaret and John Kelly, built this house at 2536 Wesley Avenue, the area was mostly undeveloped. The house was directly across from the beach, with uninterrupted views from all sides.

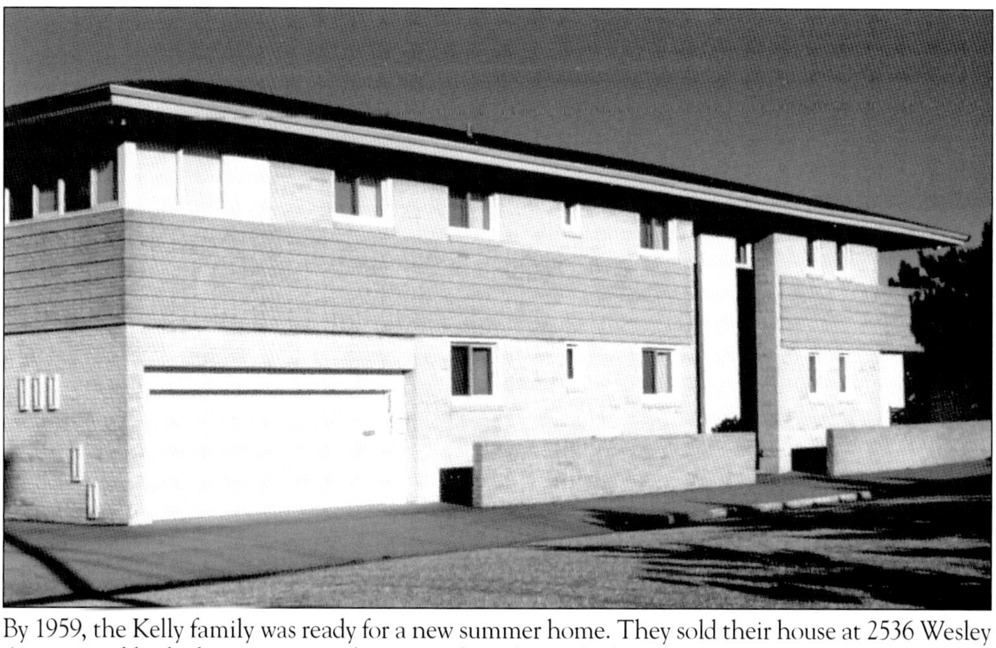

By 1959, the Kelly family was ready for a new summer home. They sold their house at 2536 Wesley Avenue and built this one across the street, directly on the beach.

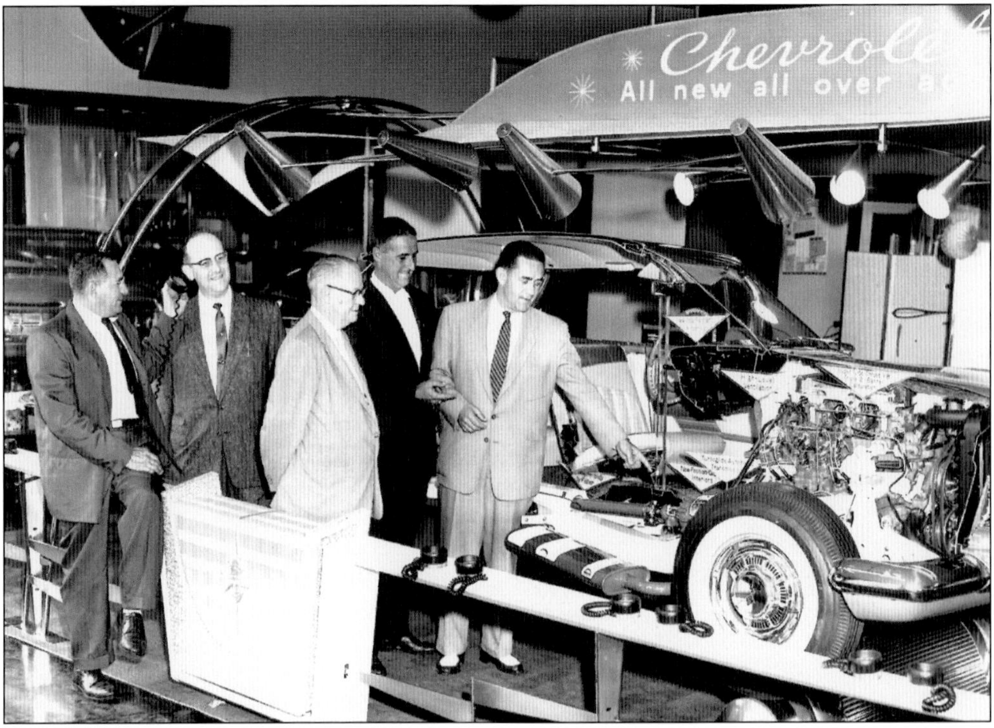

The owners of Palmer's Chevrolet and Oldsmobile at 1117–1129 Asbury Avenue were very proud of this display of a cutaway of their newest model. Shown from left to right are Louis Palmer, Commissioner D. Allen Stretch, Mayor Nathaniel C. Smith, Harry Klause, and Commissioner B. Thomas Waldman in this 1959 picture.

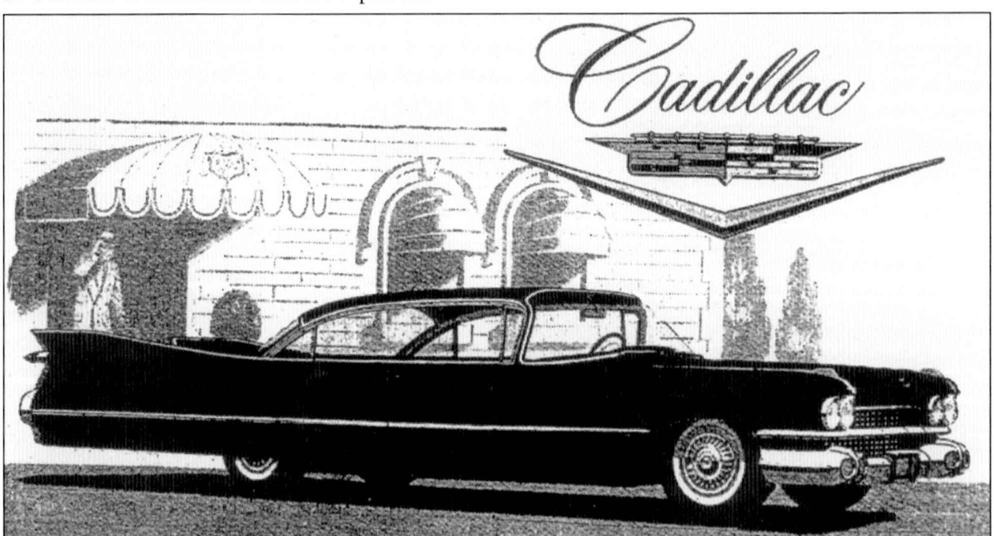

Cars in the 1950s were big, powerful, and dazzling with chrome, and none more so than the Cadillac. The Druck Motor Company at 1158 Asbury Avenue had this advertisement in the local newspaper, the *Sentinel-Ledger*, on January 8, 1959. The advertisement stated that "Radiant in its design . . . resplendent in its luxury . . . brilliant in its performance—the Cadillac for 1959 is without precedent even among Cadillacs of the past."

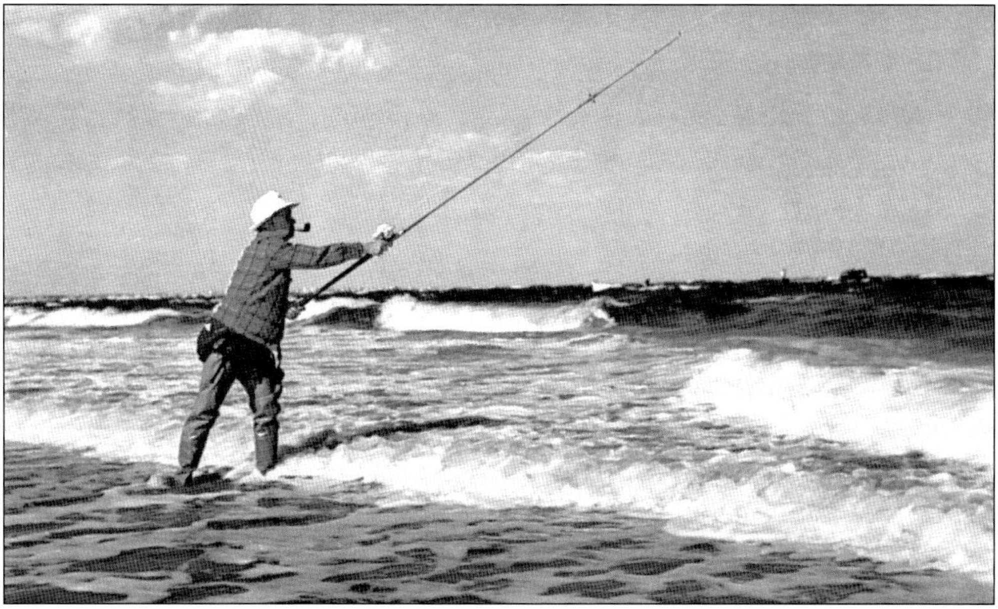

The Cape May County Fishing Contest was held every week beginning in late May. Prizes were awarded for the best fish entered in the following classes: croaker, black drum, flounder, kingfish, porgy, striped bass, bluefish, tuna, marlin, dolphin, albacore, tautog, and for the rarest fish.

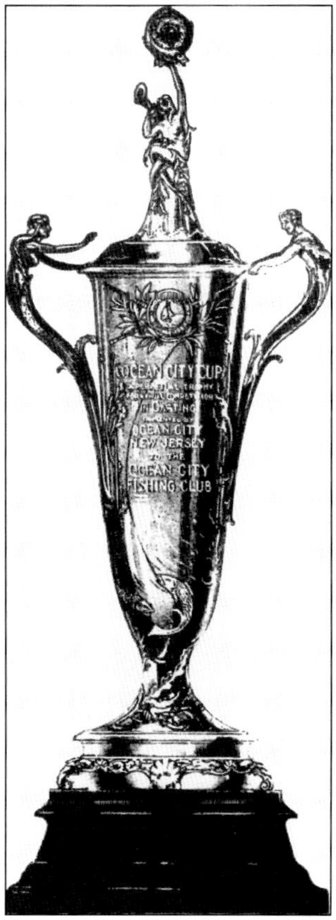

This sterling silver cup, presented to the Ocean City Fishing Club in 1916 by the city commissioners, was a perpetual trophy for winners of the Ocean City Casting tournament. In 1959, it was displayed at the New York Sportsmen's Show in the New York Coliseum.

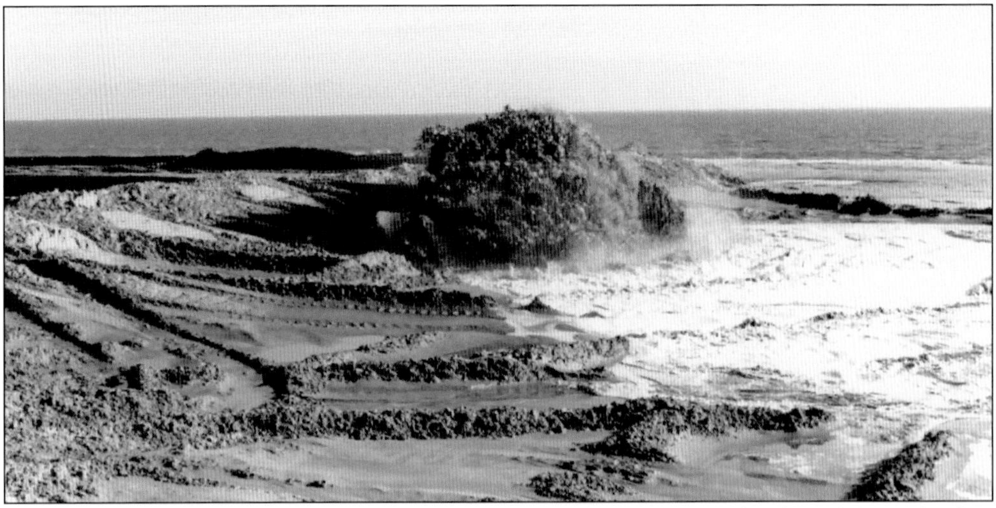

In 1959, the Hill Dredging Company pumped 1.4 million cubic yards of sand from the bay bottom, through pipes, onto the beaches from East Atlantic Boulevard to Fifteenth Street. Periodic rebuilding of the beach was necessary because of erosion. Tides and currents aggravated by storms scour sand from the beach and carry it out to sea.

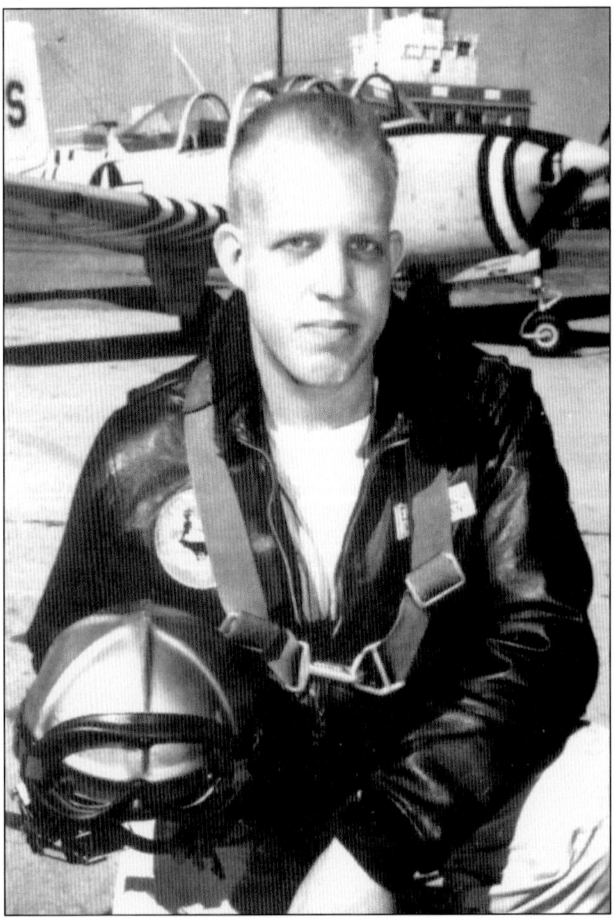

Lt. Alfred E. Senior Jr. was killed on August 6, 1959, when the navy plane on which he was copilot crashed into the Mediterranean Sea. He was a 1952 graduate of Ocean City High School and a 1957 graduate of the United States Naval Academy.

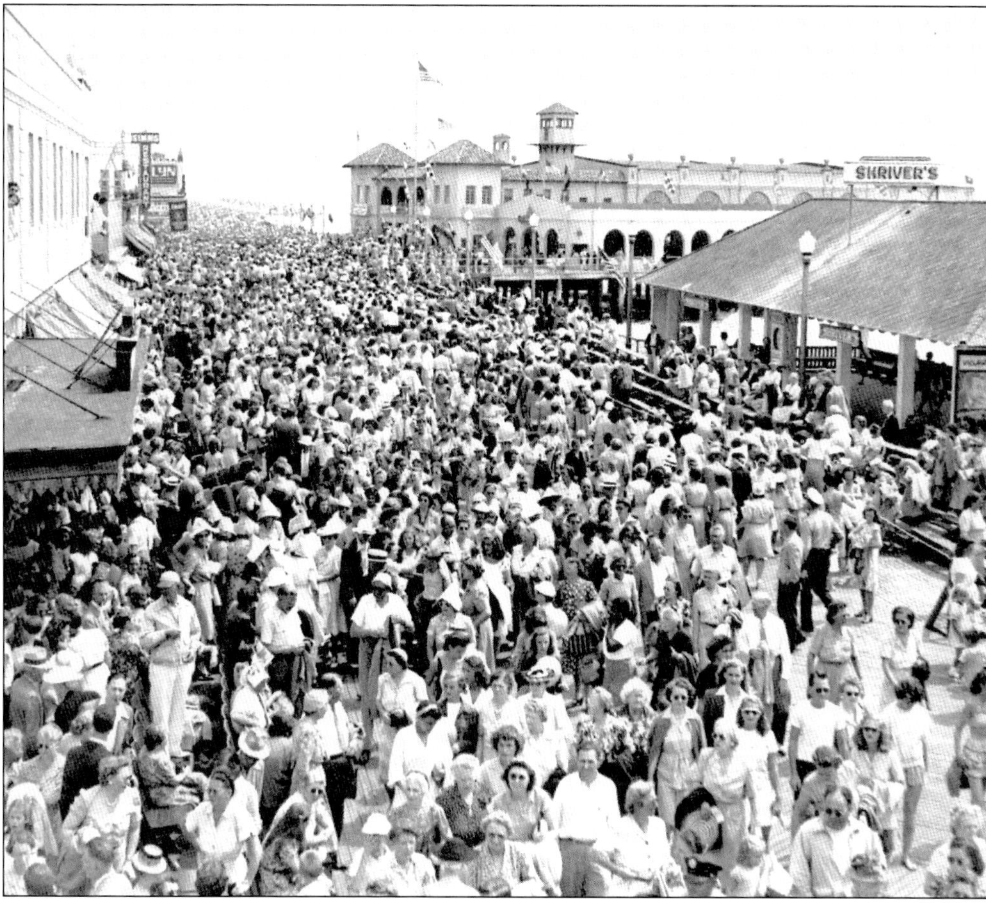

There was barely breathing room in this picture from 1958 taken on the boardwalk near Ninth Street. The building on the left is Shriver's, across from it on the right is Shriver's Pavilion with the Music Pier on the right behind the pavilion.

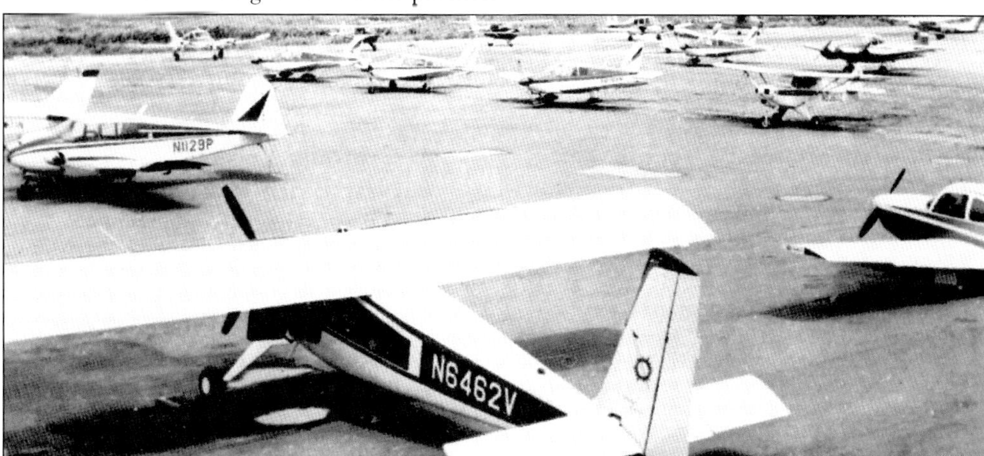

By 1959, the Ocean City Municipal Airport served an average of 2,000 small planes annually. The 25th anniversary of the airport was celebrated with a banquet held at the Flanders Hotel on Saturday, June 6, and a fly-in on Sunday with airplanes from all parts of the country.

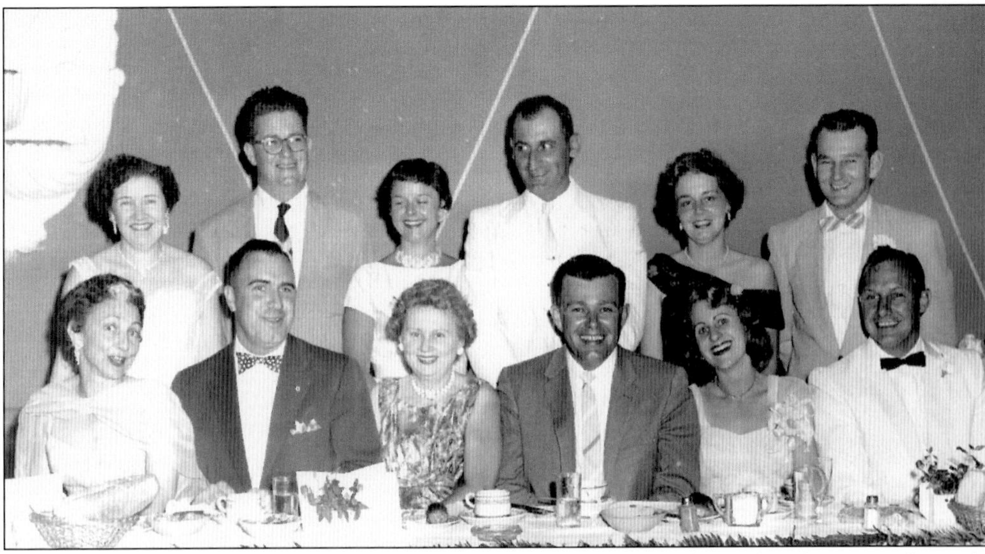

The Married Couples Club was begun by a group of young married couples who wanted a night out with friends. Each month they would plan a theme for their event. In May of each year they held a dinner dance. From left to right are (first row) Ruth Costello, Bob Mengel, Teresa McLaughlin, Chet Ferguson, Helen Foor, and Earl Shaw; (second row) Hope Shaw, George McLaughlin, Doris Ferguson, Joe Costello, Ann Mengel, and Archie Foor.

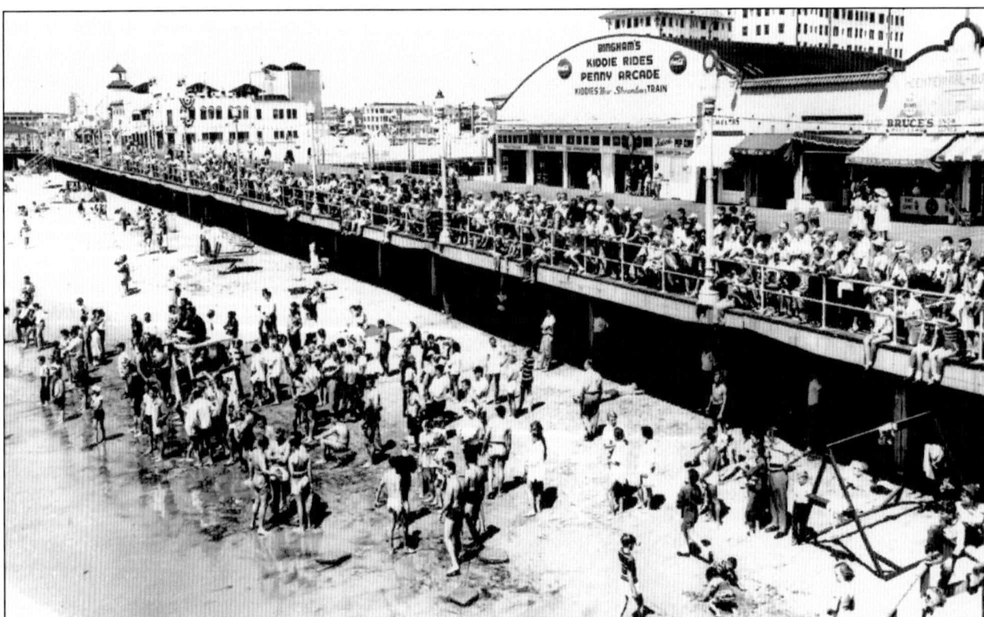

The large arched building of Bingham's Kiddie Rides, on the boardwalk between Tenth and Eleventh Streets, was first used at the 1939 New York World's Fair. In 1959, David Simpson and Fred Tarves bought the building and business, remodeled it, and renamed it Playland.

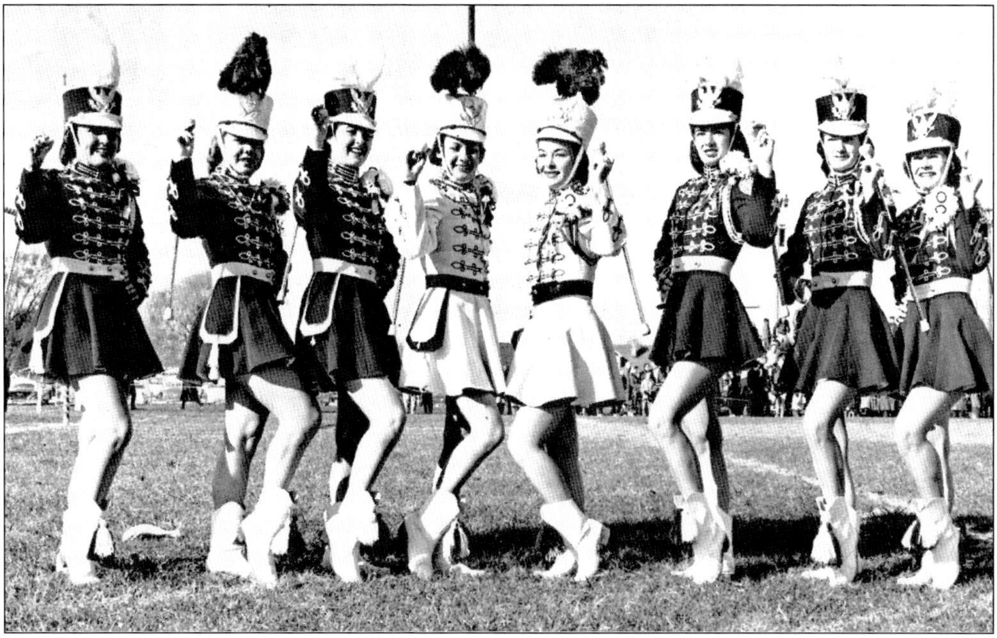

This 1959 picture shows Ocean City High School's drum majorettes. From left to right are Louise Stiles, band majorette Joyce Danner, Pat Kravitz, head majorette Sally Nania, head majorette Helen Benckert, Frannie Shaffer, Louise Baum, and Linda Smith.

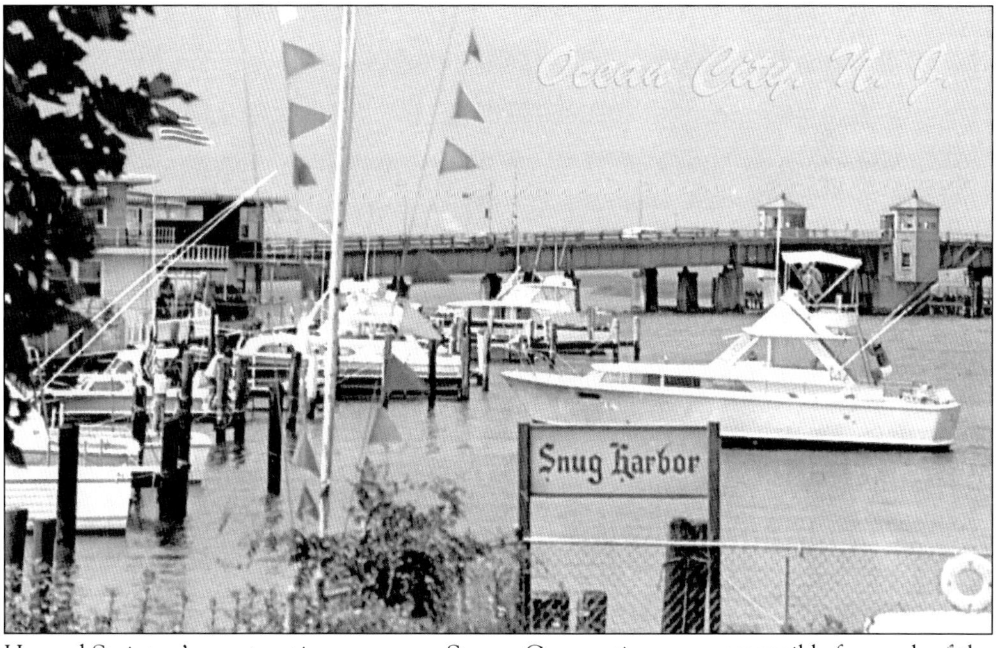

Howard Stainton's construction company, Stocco Corporation, was responsible for much of the building in Ocean City, including this lagoon, which they cut between Eighth and Ninth Streets and named Snug Harbor. The company also built motels, single-family homes, and apartments. Stainton liked to operate the company's dredge, the Dolphin, himself.

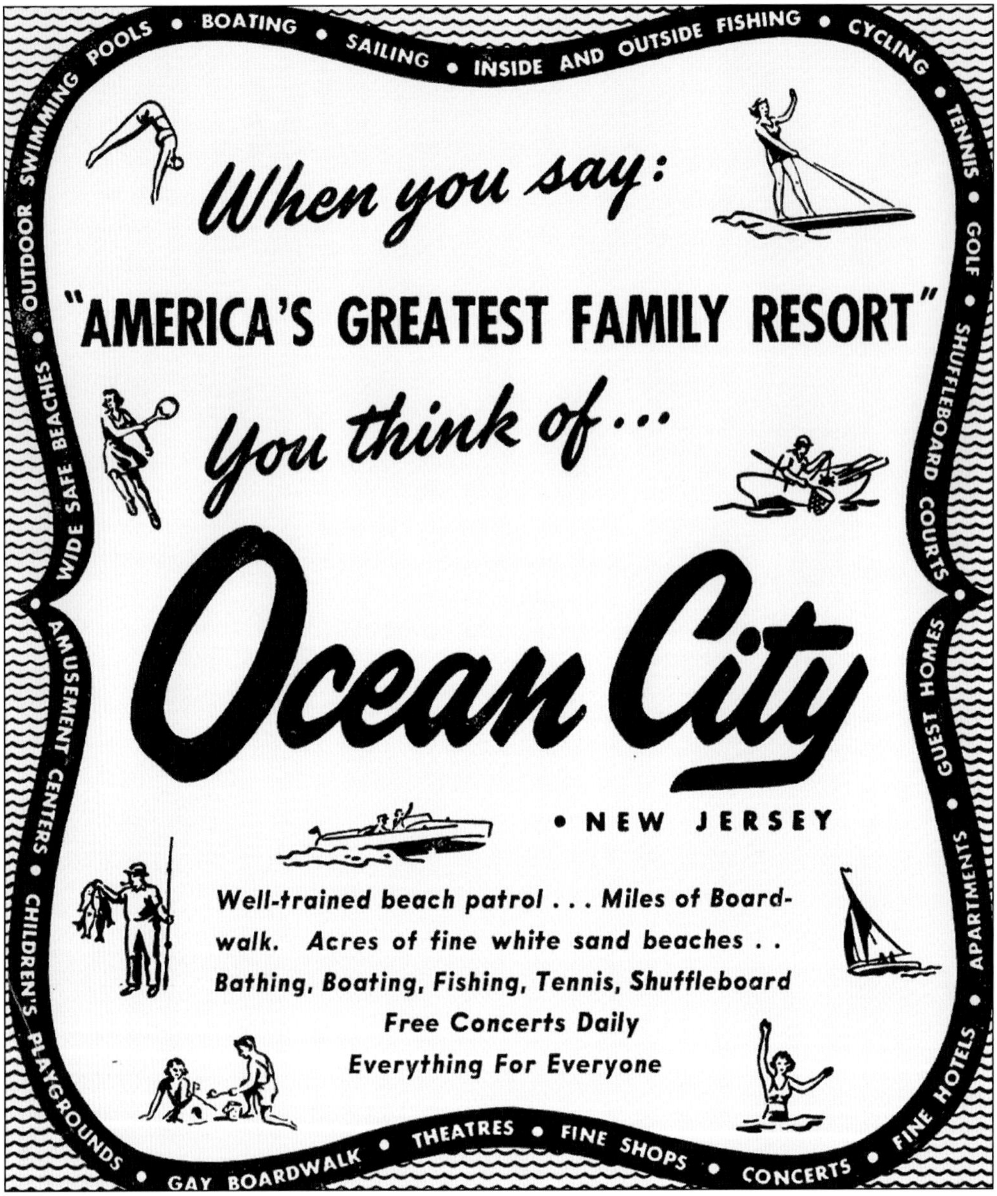

This advertisement was on the back page of Ocean City's 1959 *Official Vacation Guide*. The guide had information on hotels, motels, guesthouses, apartments, and cottages available for rent, as well as information about summer events.

Three

No Vacancy at Motels 1960–1964

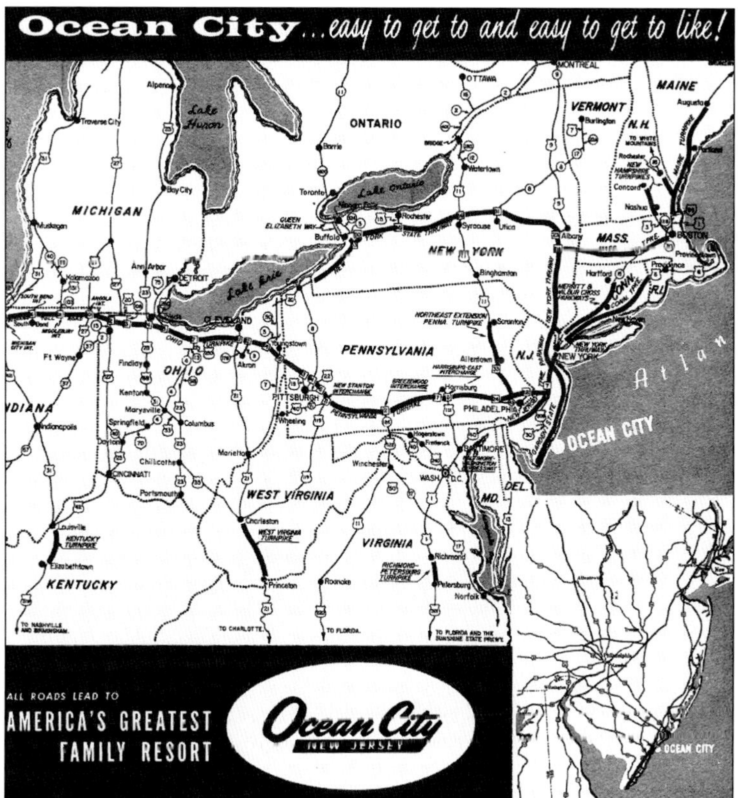

"Ocean City . . . easy to get to and easy to get to like!" was at the top of this map, a publicity piece put out by Ocean City's public relations department for the summer of 1960.

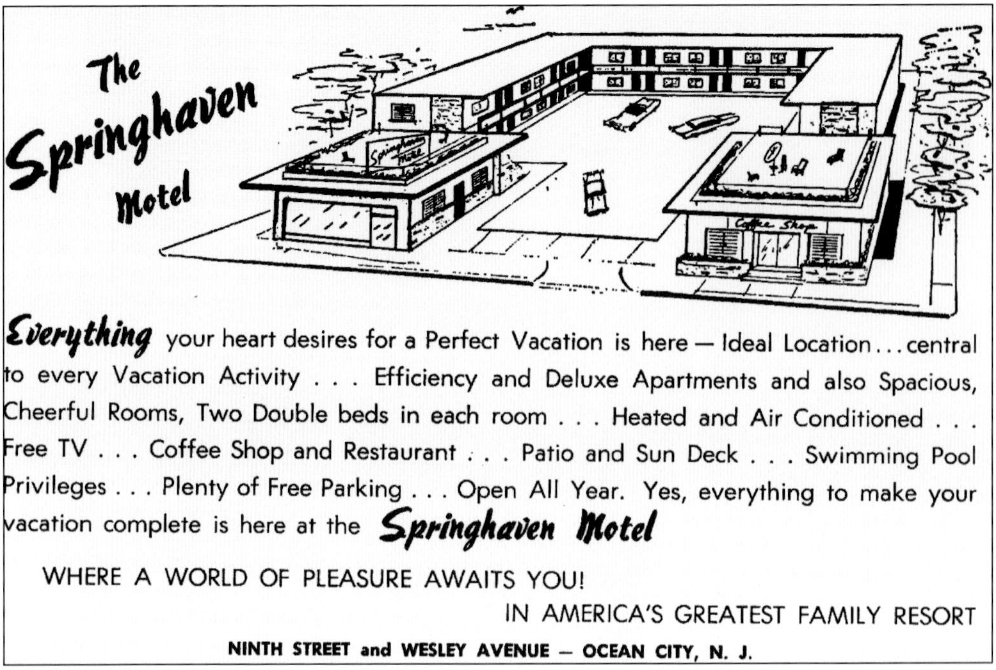

The Springhaven Motel at Ninth Street and Wesley Avenue put out this advertisement in 1961.

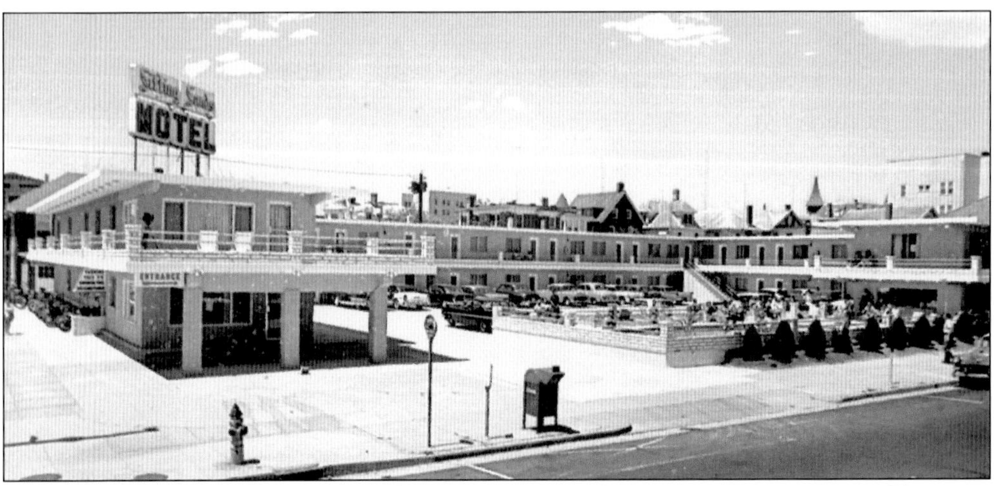

The Sifting Sands Motel on the corner of Ninth Street and Ocean Avenue was "A sparkling gem of modern architecture combining beauty and comfort." It offered a lounge room and sundeck, a snack bar, and free parking "at your door."

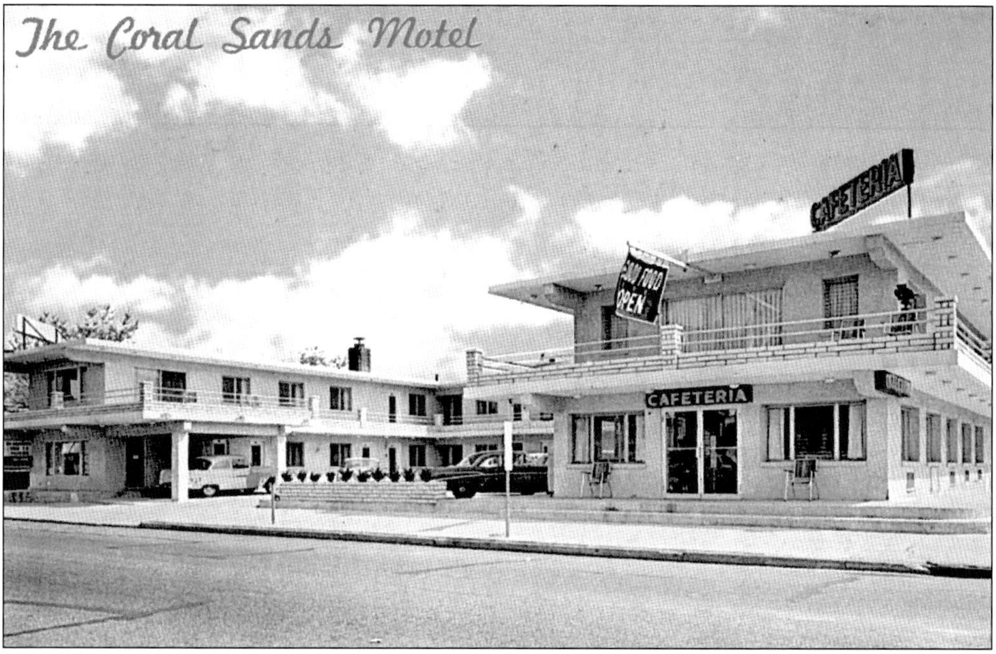

The Coral Sands Motel, on the corner of Ninth Street and Atlantic Avenue, was open all year. It advertised a "Glittering new cafeteria and dining room with quality food and courteous waitress service." It was owned and managed by Mary and Alexander Kazmarck, who also owned and managed the Sifting Sands.

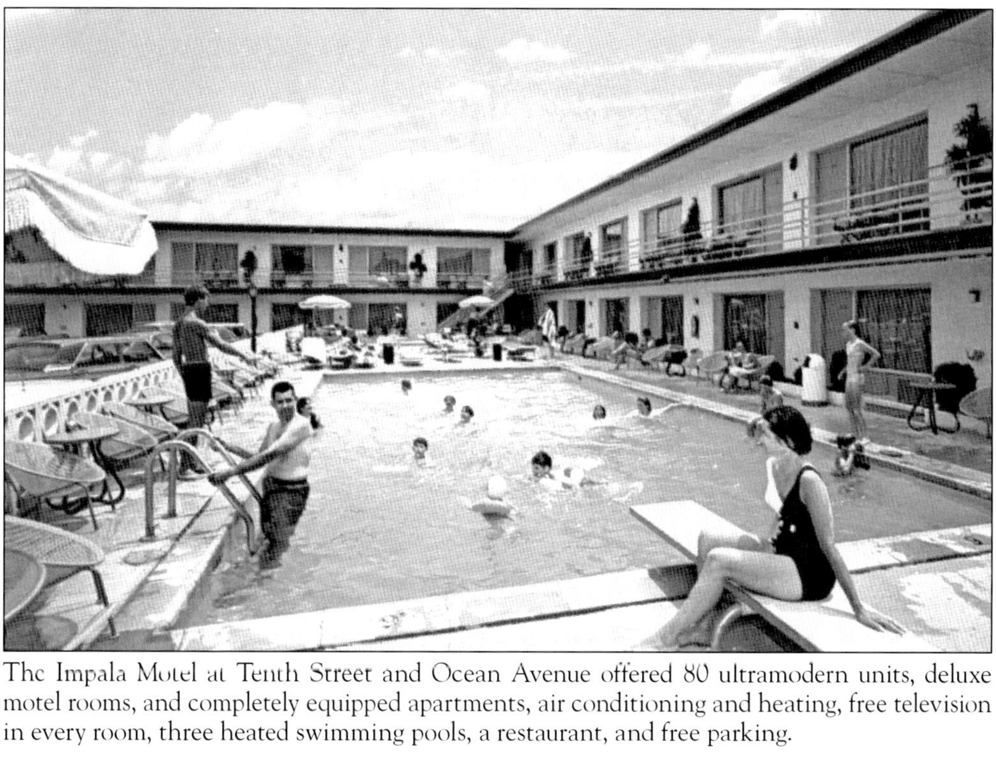

The Impala Motel at Tenth Street and Ocean Avenue offered 80 ultramodern units, deluxe motel rooms, and completely equipped apartments, air conditioning and heating, free television in every room, three heated swimming pools, a restaurant, and free parking.

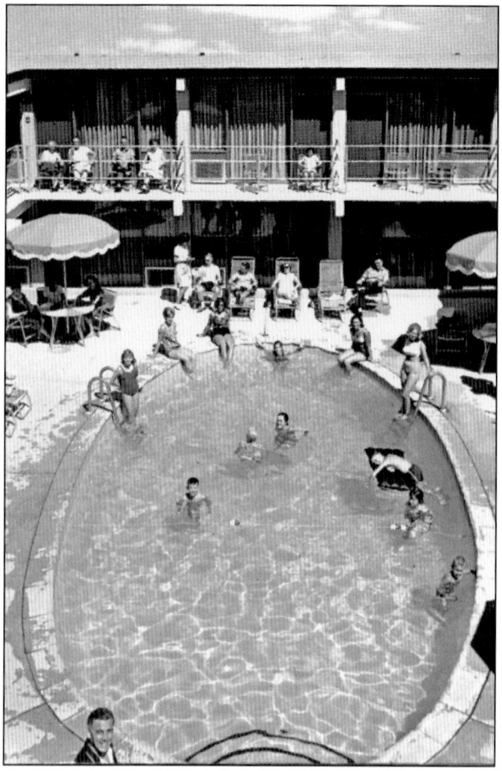

The Royal Crest Motel at Twelfth Street and Ocean Avenue advertised ceramic tile baths, wall-to-wall carpeting, television, a heated swimming pool, and individually controlled air conditioning and heat. It had 40 rooms for rent by the day or by the week.

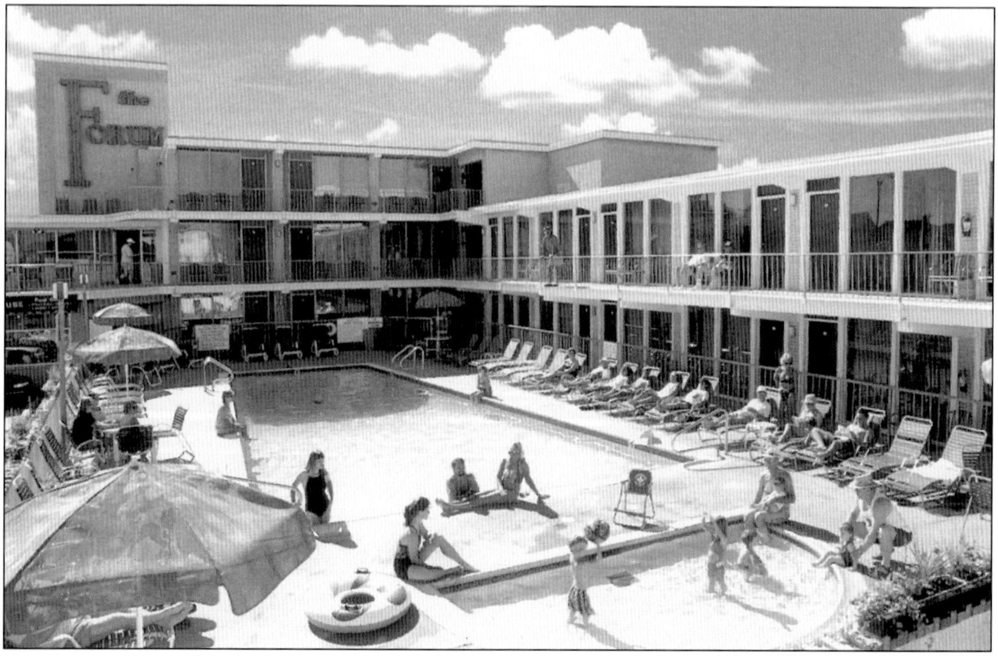

The Forum Motel at Eighth Street and Atlantic Avenue had a children's pool as well as one for adults, and advertised "Luxurious accommodations and perfect location, just one short block from the beach and boardwalk. Rooms and suites are spacious and beautifully decorated."

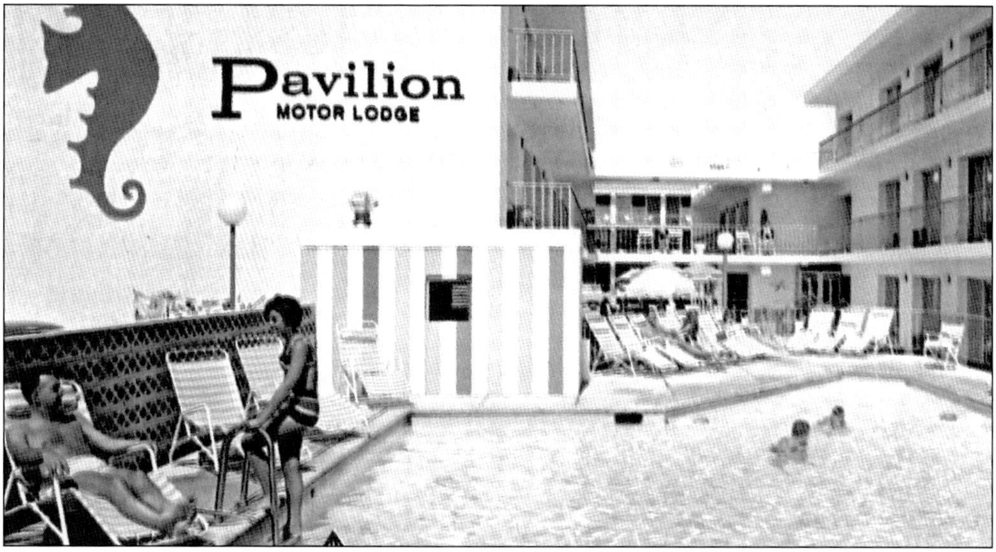

The Pavilion Motor Lodge at Eighth Street and Atlantic Avenue, "In the Heart of Ocean City," offered large, ultramodern rooms and two-bedroom apartments.

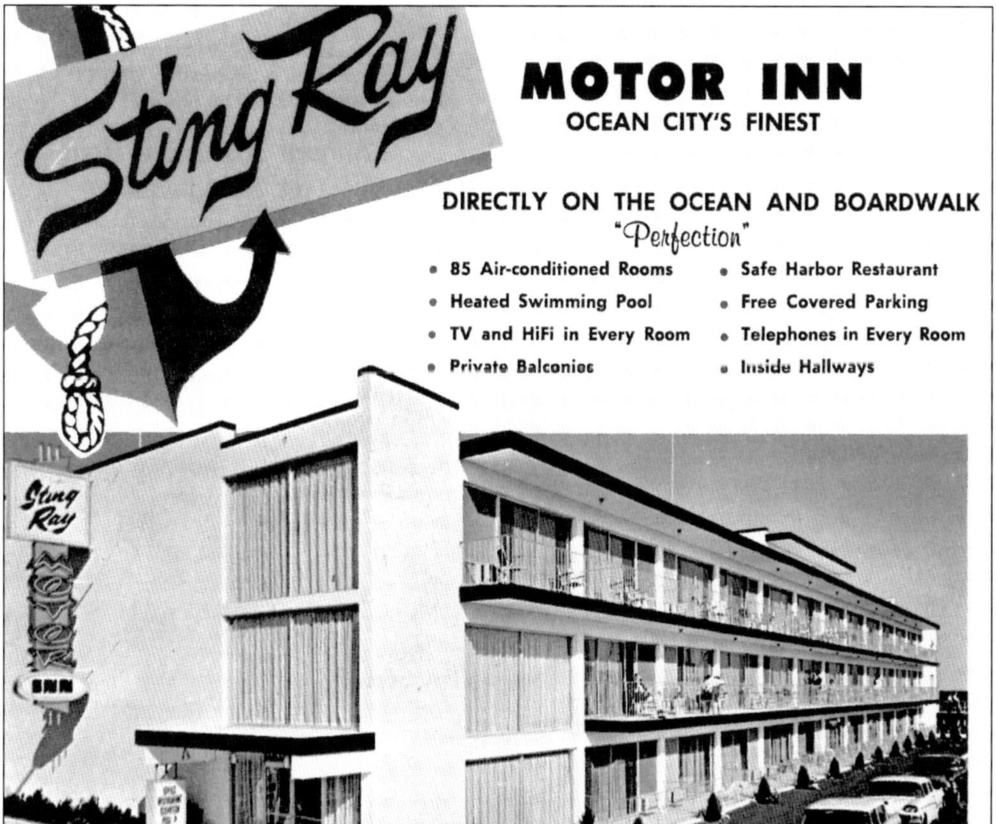

The Sting Ray Motor Inn, "Ocean City's Finest," at Thirteenth Street and Ocean Avenue, offered 85 air-conditioned rooms, the Safe Harbor restaurant, free covered parking, a telephone, television, and Hi-Fi in every room.

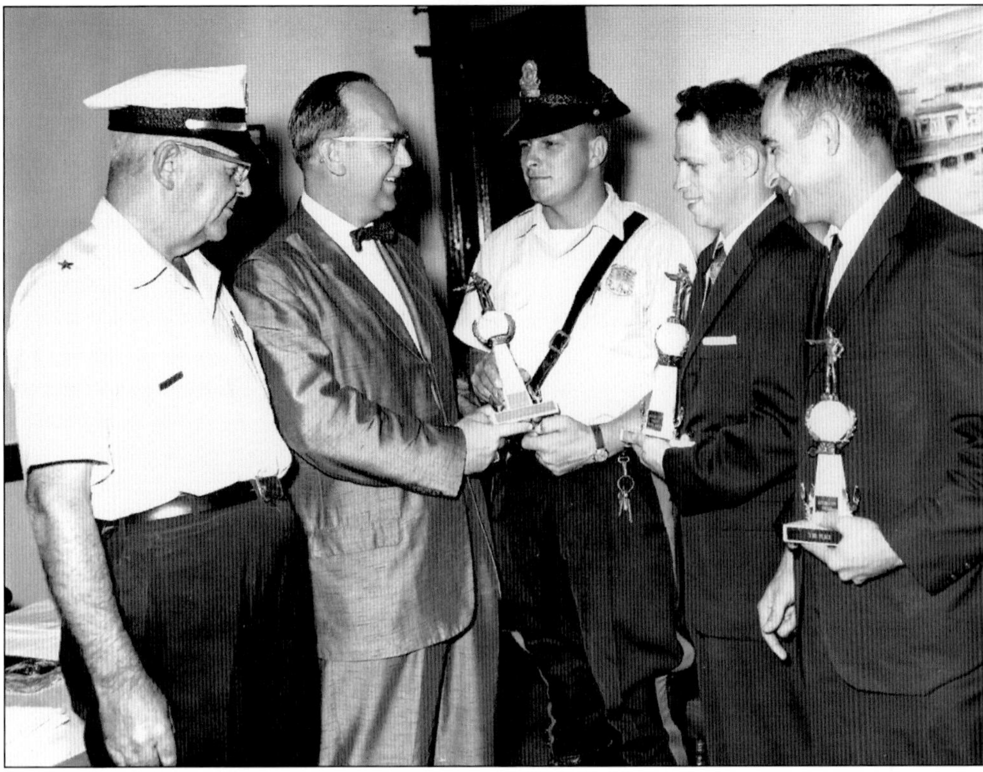

This photograph shows the 1960 police pistol championship winners and runner-up receiving their trophies. From left to right are Chief William H. Smith Jr. and Commissioner D. Allen Stretch presenting trophies to patrolman William Gannon, patrolman John Vanderpool, and detective Dominick Longo. In 1974, detective Longo was named chief of police.

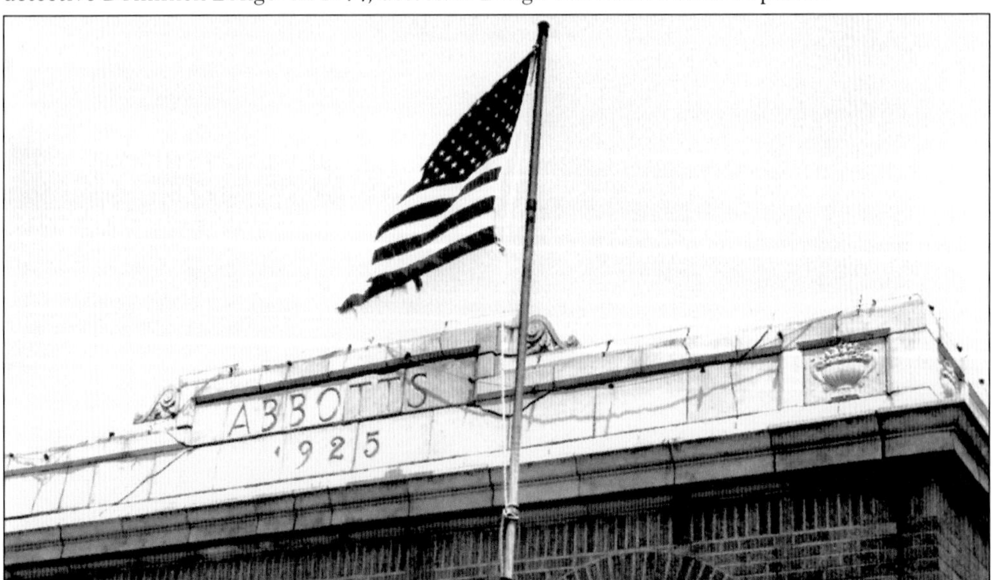

July 4, 1960, was the first time the 50-star flag was ever flown. This one is flying in front of the Abbots Dairy Building at Twelfth Street and Haven Avenue.

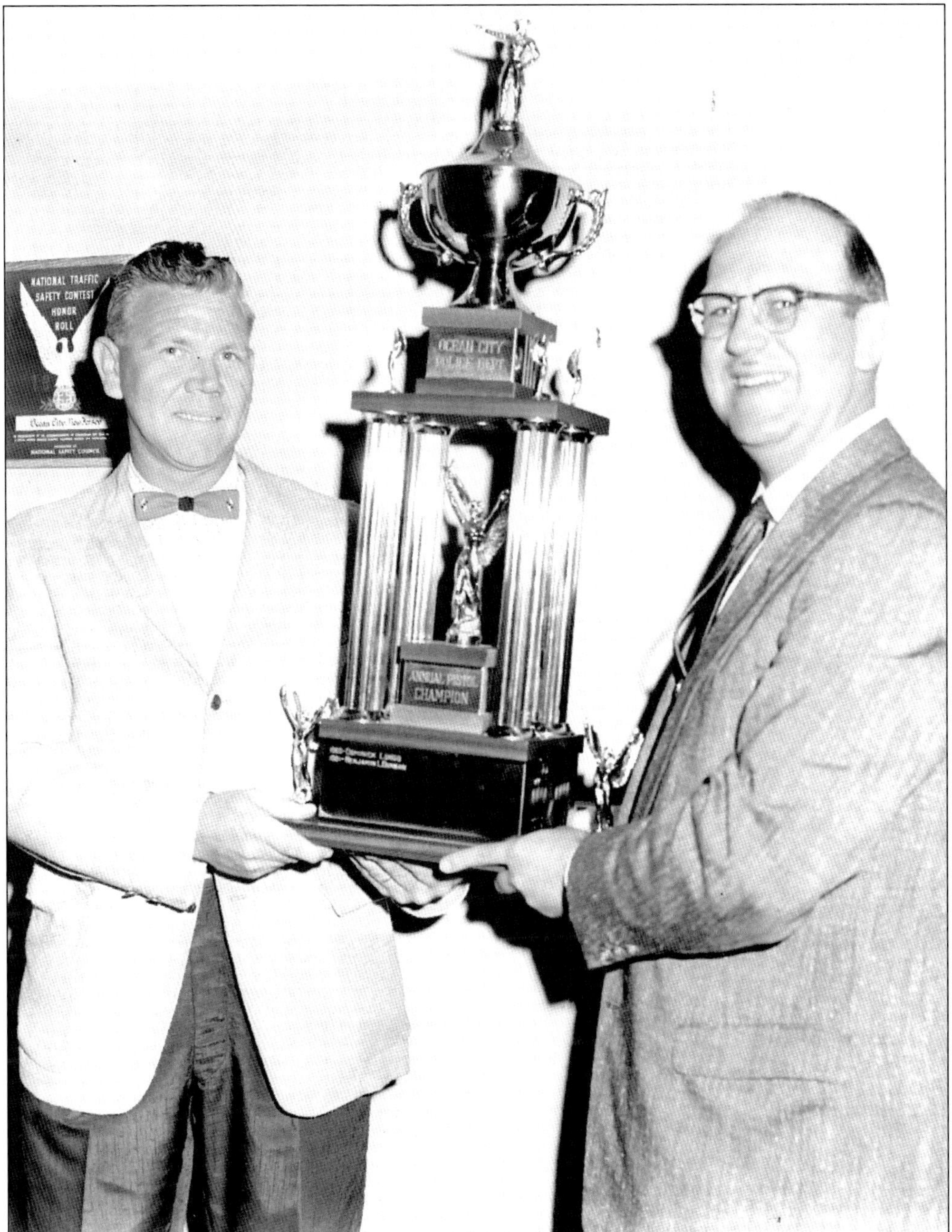

In this 1961 photograph, police captain Benjamin Dungan, left, receives his trophy as police pistol champion from director of public safety D. Allen Stretch. In 1965, Captain Dungan became Chief Dungan.

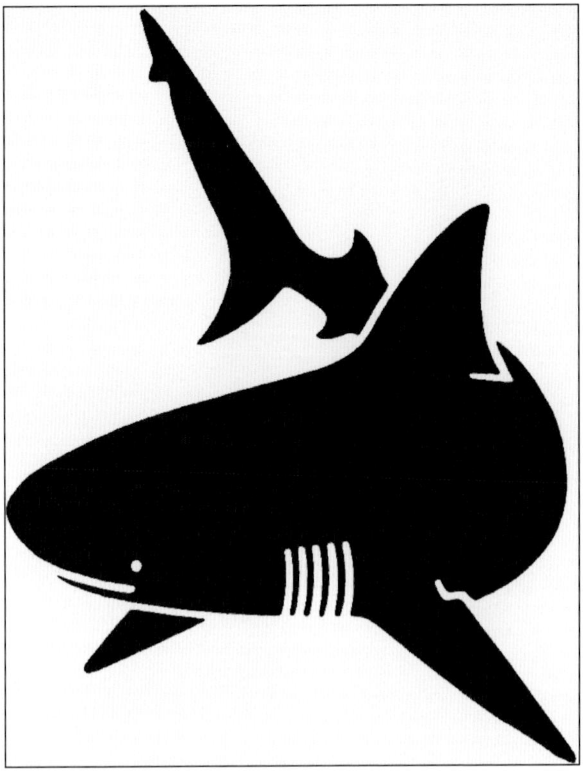

On August 25, 1960, a few days after a shark attacked a swimmer in Sea Girt, New Jersey, Ocean City public safety director D. Allen Stretch scoffed at the idea that sharks that were menacing bathers in North Jersey would find their way to South Jersey. Five days later, medical student Richard Chung was swimming a quarter-mile off the beach at Sixth Street when attacked by a shark. Two off-duty lifeguards, Larry Stedem and Richard Clune, quickly rowed to him, pulled him into their boat, and raced to the beach. He was taken to Shore Memorial Hospital in Somers Point where surgeons operated and were able to save his leg. This story made national news and was even written up in the July 1961 *Reader's Digest*.

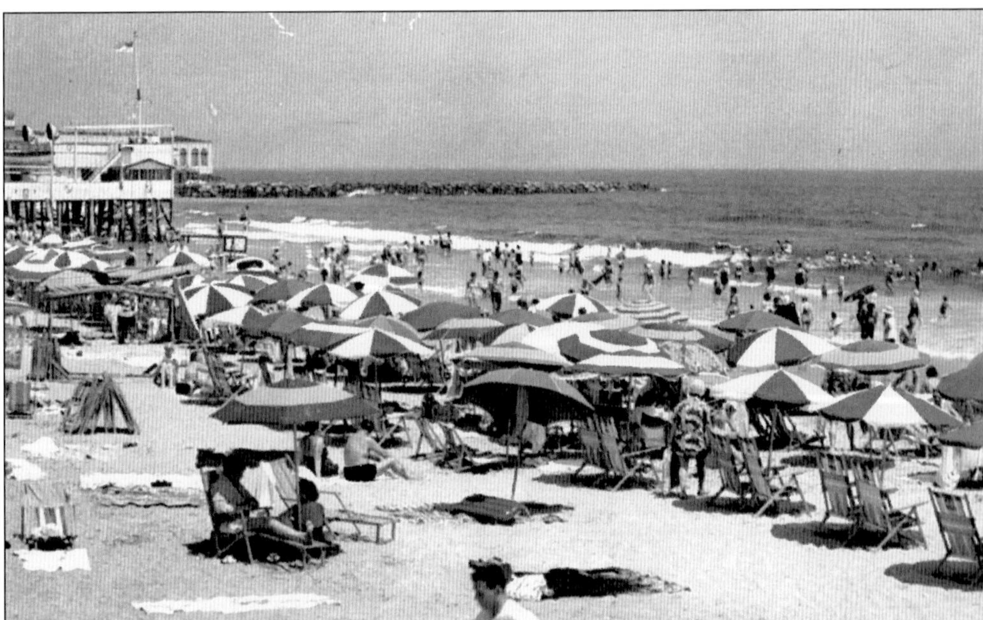

The shark attack of 1960 did not thin the crowds on the beaches or in the ocean during the summer of 1961.

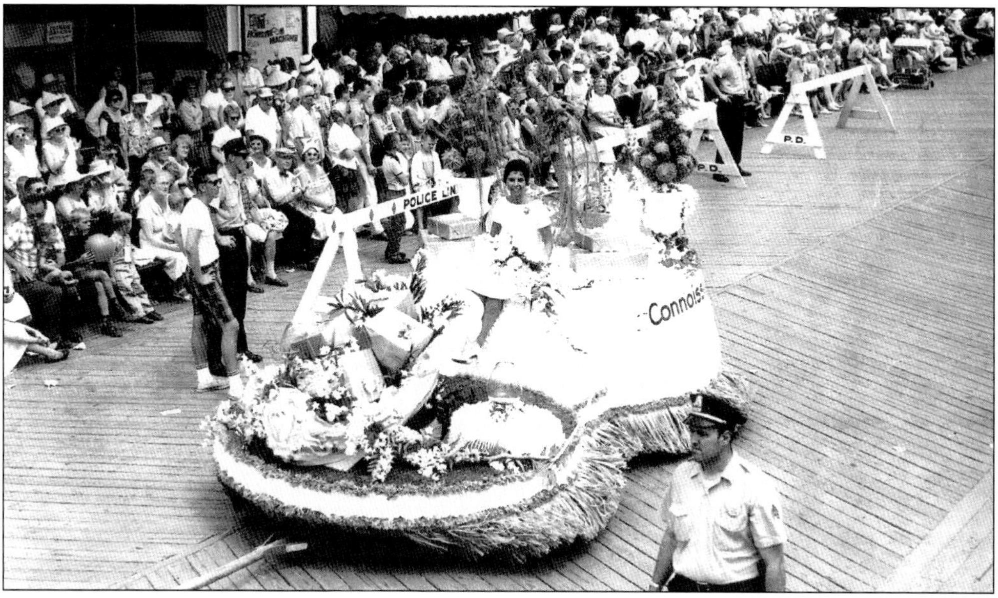

During the summer of 1956, Jim Penland opened the Connoisseur Shop in the landmark Golden Galleon Building on the boardwalk between Eleventh and Twelfth Streets. A creative and talented man, Penland loved his adopted city and participated in many activities. In 1961, he entered this float advertising his shop in the baby parade.

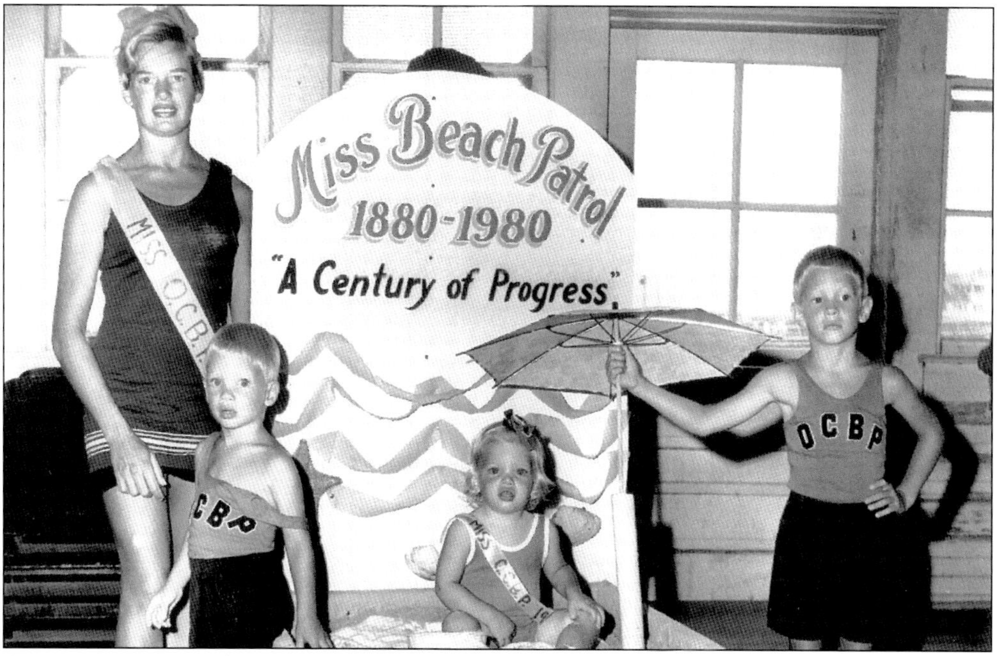

On August 9, 1962, the Raab family, from left to right, Mother Dottie, Gary, Diane, and Jerry, took a look into the future with this prize-winning float in the baby parade. The baby parade, one of the most colorful and entertaining events of the summer season, was held each year on the boardwalk on the second Thursday in August. Spectators lined the boardwalk to enjoy the floats and marching bands. Prizes were awarded in many categories, and each child entered would receive a small trophy or ribbon.

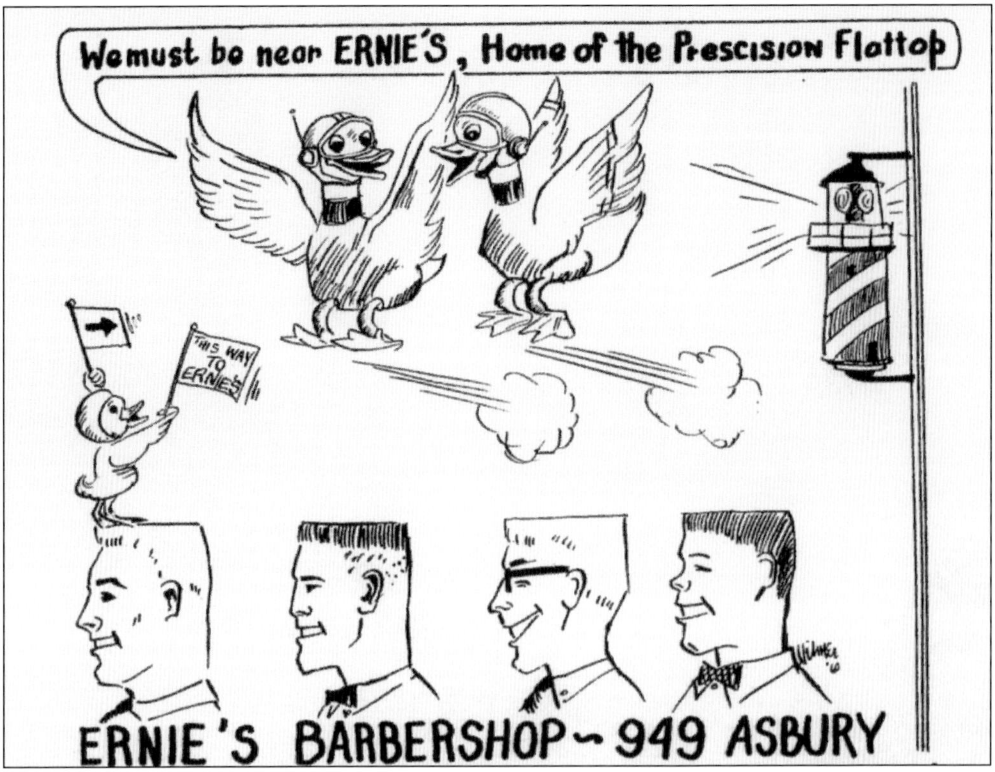

The Beatles had not yet arrived, and the flat top hair style was still in vogue when Ernie's Barbershop at 949 Asbury Avenue placed this advertisement in the 1961 *Ocean City Weekly Guide*.

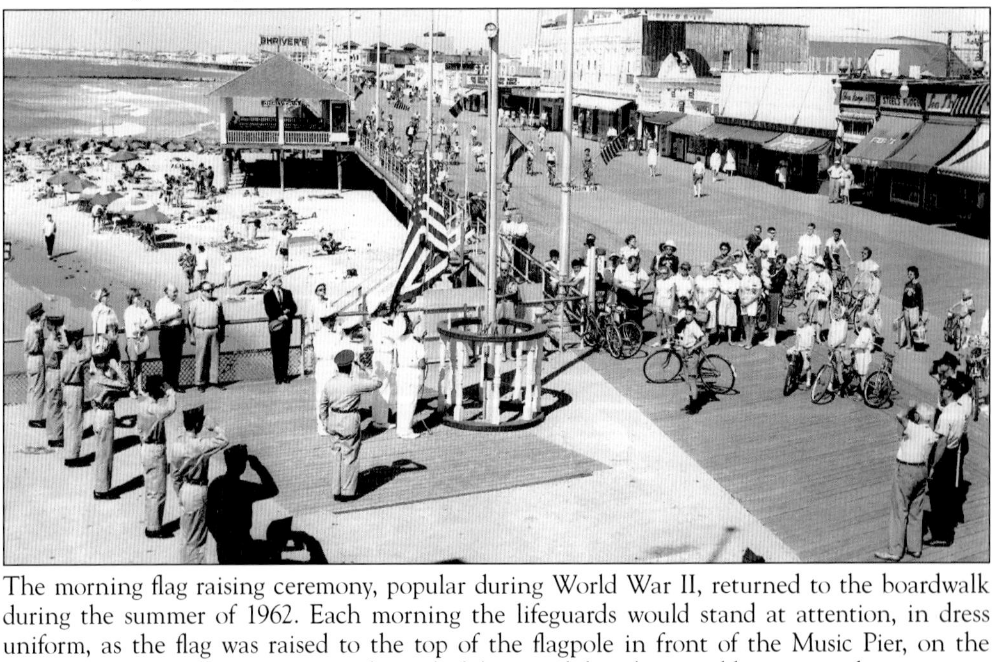
The morning flag raising ceremony, popular during World War II, returned to the boardwalk during the summer of 1962. Each morning the lifeguards would stand at attention, in dress uniform, as the flag was raised to the top of the flagpole in front of the Music Pier, on the boardwalk at Moorlyn Terrace. At the end of their workday, they would again stand at attention as the flag was lowered.

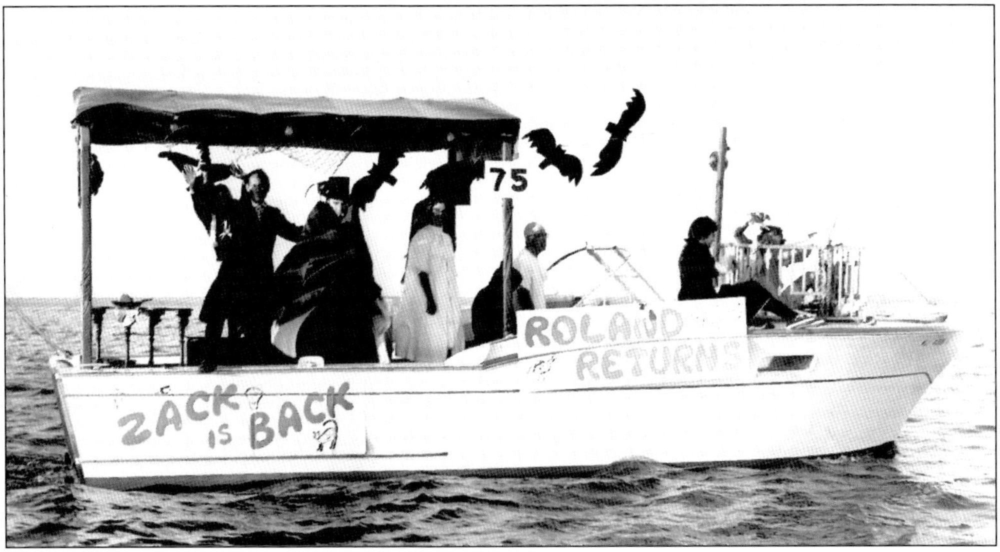

The Derr family entered this award-winning float in the 1962 Night in Venice parade. Each year in July, on a Saturday evening partly determined by the tides, the city held its famous boat parade, Night in Venice. The decorated boats started from the Ocean City Yacht Club on the bay off Battersea Road in the north end of town and went south, in and out of the lagoons. Prizes were offered in many categories.

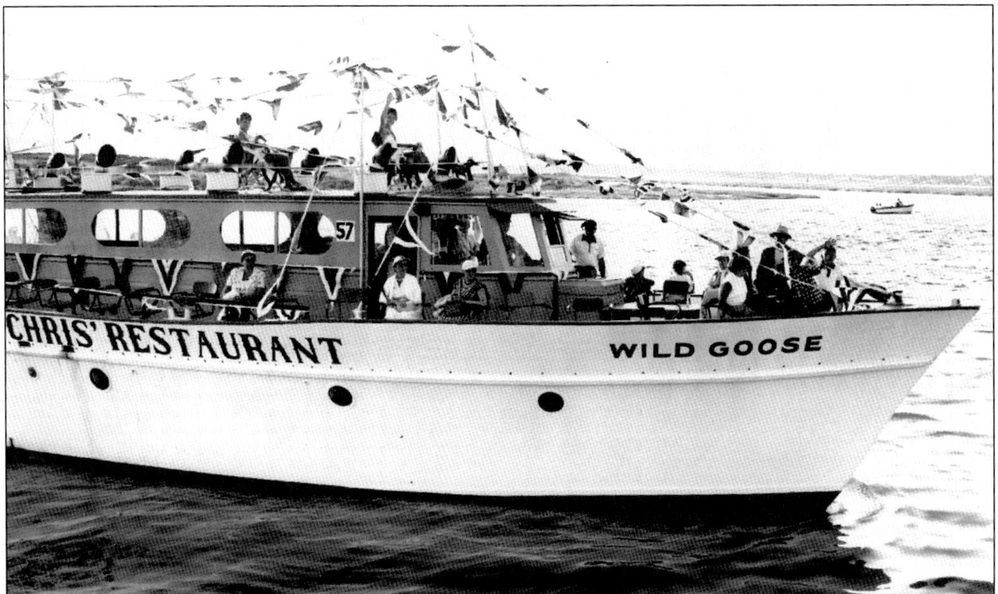

Chris' Seafood Restaurant and Seafood Market on the bayfront near Ninth Street offered not only great seafood, but also rides on Chris Montagna's fleet of pleasure boats. He offered half-day trips on the *Wild Goose*.

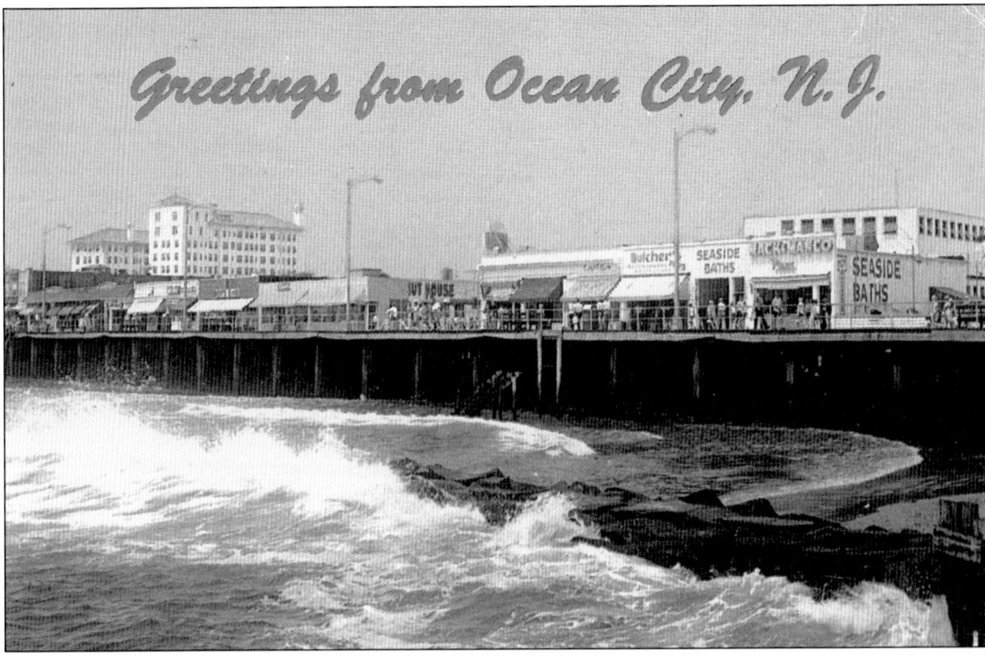

The Manco family started Mack and Manco's Pizza at 914 Boardwalk in 1956. By the time they opened their second shop five years later at 758 Boardwalk, they had become an Ocean City tradition.

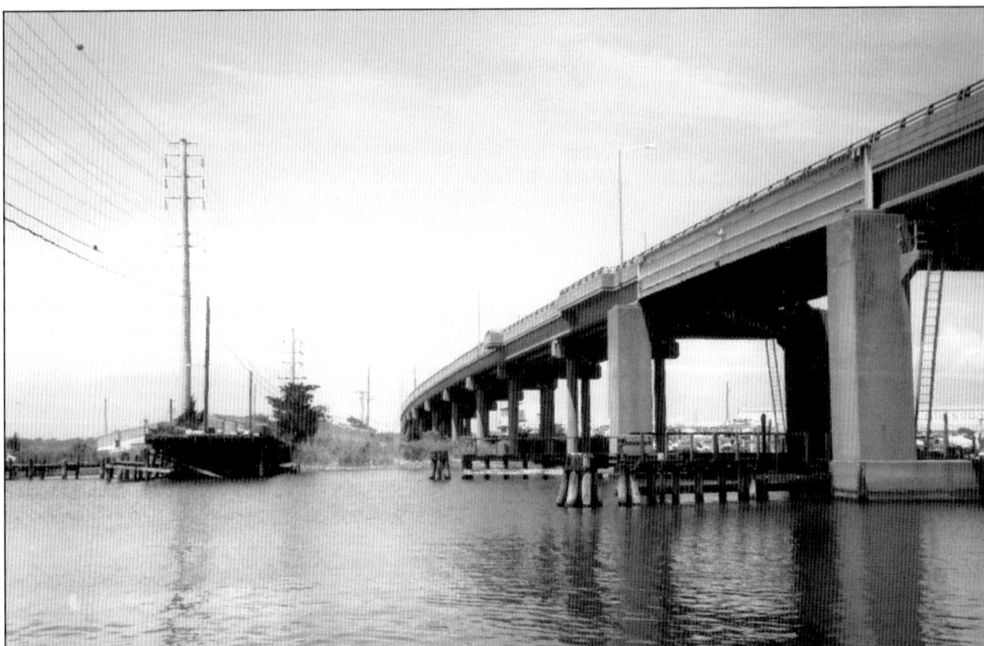

On July 4, 1962, the new $1,243,000 Roosevelt Boulevard Bridge connecting Ocean City with Marmora at Thirty-fourth Street opened. Construction began in November 1960 on the 1,625-foot span. The cost of the high level bridge was paid by the county and federal governments.

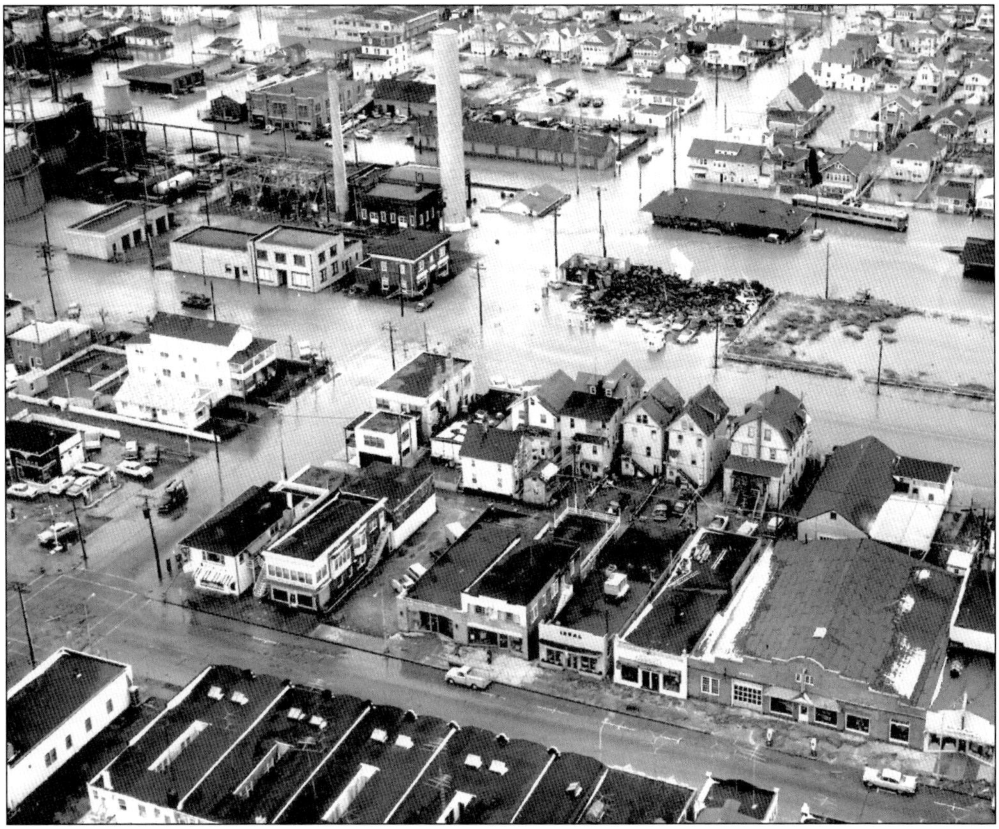

The most disastrous storm in Ocean City's history struck on March 6, 1962, and raged unabated for two days. Fortunately there were no lives lost, although the property damage was enormous. Most of the boardwalk and the fishing piers were washed away. The central business district was flooded, and most stores and businesses sustained damage. This photograph is from Tenth Street and West Avenue looking toward the bay.

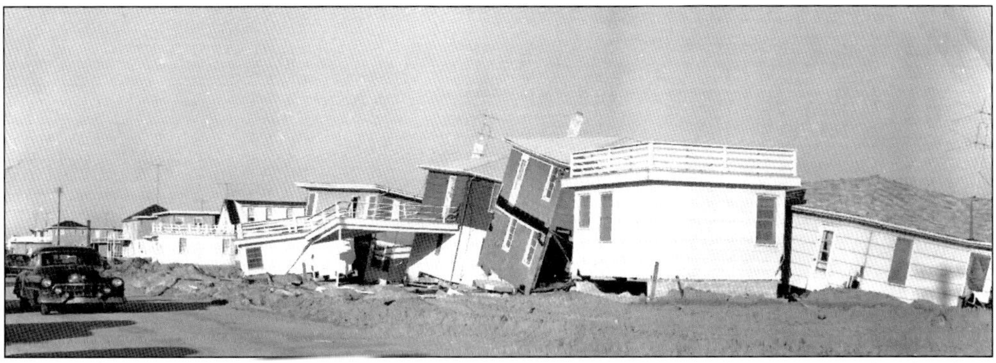

During the March 6, 1962, storm, the area south of Thirty-fourth Street was hit hardest. Hundreds of houses were so badly damaged that they had to be demolished.

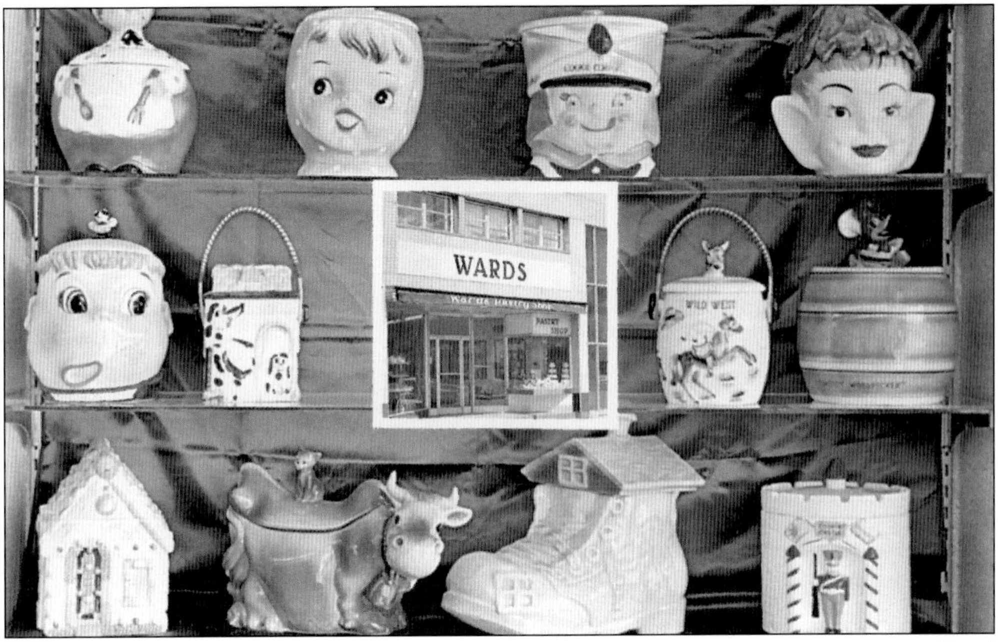

In 1963, Charles and John Hohman, owners of Wards Pastry at 724–726 Asbury Avenue, offered their patrons free parking at 727 West Avenue and a look at their famous cookie jar display, "The largest known collection of cookie jars." They also offered delicious cakes, cookies, pies, and pastries.

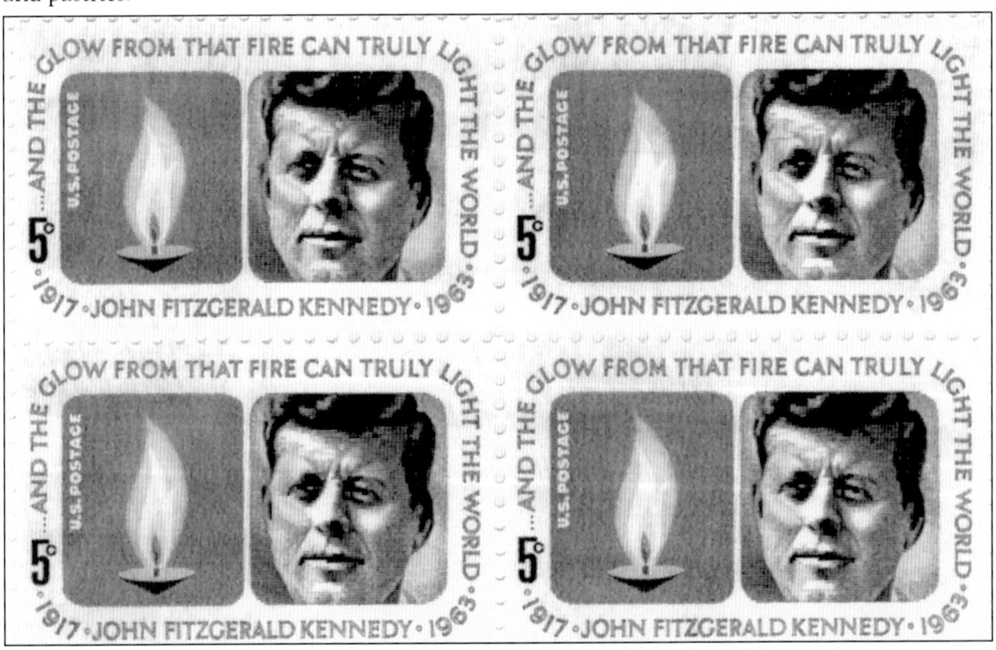

This stamp, issued as a memorial tribute to the 35th president of the United States, who was assassinated on November 22, 1963, was released on May 29, 1964, the late president's 47th birthday. Commissioner D. Allen Stretch, head of the Democratic Party in Ocean City, often reminisced about the time he had greeted Sen. John F. Kennedy when the presidential hopeful arrived in Atlantic City in 1960.

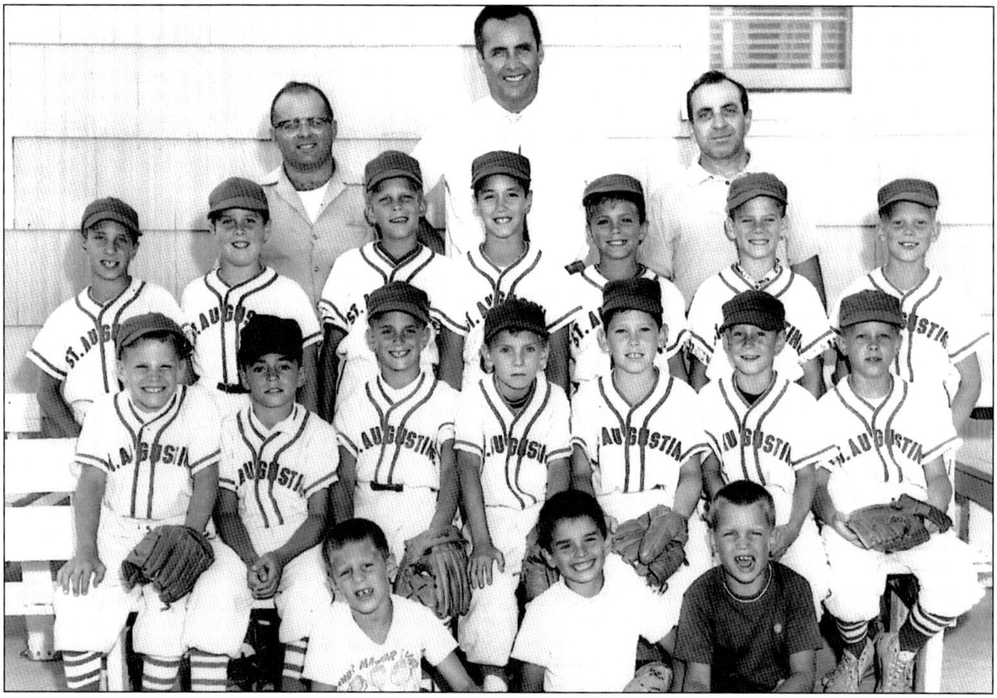

This photograph of an Ocean City junior baseball team sponsored by St Augustine's Church was taken in 1964. Pictured left to right are (first row) Michael Sannino, Carmen Costanzo, and Scott Vanderslice; (second row) John Andrews, Joe Allegretto, Dave Andrews, Jim Marshall, George Duncan, Dave Clunn, and John Vanderpool; (third row) Frank Sannino, Larry Pardee, Harry Vanderslice, Joe Florentine, Bill Lefleur, Steve Kyle, and Don Johnson; (fourth row) coach Naz Costanzo, coach Harry Vanderslice, and coach Frank Sannino.

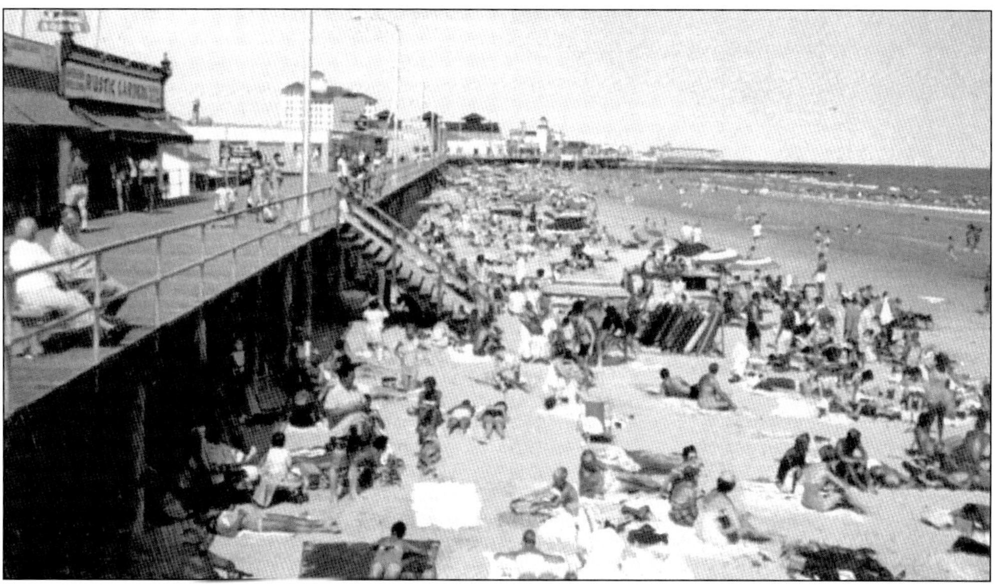

When the Drifters' recording of "Under the Boardwalk" hit number four on the billboard charts during the summer of 1964, everyone in Ocean City thought the song had been written for them.

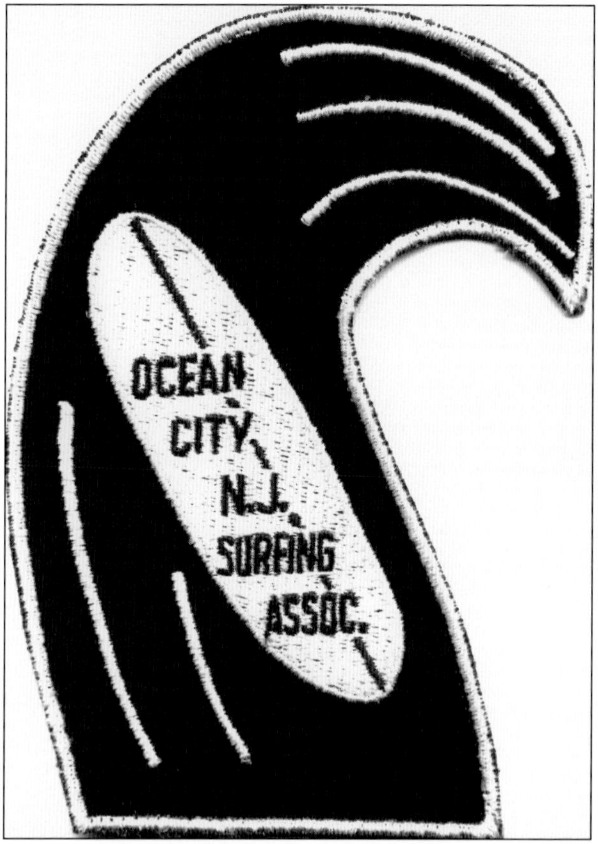

T. John Carey and recreation director Donald M. Pileggi founded the Ocean City Surfing Association in 1963. Carey had been the national champion in surfboard rescue in 1935 and 1936, when he was an Ocean City lifeguard, and wanted to bring the sport to the youth of Ocean City.

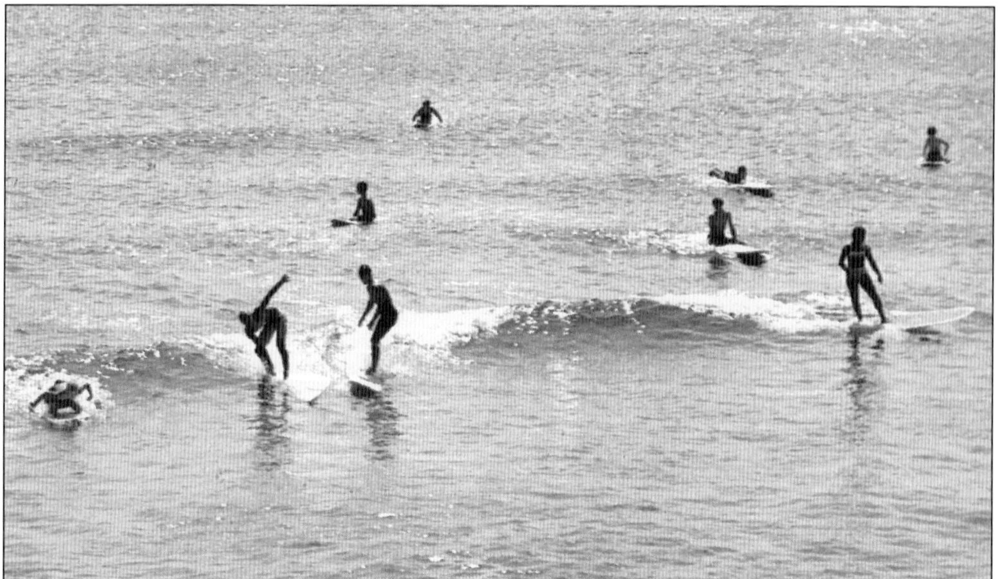

T. John Carey taught free training classes for Ocean City surfboarders during the summer of 1964 off the Fourteenth Street beach in front of Bob's Grill. Those on the beach could hear the Beach Boys singing "Surfin' U.S.A."—the music coming from the restaurant!

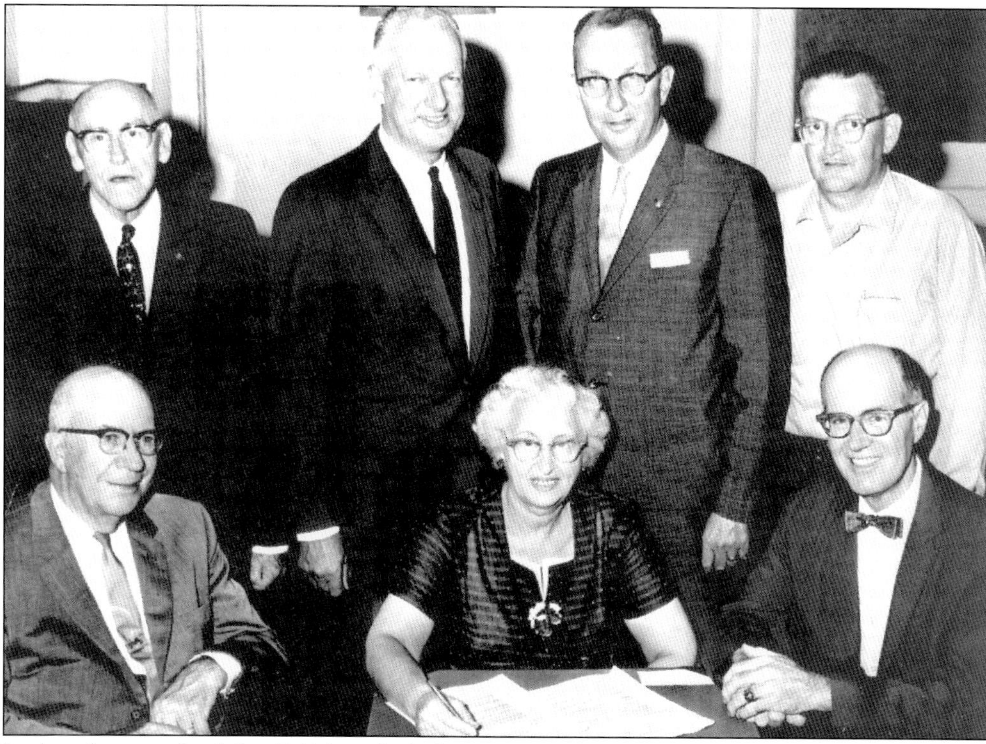

In this photograph of the 1964 board of education are, from left to right, (first row) Dr. Herschel Pettit, secretary of the board Alice Garretson, and Floyd W. Townsend; (second row) Dr. Thornley Hughes, Bruce P. Dimon, superintendent of schools Dr. Charles B. Pierce, and Herbert Brownlee.

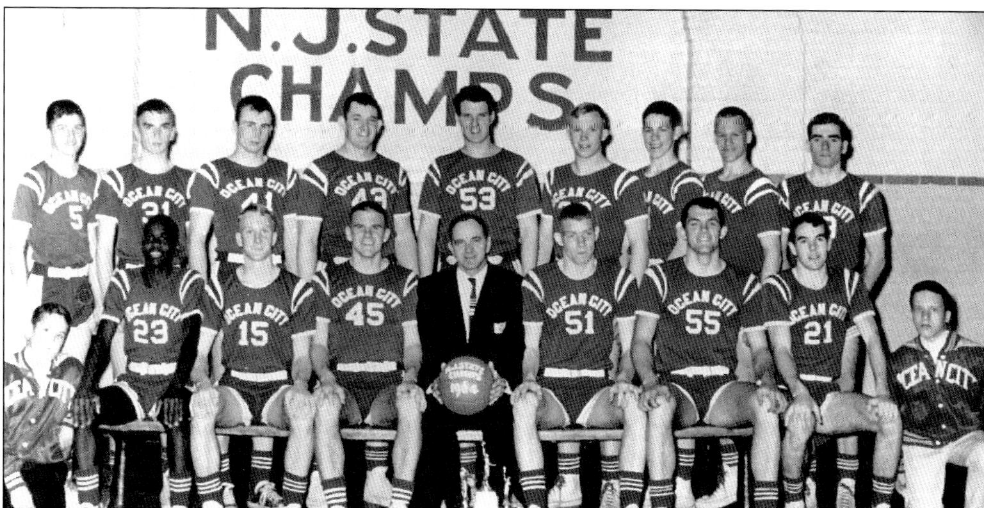

This is a photograph of Ocean City High School's 1964 state championship basketball team. From left to right are (first row) manager Mark Graham, Barry Banks, Randy Fox, captain John Cranston, coach Fred "Dixie" Howell, Ed McClain, Bill Haynes, John Laudenslager, and manager Fred Moyer; (second row) Ricky Howell, John Gleason, Craig French, Jim Wimberg, Dave Mazzoni, Don Swan, John Steumpfig, Ronnie Fox, and Ken Holland.

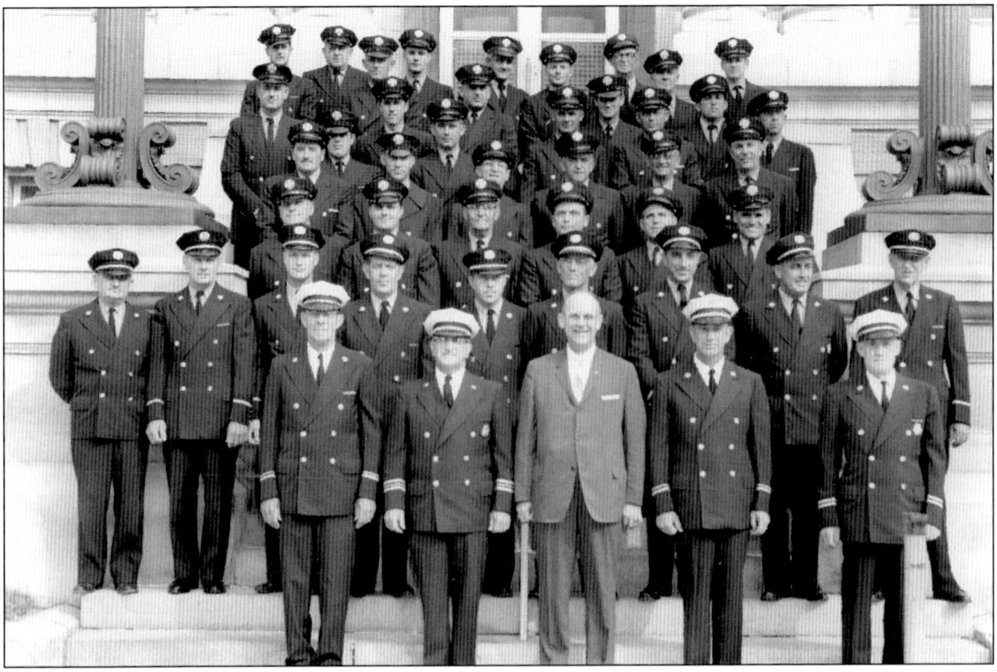

In this 1964 picture of the fire department, Chief Ferdinand A. Taccarino is standing left of Commissioner D. Allen Stretch (in suit).

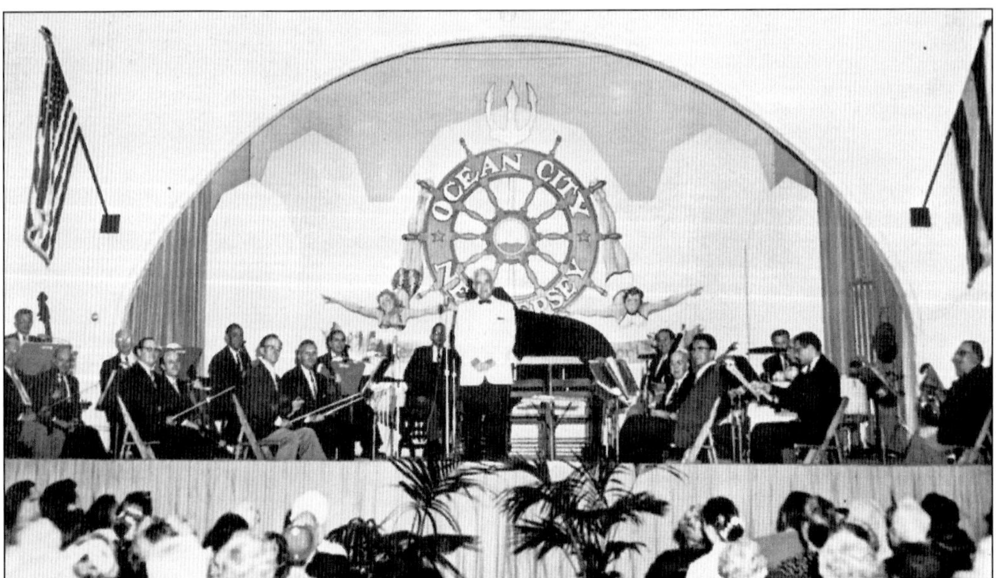

Clarence Fuhrman returned for his 18th season conducting the Ocean City Municipal Orchestra in 1964. The orchestra performed nightly concerts in the Music Pier on the boardwalk during the summer season. The concerts were free to the public.

Ocean City native Gay Talese began his writing career when he was a student at Ocean City High School, writing a column called "Sportopics" for the local newspaper, the *Sentinel-Ledger*. He left the newspaper to major in journalism at the University of Alabama. Talese later wrote for the *New York Times* and for *Esquire* magazine and has authored eight books.

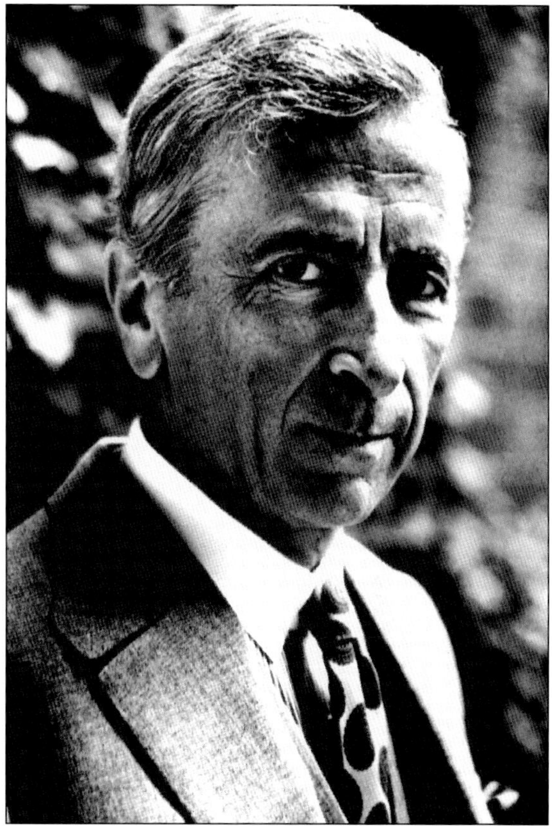

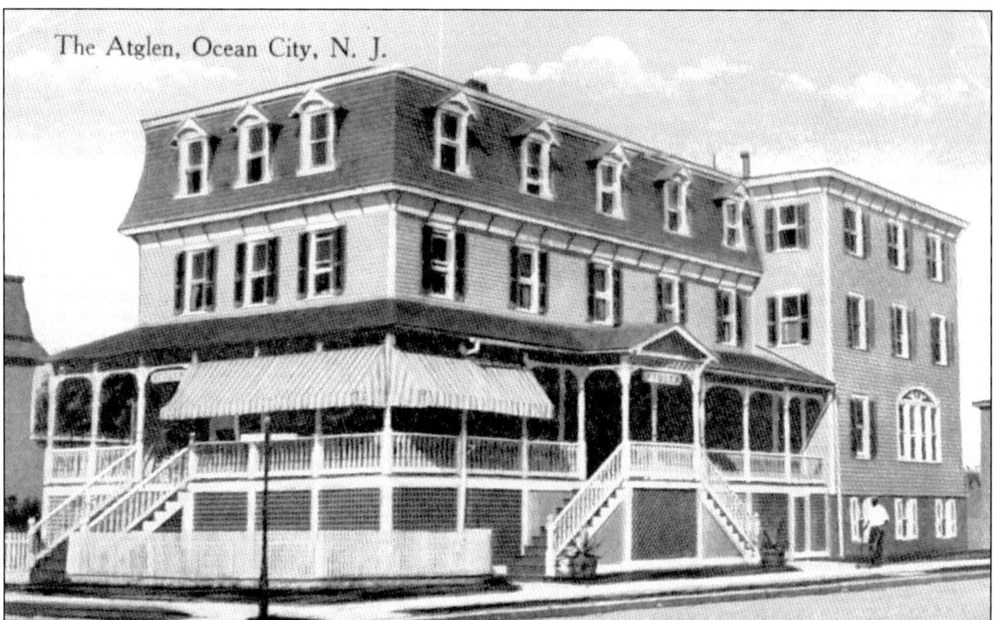

The Surf Hotel, called the Atglen when it was built in 1897, was demolished in 1964 after it was heavily damaged by fire. It stood at Ninth Street and Central Avenue.

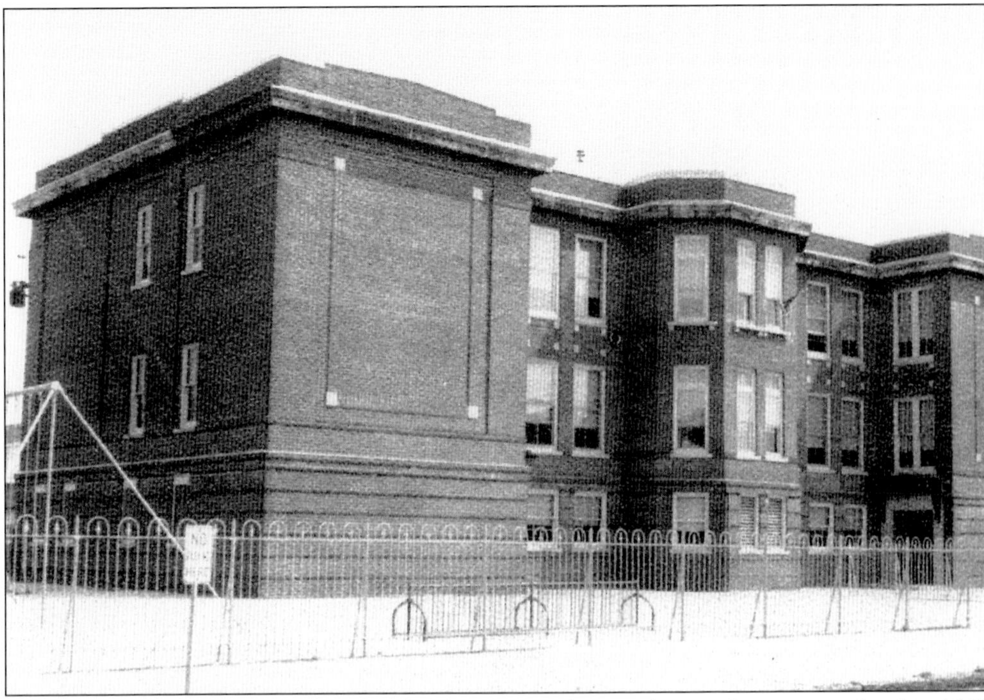

The Wesley Avenue School at 409 Wesley Avenue was last used as an elementary school in 1965. It then housed the Ocean City Creative Arts Center and the Ocean City Historical Museum.

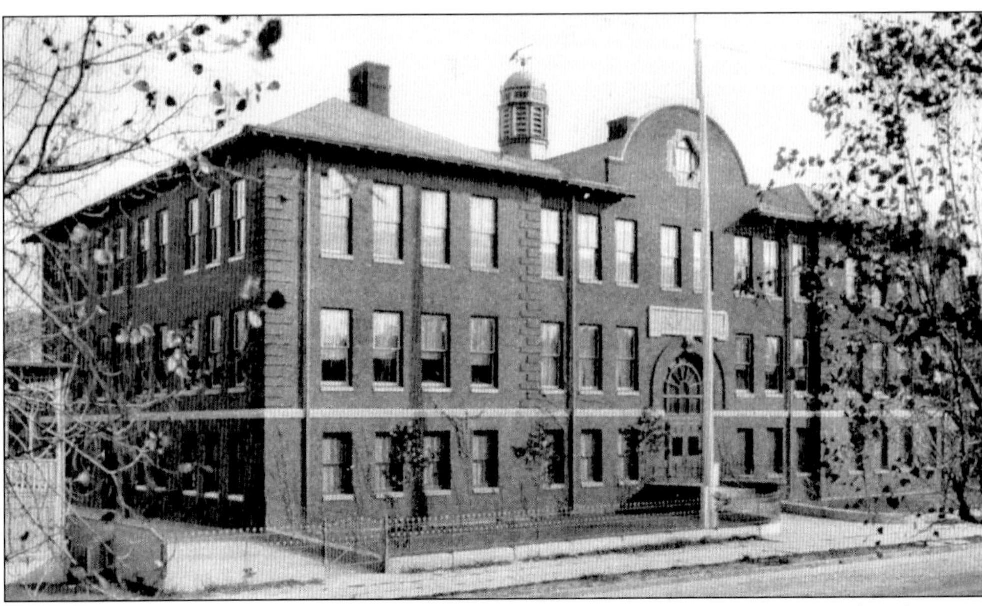

The Central Avenue School at 835 Central Avenue became the police department headquarters when it was no longer needed as an elementary school.

Four

Ocean City Prospers 1965–1969

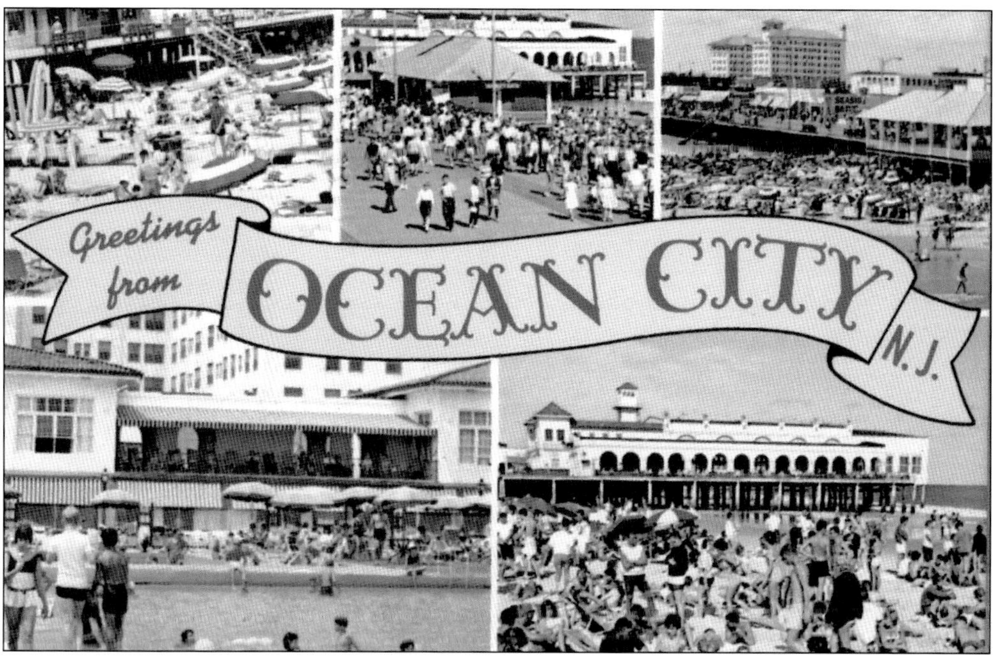

These scenes of the crowds on the beach, boardwalk, and Flanders Hotel pool are similar to many taken during the 1960s.

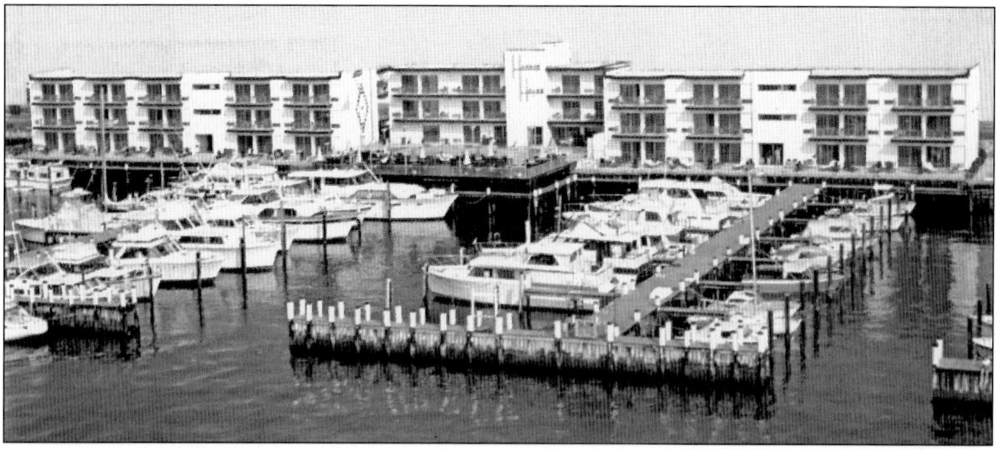

Opened in 1965, the Harbor House Motel and Marina, at Second Street on the bay, was the first motel built on the bay. It advertised "A unique motel and marina with deluxe bay front air conditioned and heated units, heated swimming pool and children's wading pool, shuffleboard courts, elevator, coffee shop and snack bar." It also had 150 boat slips available for rent and a bait and tackle shop.

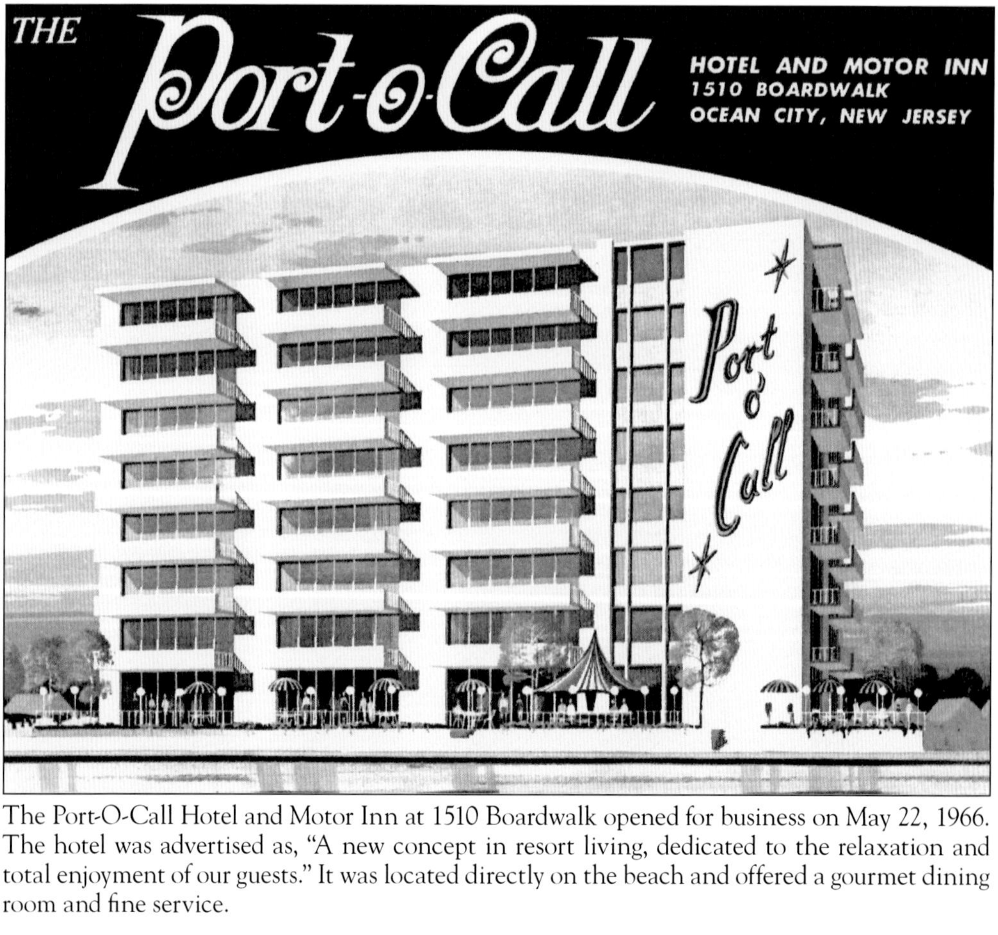

The Port-O-Call Hotel and Motor Inn at 1510 Boardwalk opened for business on May 22, 1966. The hotel was advertised as, "A new concept in resort living, dedicated to the relaxation and total enjoyment of our guests." It was located directly on the beach and offered a gourmet dining room and fine service.

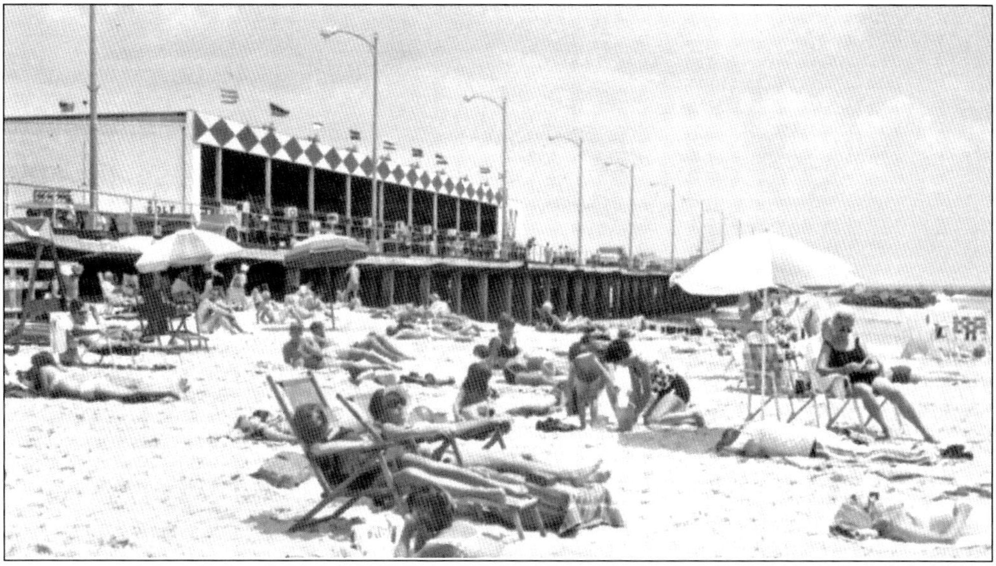

On June 12, 1965, Wonderland, a modern and colorful family amusement center, opened at Sixth Street and the boardwalk. The arcade type building was designed to accommodate a monorail ride and 10 other rides under a roof. The amusement center was owned and operated by Roy Gillian. His father, David Gillian, had opened the Fun Deck Amusement Center at Plymouth Place and the boardwalk in 1930.

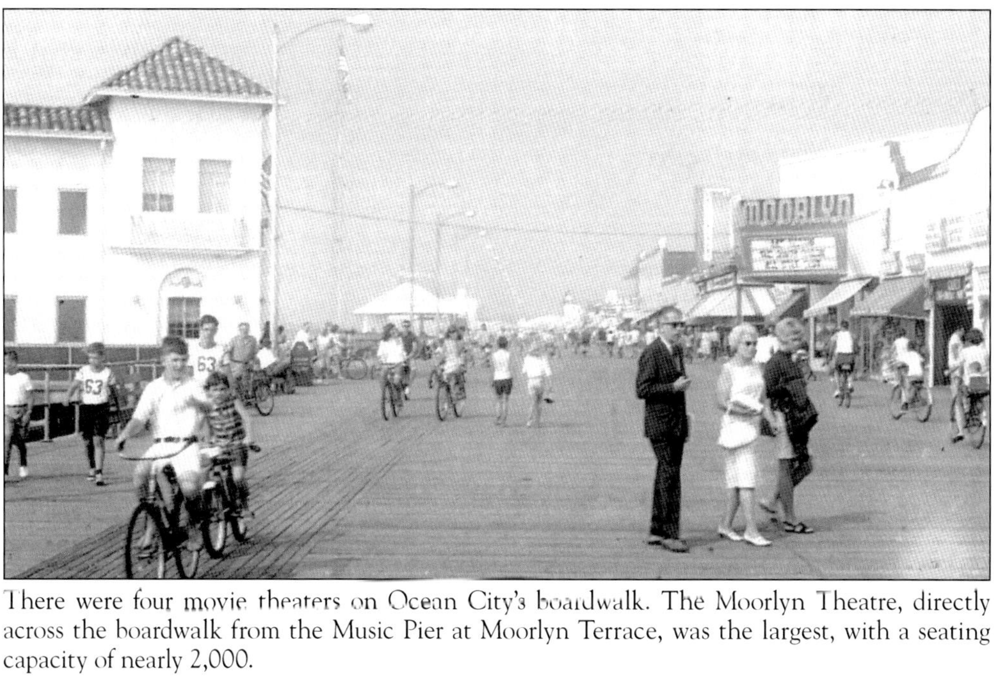

There were four movie theaters on Ocean City's boardwalk. The Moorlyn Theatre, directly across the boardwalk from the Music Pier at Moorlyn Terrace, was the largest, with a seating capacity of nearly 2,000.

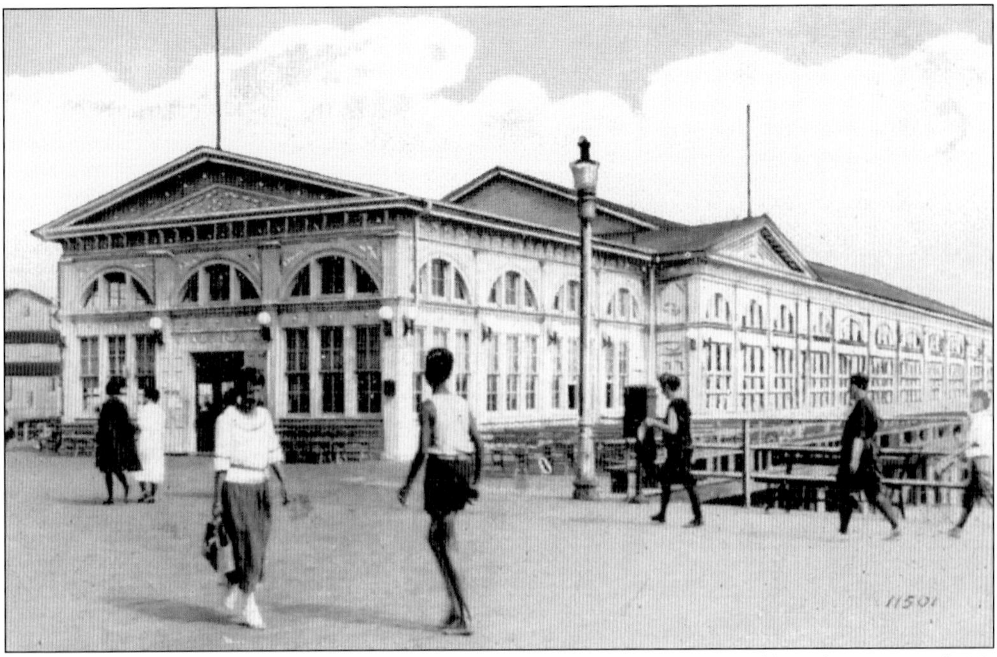

Convention Hall, at Sixth Street and the boardwalk, was totally destroyed by a fire on March 20, 1965. The flames were so intense that the firemen were unable to enter the building for hours. Fortunately, a strong west wind blew the flames, smoke, and burning embers seaward.

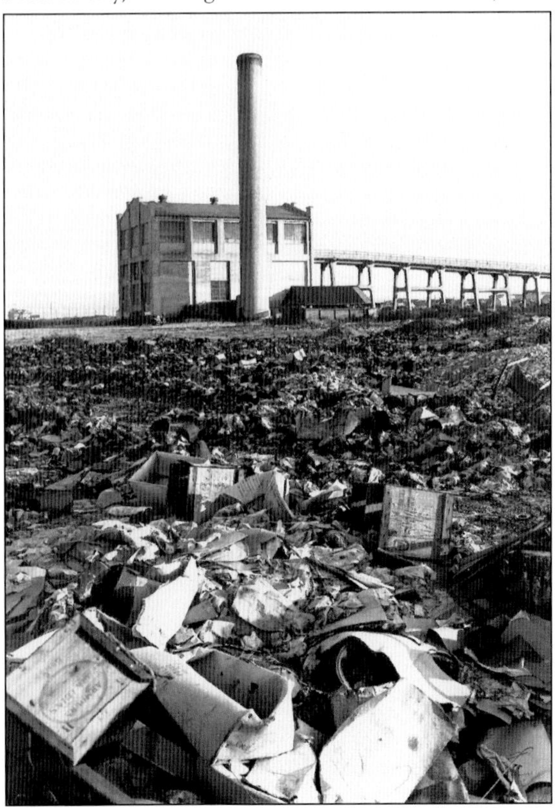

The Municipal Incinerator Plant, west of Bay Avenue near Twenty-fourth Street, considered by many to be a 25-year-old "white elephant," was demolished in March 1965. The incinerator was built as a means of doing away with open dump burning. It was supposed to be of sufficient capacity to reduce all waste paper and garbage collected from the homes of the entire city to ash, but it did not work. Open dump burning resumed while the building stood vacant. The tall smokestack did, however, become a landmark.

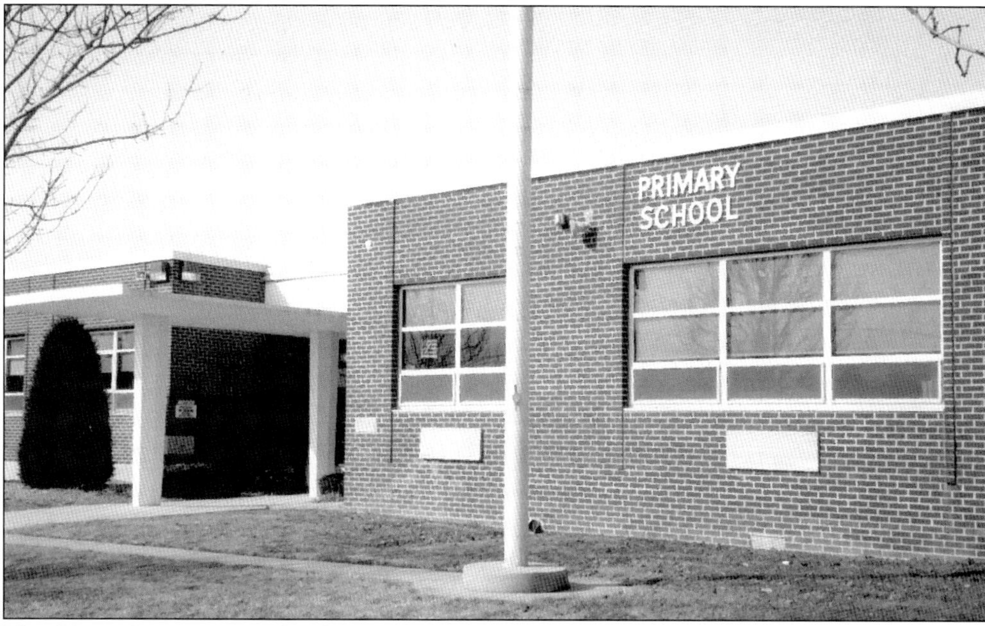

The Ocean City Primary School on West Avenue between Fifth and Sixth Streets opened in 1965.

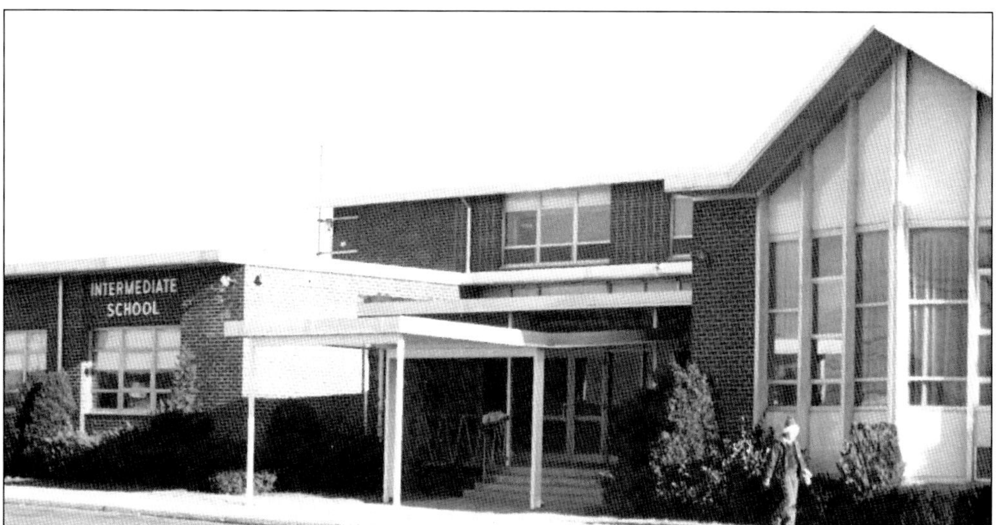

The Ocean City Intermediate School on Bay Avenue between Eighteenth and Nineteenth Streets opened in 1965. A few years later it was enlarged by the addition of more classrooms and a gymnasium. At that time, the seventh and eighth graders were brought down from the high school where they had been housed in one wing.

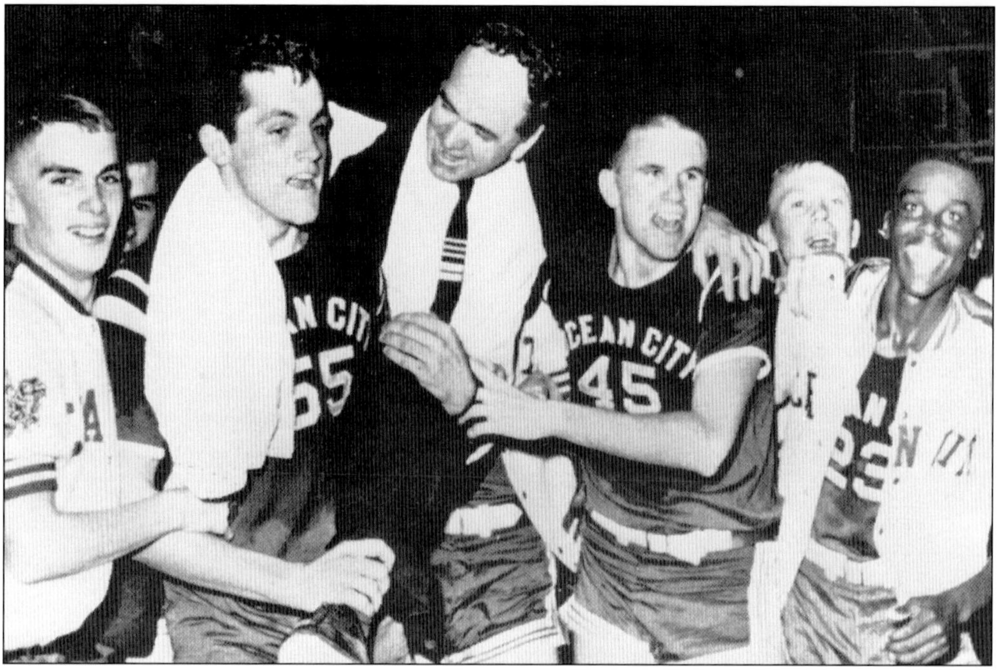

The 1965 senior class of Ocean City High School dedicated their yearbook, *The Caravel*, to Fred "Dixie" Howell with "Admiration and deep affection." Howell was a longtime teacher and coach who instilled in his students a desire to become well-rounded and worthwhile citizens.

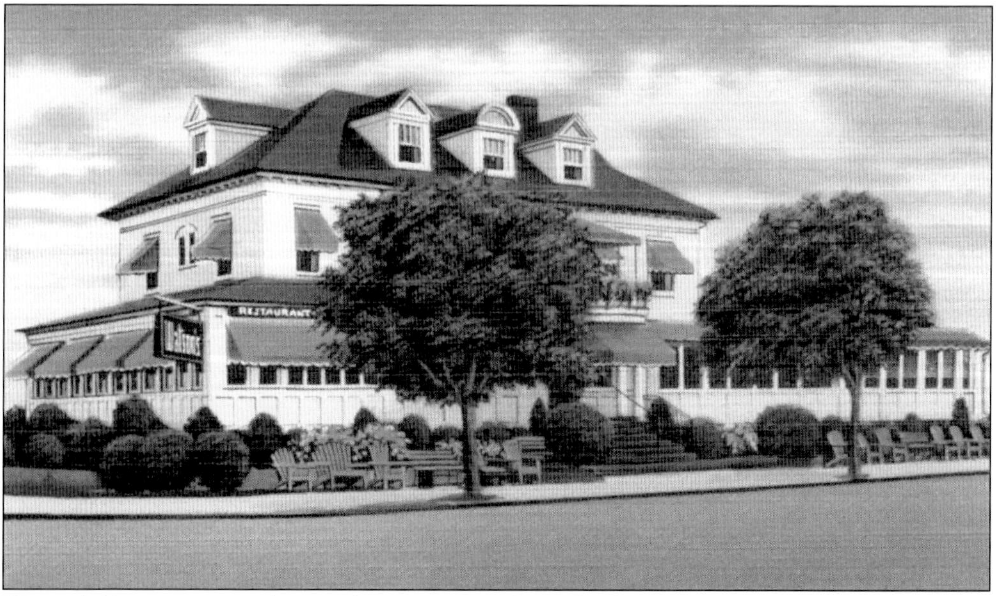

Watson's Restaurant on the southeast corner of Ninth Street and Ocean Avenue was built in 1914 as a private home for Albert Fogg. It had 10 bedrooms and a maid's quarters. It was converted to a restaurant in 1934.

Lifeguard Fred Miller was one of the best rowers on the Ocean City Beach Patrol during the summer of 1965.

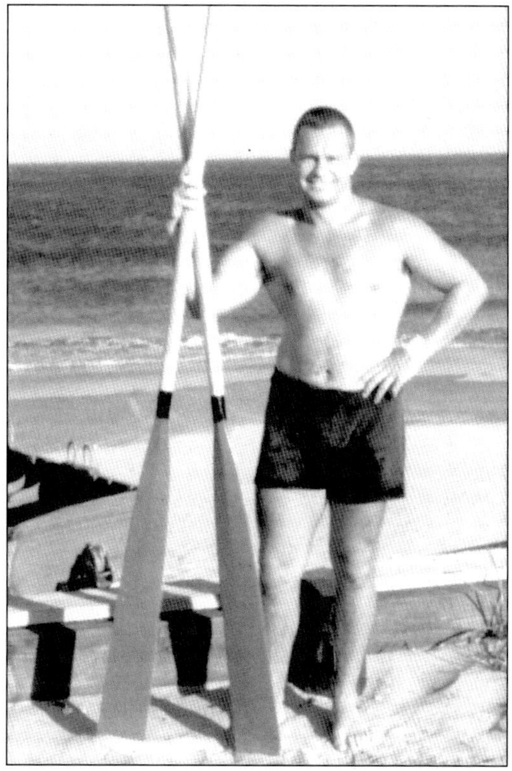

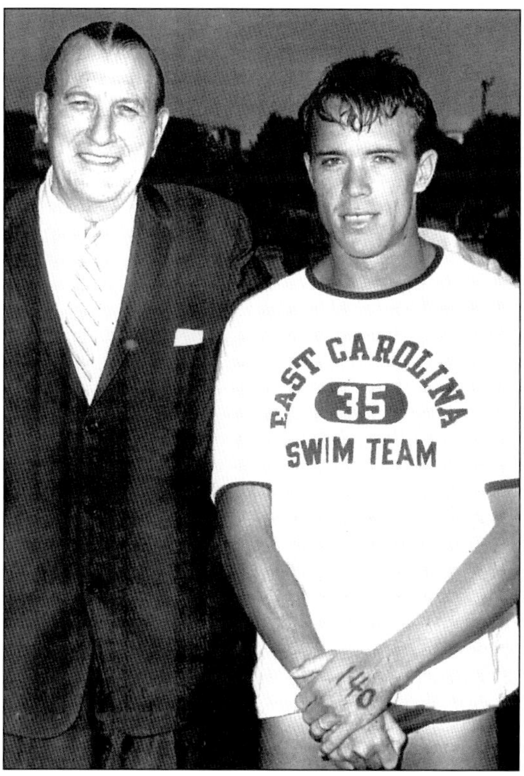

Sen. Frank S. "Hap" Farley congratulates Ocean City Beach Patrol's Mike Hamilton for winning the 1965 Farley Bay Swim.

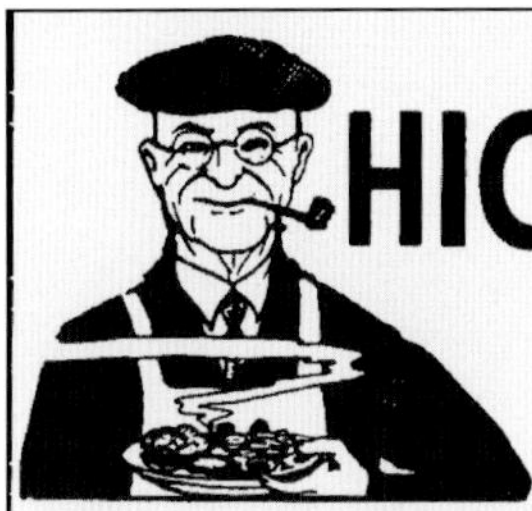

OPEN ALL YEAR

HICKMAN'S SEA FOOD

IN BUSINESS SINCE 1895

1155 ASBURY AVENUE

PHONE 399-1515

COOKED TO TAKE OUT

		Order	Platter
IMPERIAL CRAB		$ .95	$1.50
DEVILED CRAB PATTY		.60	1.25
SOFT CRAB		.75	1.45
DEVILED CLAM		.30	1.25
FISH CAKE		.25	1.00
FRIED SCALLOPS	½ lb.	.75	1.25
FRIED SHRIMP	½ lb.	.90	1.35
FRIED OYSTERS	½ Doz.	1.20	1.50
FRIED FLOUNDER		.30 & .45	1.00
FRIED THICK FLOUNDER		1.00	1.50
STUFFED FLOUNDER		1.00	1.60
STUFFED SHRIMP WITH CRABMEAT	3 for	.70	1.35
BROILED FISH		1.00	1.60
SEA FOOD COMBINATION (Fish, Clam, Oyster, Shrimp, Scallop & Crab)		1.25	1.50
BROASTED CHICKEN	4 Pieces	1.00	1.45
Small Tub 12 Pieces $2.85 — Large Tub 20 Pieces $4.35			
BREADED VEAL CUTLET		.70	1.25
BROILED LOBSTER TAIL		2.00	2.50
BROILED MAINE LOBSTER		2.95	3.45
SHRIMP COCKTAIL		1.00	1.60

	½ Pt.	1 Pt.	
LOBSTER SALAD	$1.25	$2.50	$1.75
CHICKEN SALAD	1.25	2.50	1.75
SHRIMP SALAD	1.25	2.50	1.75
CRAB SALAD	1.25	2.50	1.75

Platters Include: Cole Slaw, Lettuce & Tomato, Pickle, Tartar Sauce.
Choice of: F. F. Potatoes, Potato Salad, Baked Potato, Macaroni Salad, Pepper Hash or Vegetable.

	½ Pt.	1 Pt.	1 Qt.
F. F. POTATOES	.35	.45	.75
F. F. ONIONS		.40	.75
PEPPER HASH	.25	.50	1.00
COLE SLAW	.25	.50	1.00
POTATO SALAD	.25	.50	1.00
MACARONI SALAD	.25	.50	1.00
CLAM CHOWDER		.35	.70
SNAPPER SOUP		.50	1.00

BAKED POTATO 25¢ each

OUT OF OUR FISH DEPARTMENT
Soft Crabs — Live Maine Lobsters — Crab Meat & Claws
All Kinds of Fresh Fish in Season

PRICES SUBJECT TO CHANGE.

When Pope Paul VI declared the end to meatless Fridays in 1966, Hickman's Sea Food at 1155 Asbury Avenue noticed a drop in business for Friday dinners.

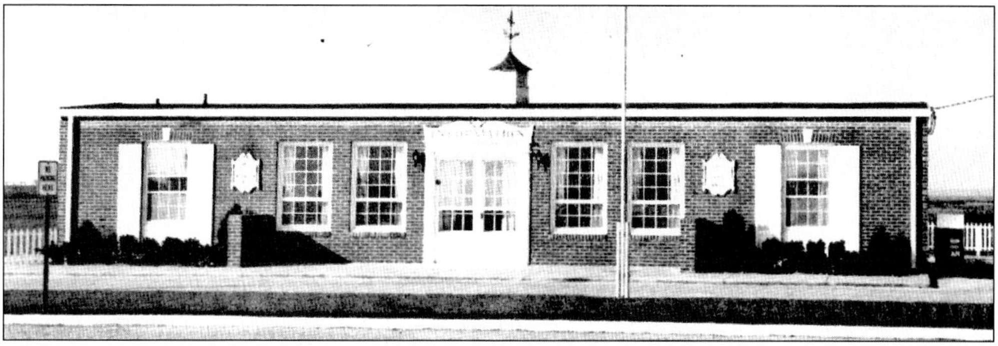

The Ocean City Chamber of Commerce opened an information and greeting center on the Somers Point-Ocean City Causeway during the summer of 1966. It was maintained year-round by the chamber and the City of Ocean City.

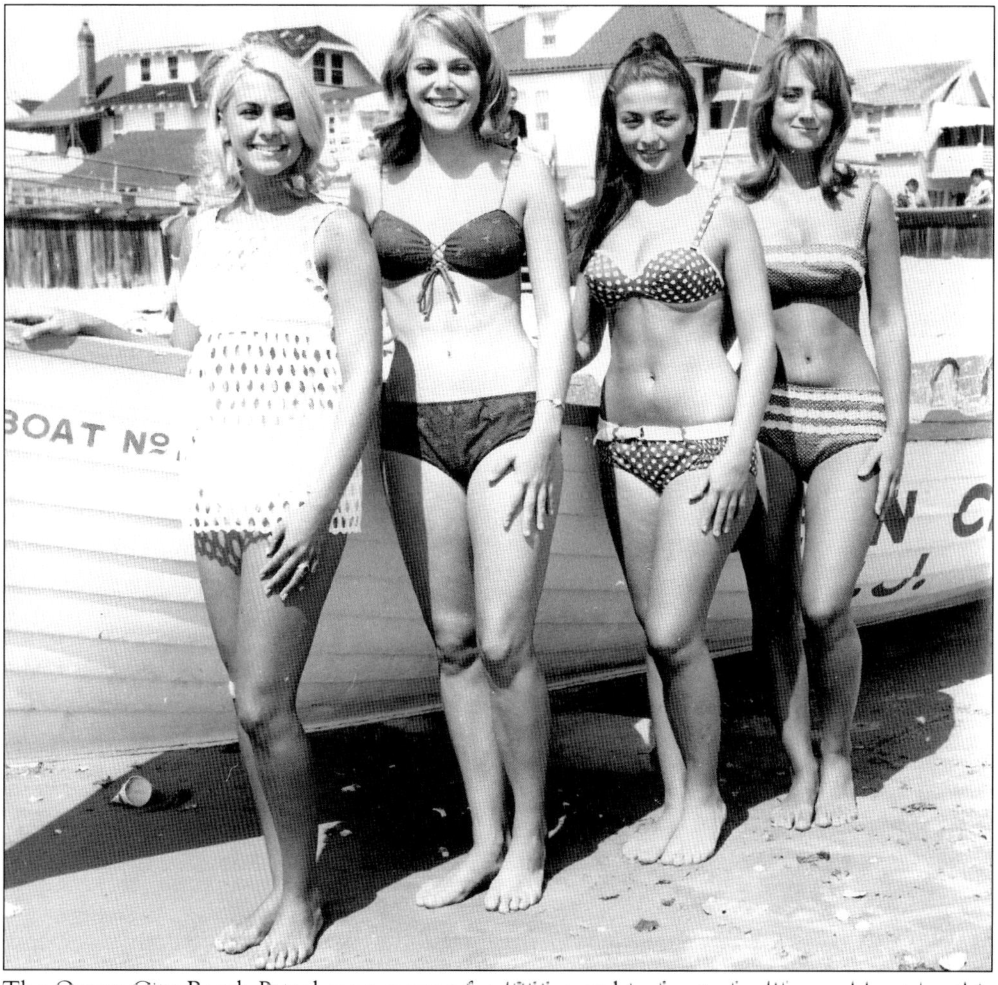

The Ocean City Beach Patrol zone queens for 1966 posed in front of a lifeguard boat for this photograph. From left to right are Marie Mercaldo, Martha McKelvey, Maria Ciccone, and Diane Eurer. Mercaldo was crowned Miss Ocean City Beach Patrol.

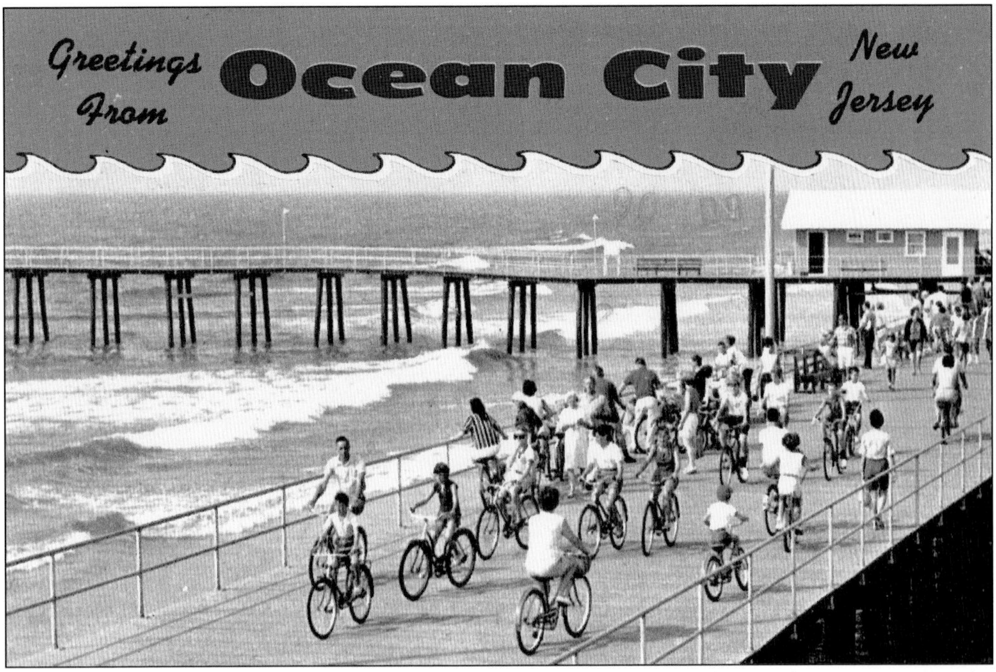

Bicycle riding on Ocean City's two-and-a-half-mile-long boardwalk is a favorite pastime for residents and visitors. During the summer season, biking is allowed on the boardwalk in the morning only.

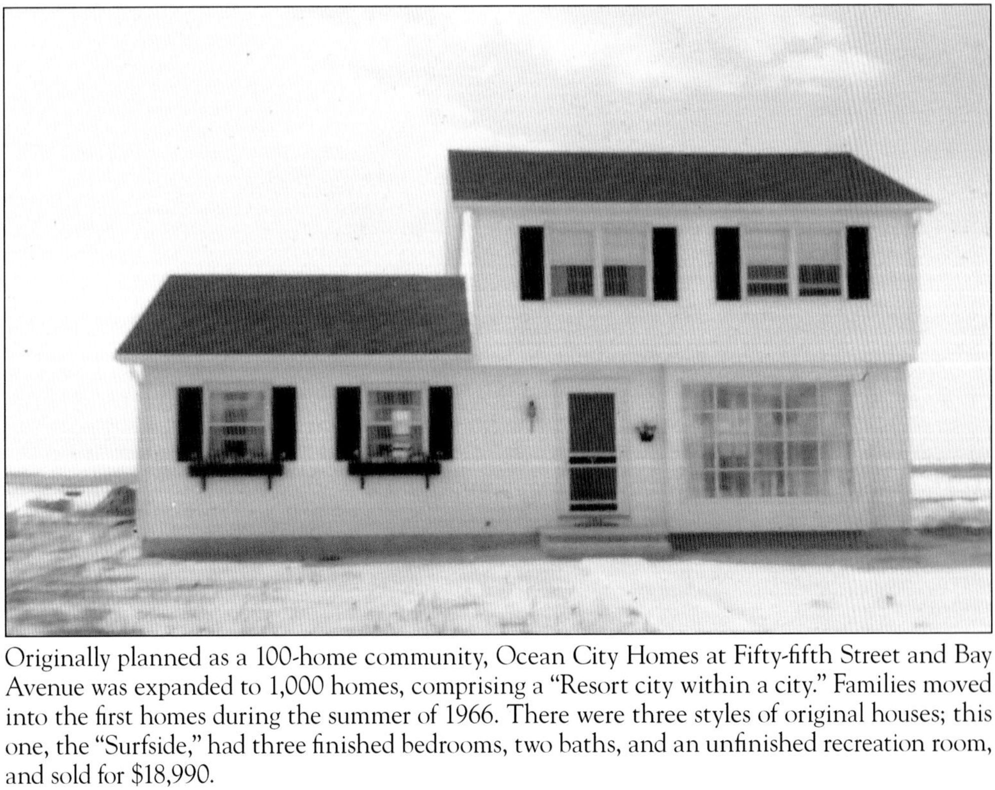

Originally planned as a 100-home community, Ocean City Homes at Fifty-fifth Street and Bay Avenue was expanded to 1,000 homes, comprising a "Resort city within a city." Families moved into the first homes during the summer of 1966. There were three styles of original houses; this one, the "Surfside," had three finished bedrooms, two baths, and an unfinished recreation room, and sold for $18,990.

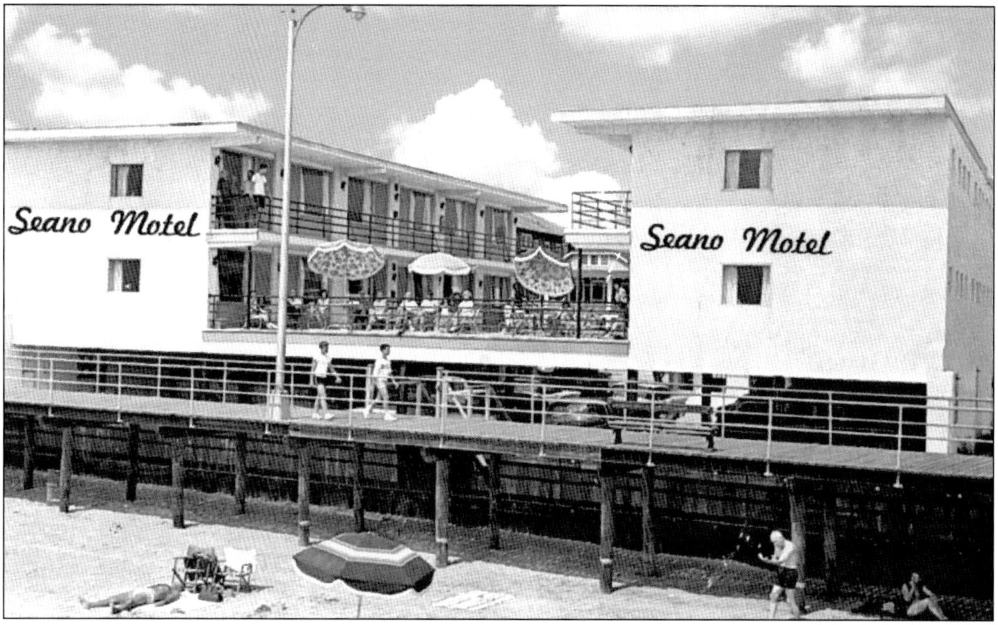

The Seano Motel at 1417 Ocean Avenue was "Completely Air-Conditioned and Heated" and offered "Large Luxurious Guest Rooms. Ceramic Tile Bath and Dressing Rooms."

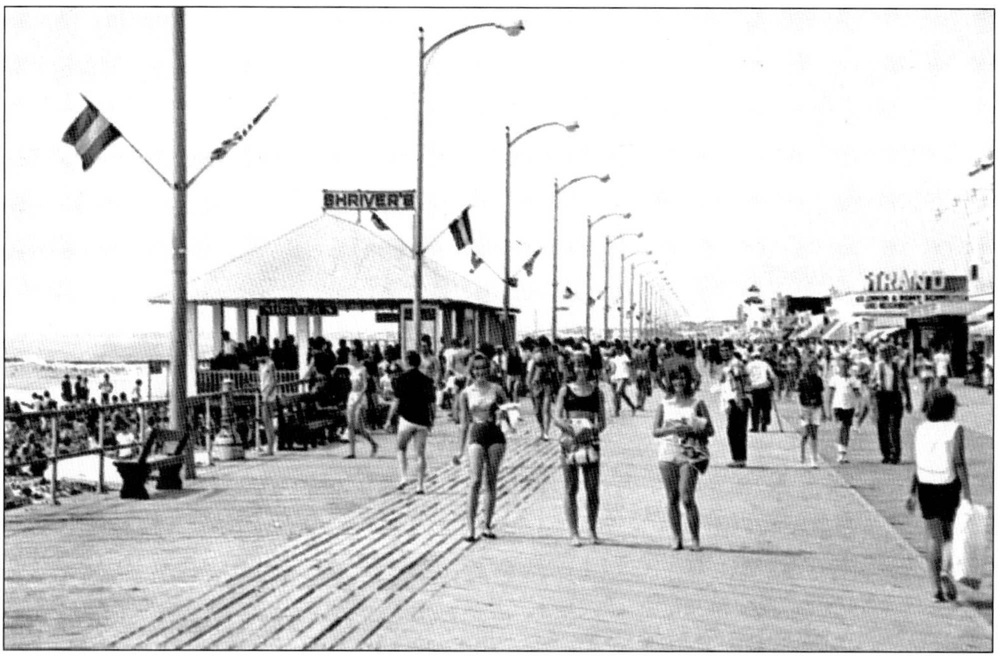

This crowd on the boardwalk, looking south from Moorlyn Terrace, was typical of a mid-afternoon crowd in July.

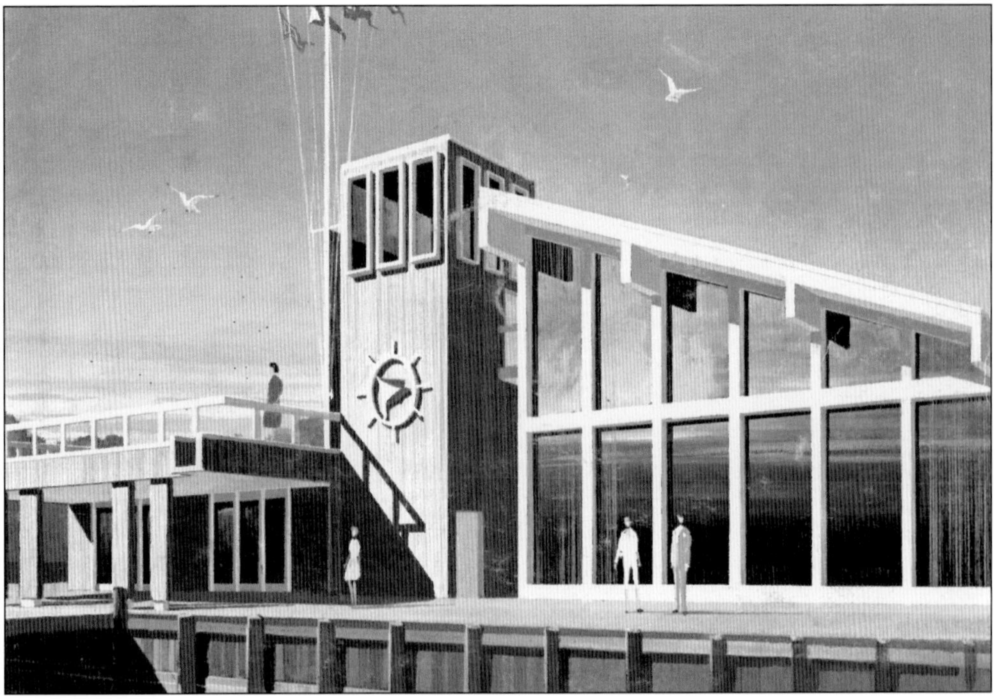

Between 1964 and 1967, substantial renovations were undertaken to improve the Ocean City Yacht Club building at Battersea Road and the bayfront. An all-glass, two-story bayfront addition was added with an adjoining tower where the "tower ladies" watched the progress of sailboat races. Members referred to it as the "Cathedral Club House."

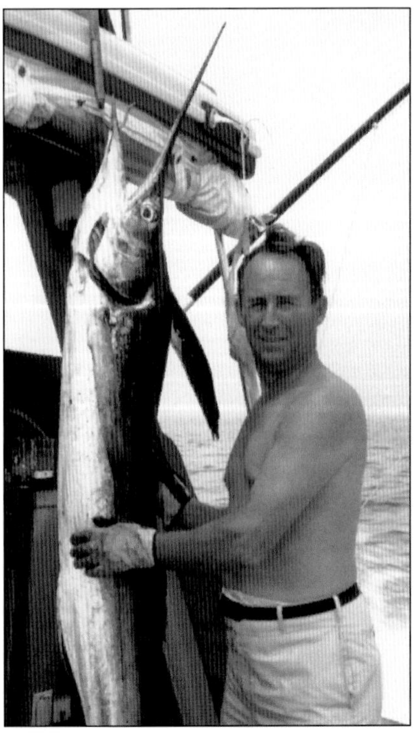

On July 17, 1968, Bob French caught this seven-foot-one-inch, 50-pound white marlin.

Princess Grace was featured on the cover of the August 2, 1967, *Ocean City Weekly Guide*. The caption read, "Princess Grace of Monaco spent a week resting in Ocean City at the summer home of her mother, Mrs. John B. Kelly, on Wesley Avenue and 26th Street. Princess Grace is pictured in the patio with her two daughters, Caroline, 10, and Stephanie, 2. She has been a summer visitor to Ocean City all her life."

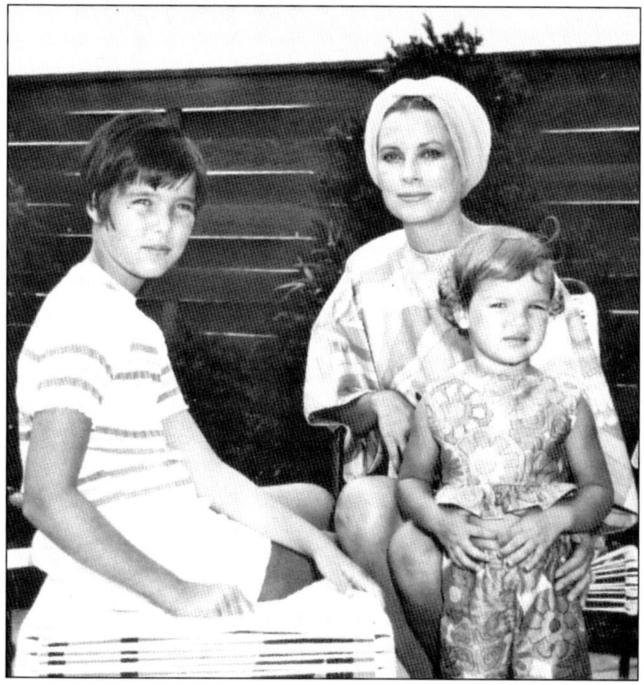

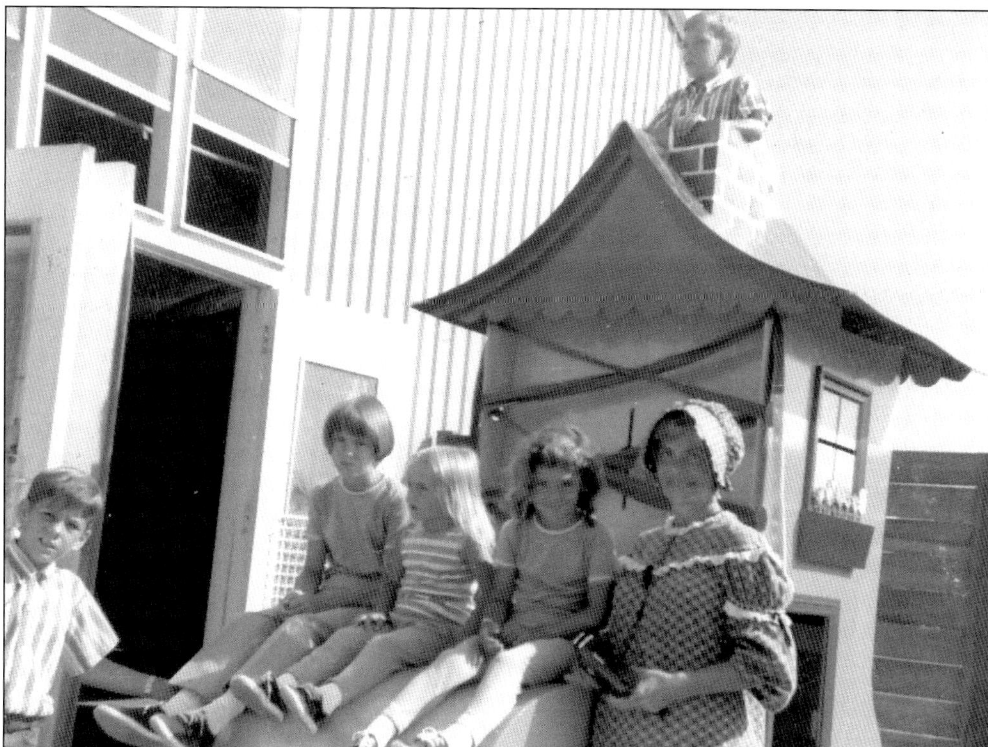

The Madera Family of Pittsburgh won first place for this float in the 59th annual baby parade held August 8, 1968. From left to right are Bruce, Linda, Diane, Laura, and mother Carol Madera. Jimmy Madera is peeking from the chimney.

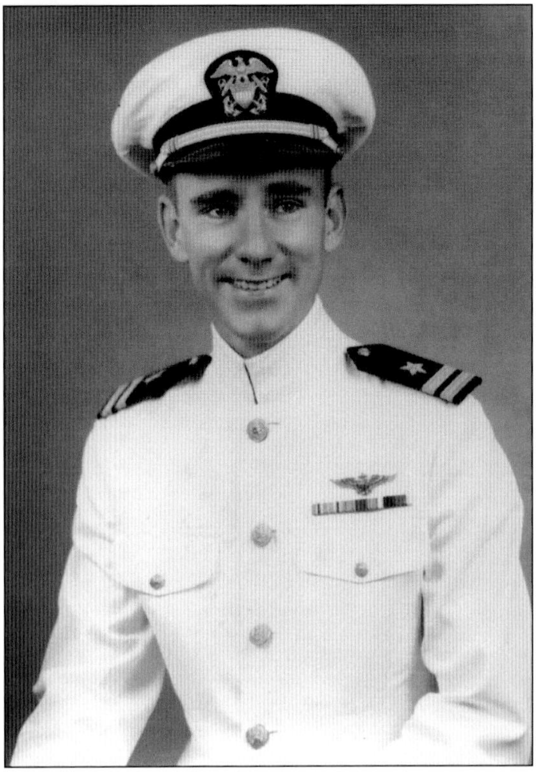

Robert S. Marts, a graduate of Ocean City High School class of 1943 and United States Naval Academy class of 1947, retired from the navy in June 1967 with the rank of lieutenant commander. After his retirement, he began a second career as a photographer at his father-in-law's Senior Studios.

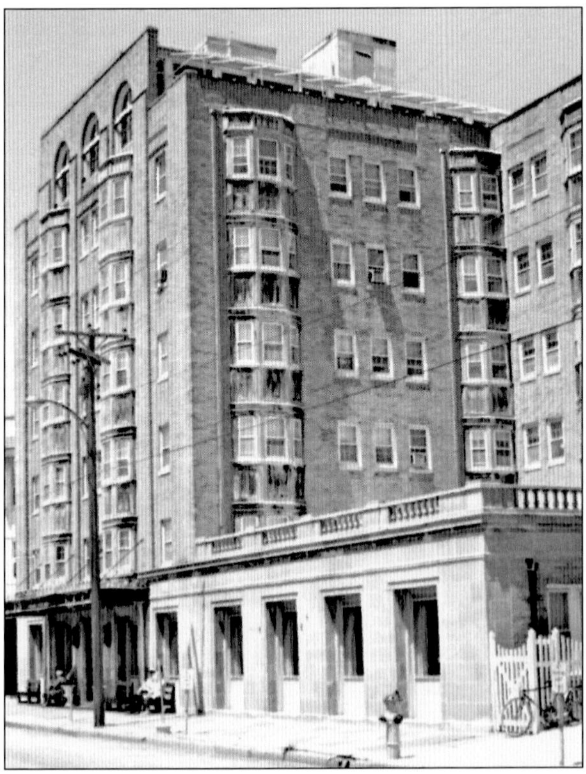

The Hanscom Hotel at Eighth Street near Atlantic Avenue was bought in the spring of 1968 by a group of Methodist laymen from Philadelphia and renamed the Homestead. It was remodeled and became a retirement home for senior citizens.

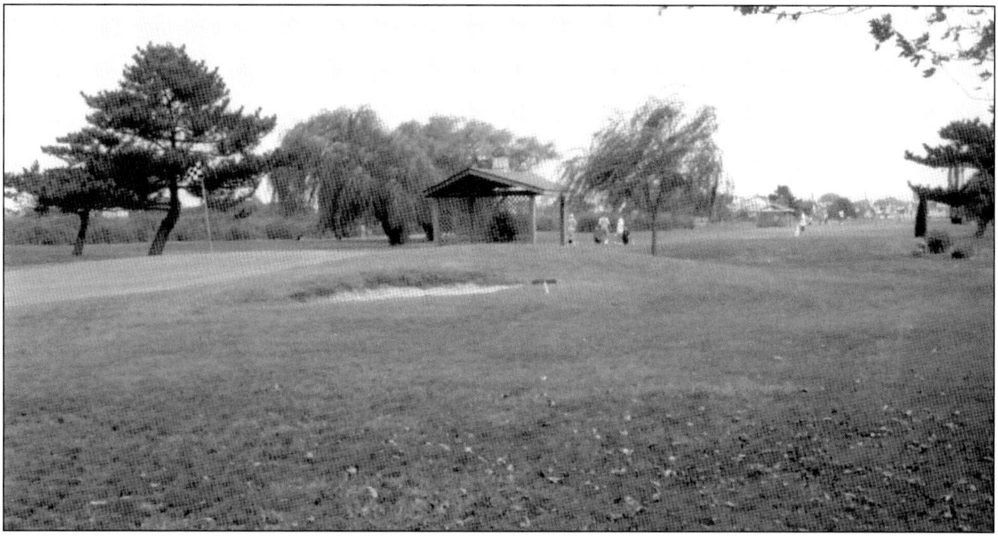

On May 16, 1968, Ocean City opened the public golf course at the edge of the Municipal Airport runway at Twenty-sixth Street and Bay Avenue. A one-story combination golf "pro" shop and airport terminal building made of prefabricated steel was also opened at that time.

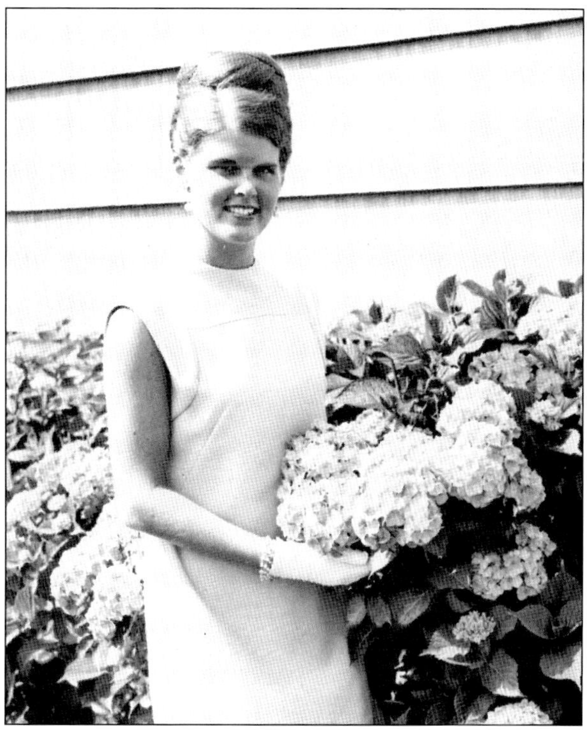

Hydrangeas are prolific bloomers in Ocean City and can be seen in many gardens. The resort was part of the "Hydrangea Trail," which started in Atlantic City and continued through most of the shore communities south to Wildwood Crest, awarding prizes for the best displays. Pamela Whittaker was selected as Miss Ocean City Hydrangea Trail Queen for the annual Hydrangea Festival in 1968.

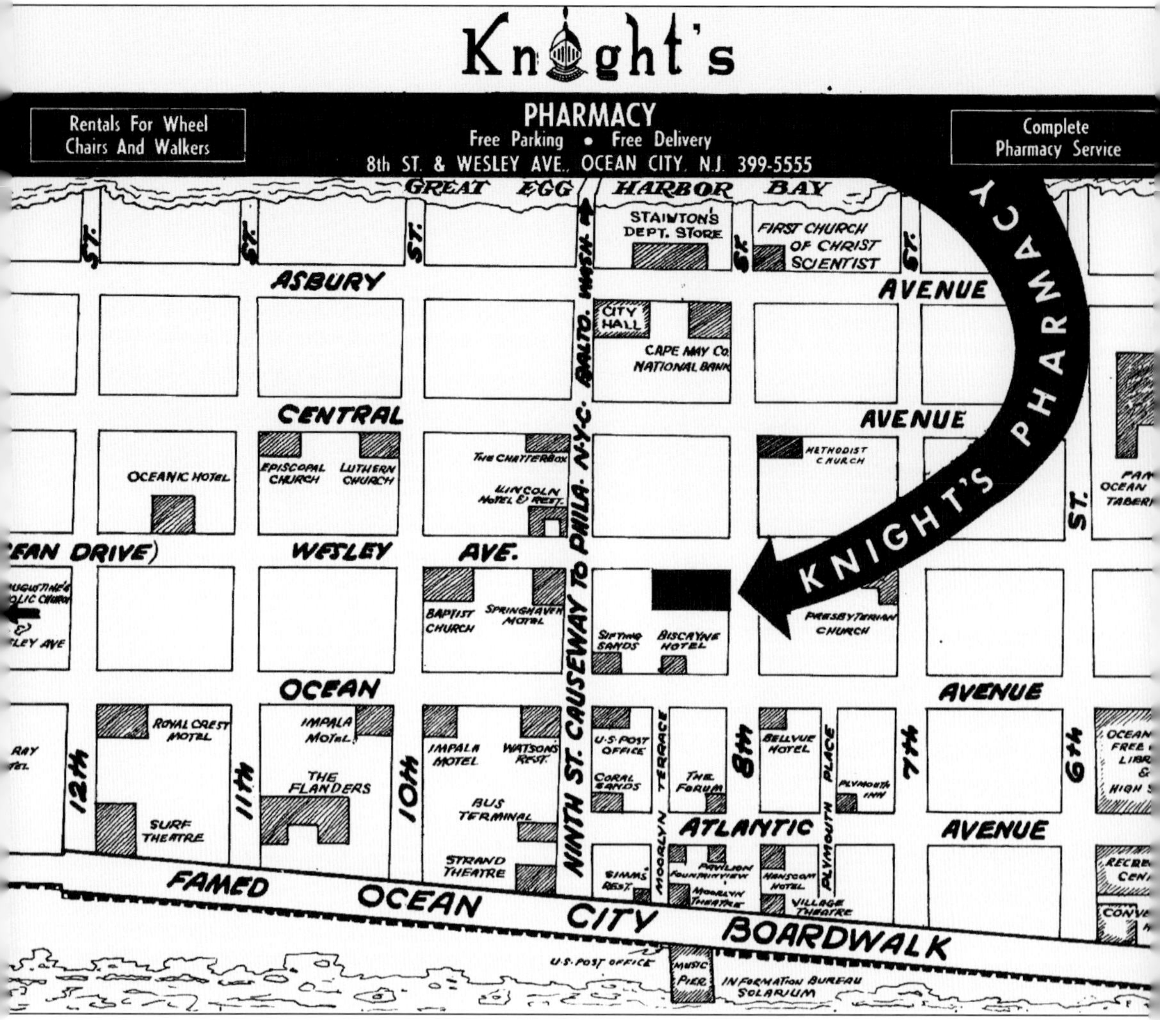

This Knight Pharmacy advertisement was in the 1969 *Ocean City Vacation Guide*. It not only showed where Knight's Pharmacy was, at Eighth Street and Wesley Avenue, but other points of interest as well.

During his tenure as mayor, from 1967 through 1971, Robert L. Sharp had the pleasure of presenting many trophies to the Ocean City lifeguards. In this 1967 photograph, Mayor Sharp (left) is presenting the Frank "Dutch" Hoffman Memorial trophy to Ocean City Beach Patrol captain George T. Lafferty.

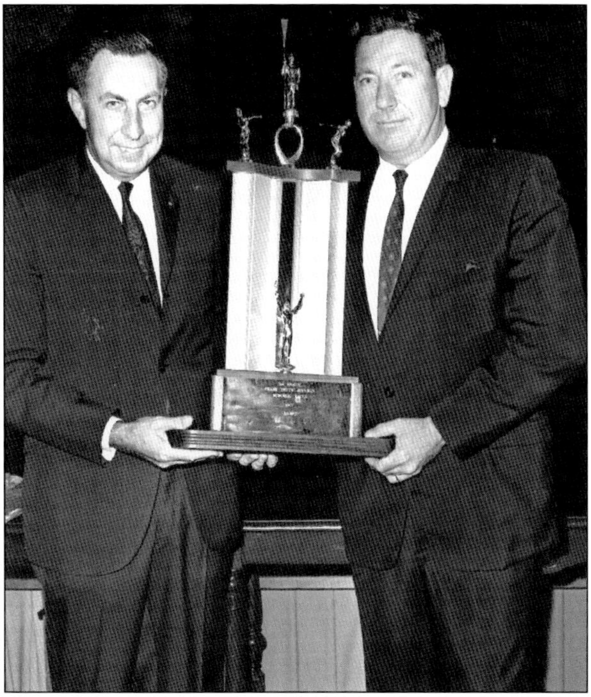

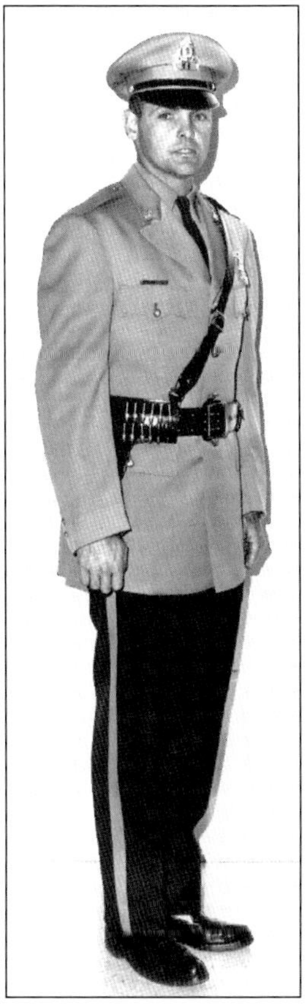

On April 29, 1968, patrolman James P. Finnegan modeled the Ocean City Police Department's new uniform.

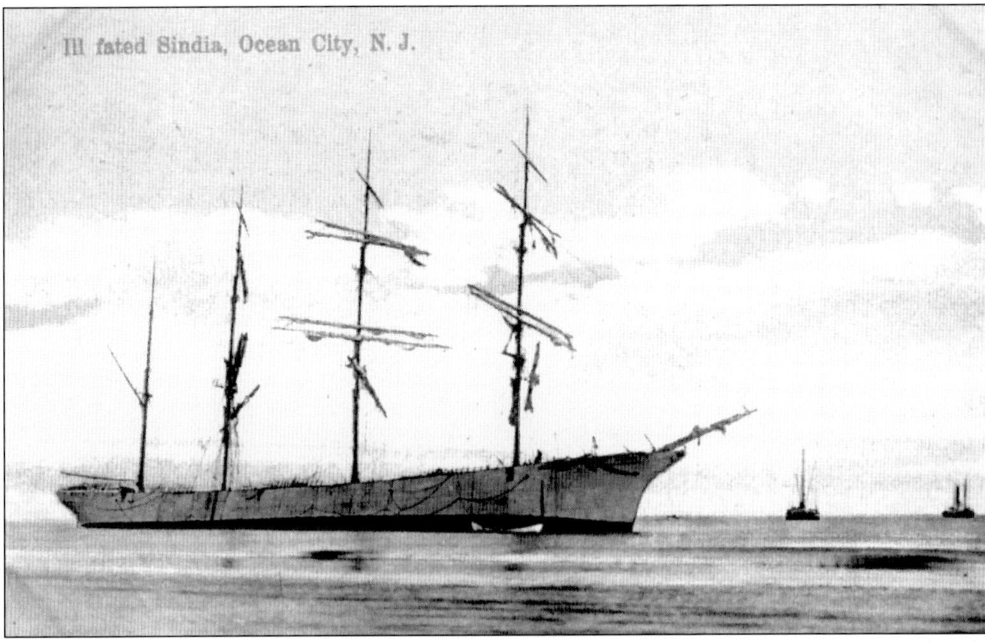

The site of the wrecked four-masted sailing bark, the *Sindia*, off the Seventeenth Street beach, became the first shipwreck in New Jersey designated a historic site on December 15, 1967.

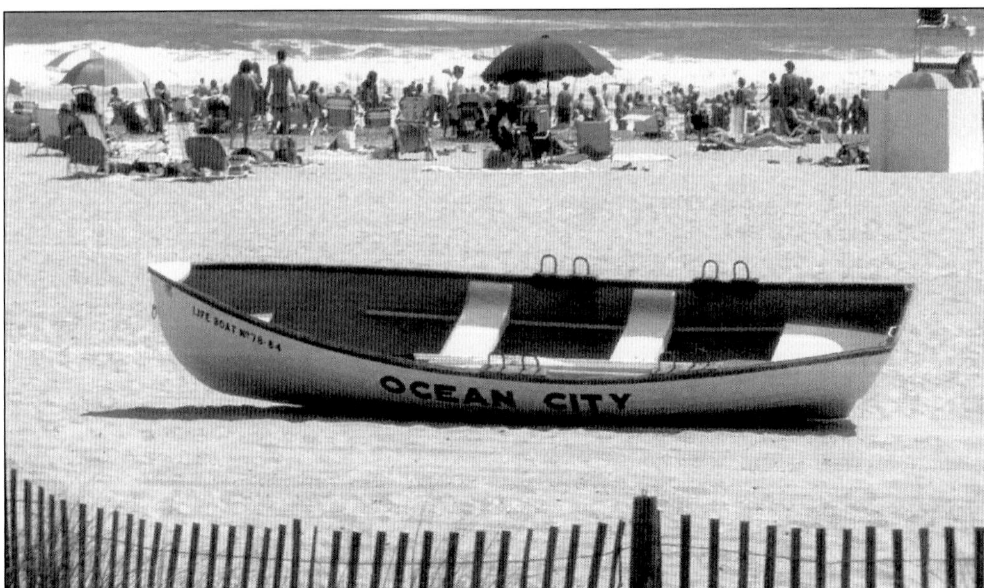

In 1968, the Ocean City Beach Patrol bought its first fiberglass boat. Built by the Van Duyne family, it had the classic design of the wood surfboats used by the patrol since the 1890s.

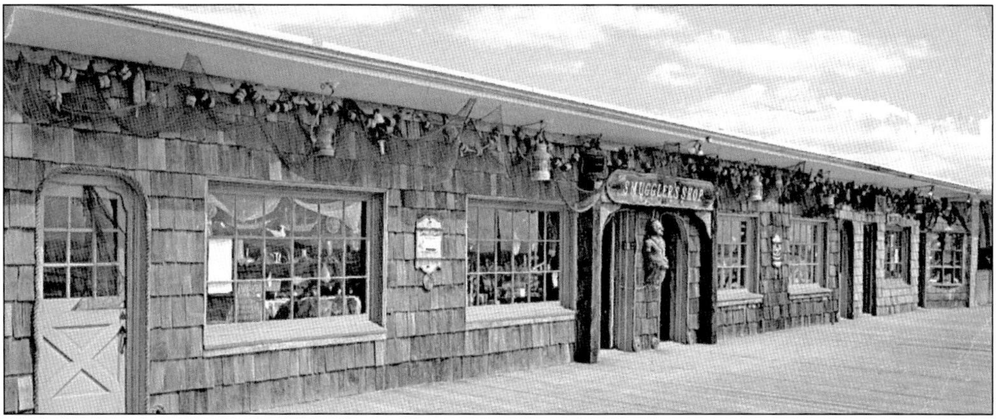

The Smugglers Shop at 1314 Boardwalk was kept open from June 1 through October 1 by owner Sam McDowell.

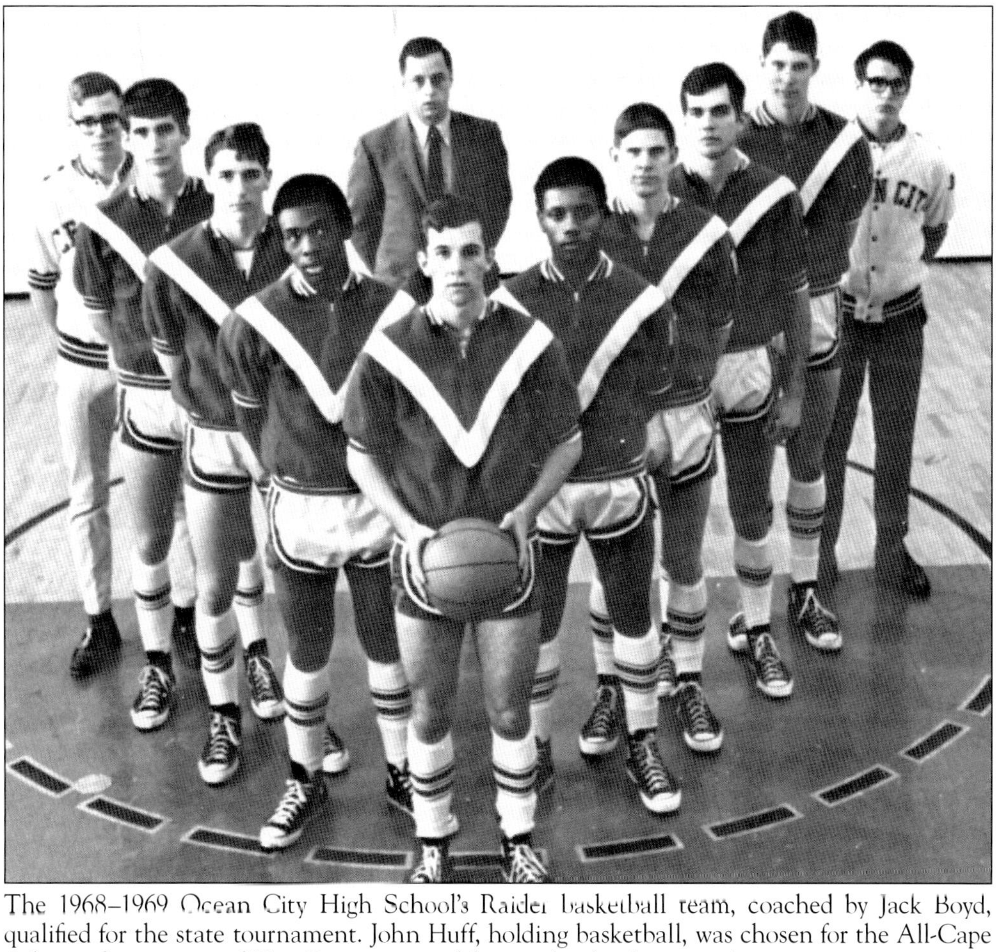

The 1968–1969 Ocean City High School's Raider basketball team, coached by Jack Boyd, qualified for the state tournament. John Huff, holding basketball, was chosen for the All-Cape Atlantic first team, and Tom Bowen, second from right, for the second team.

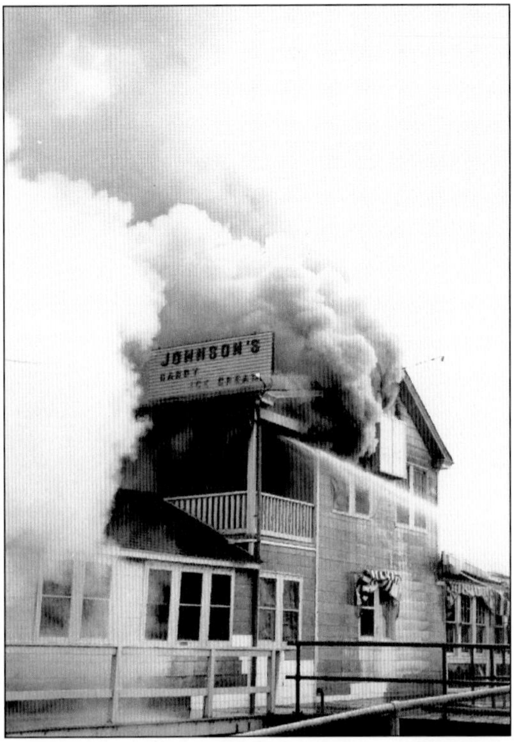

Johnson's Ice Cream and Candy Store at Brighton Place and the boardwalk had been in business in the same location since 1930. An early morning fire on September 2, 1969, caused the death of 15-year-old James Johnson, who had been asleep with his family in the apartment above the store. The rest of the family was rescued.

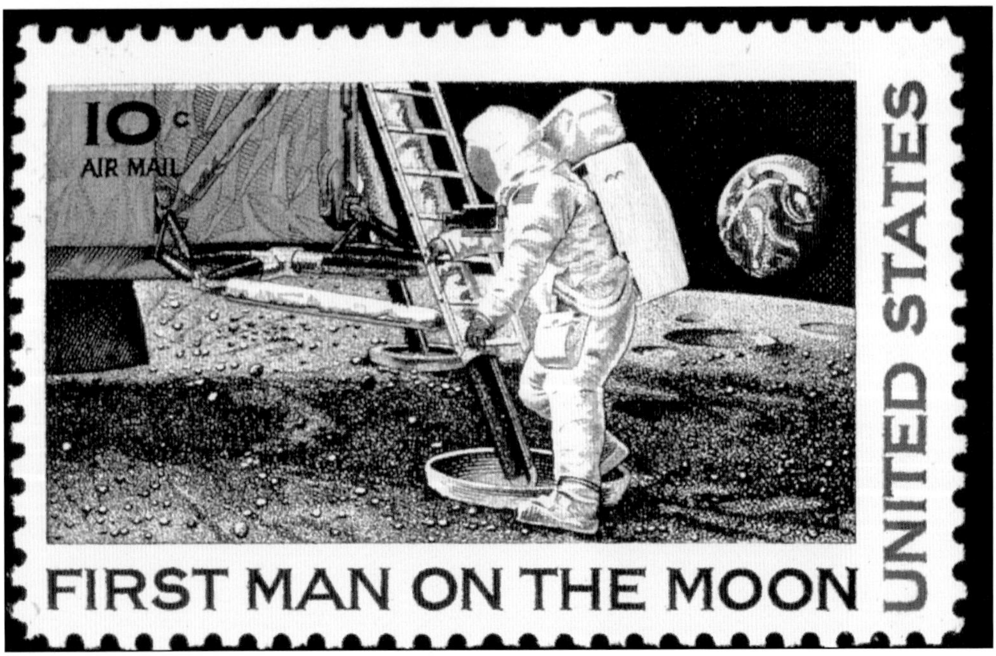

On July 20, 1969, people in Ocean City gathered in front of television sets to watch Neil Armstrong and Edwin Aldrin walk on the moon. Carolyn and Charles Murphy, owners of Boyd's Radio and Television Store at 920 Asbury Avenue, left a television set on all night in the window of the store so people would be able to see this historic event. This "First Man on the Moon" stamp was issued on September 9, 1969.

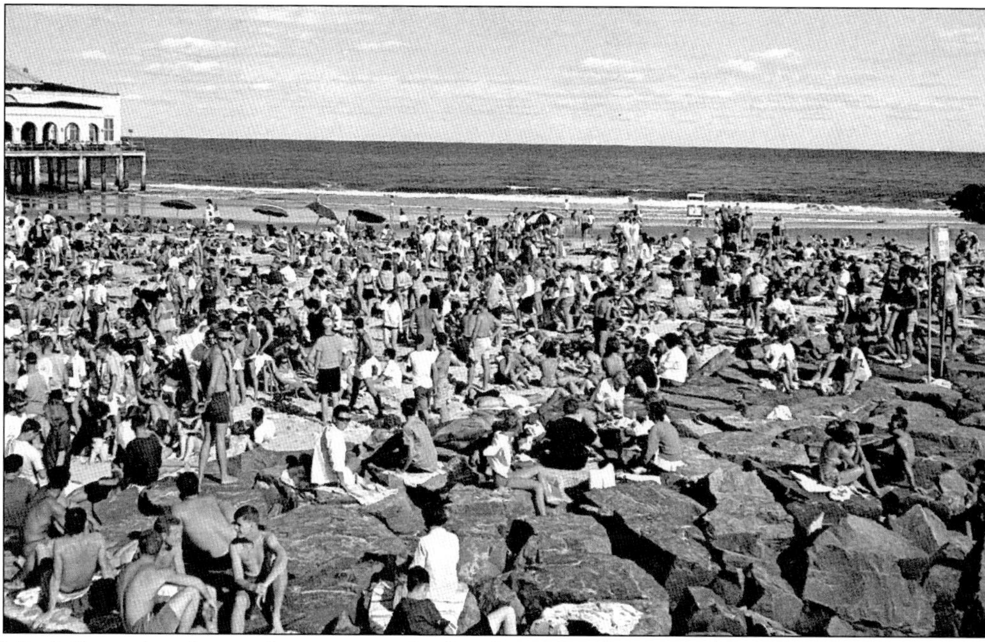

Ninth Street beach was the most popular beach in New Jersey for the collegiate crowd. It was nicknamed "Little Fort Lauderdale."

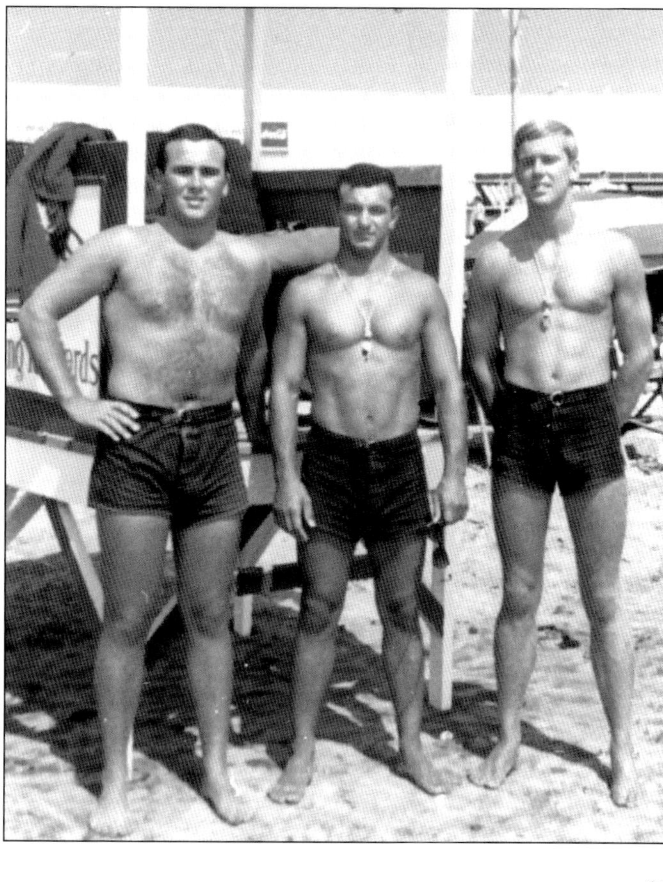

These men guarding the busy Ninth Street beach, from left to right, are Vince Hink, Angelo Psaltis, and Mike Bradley.

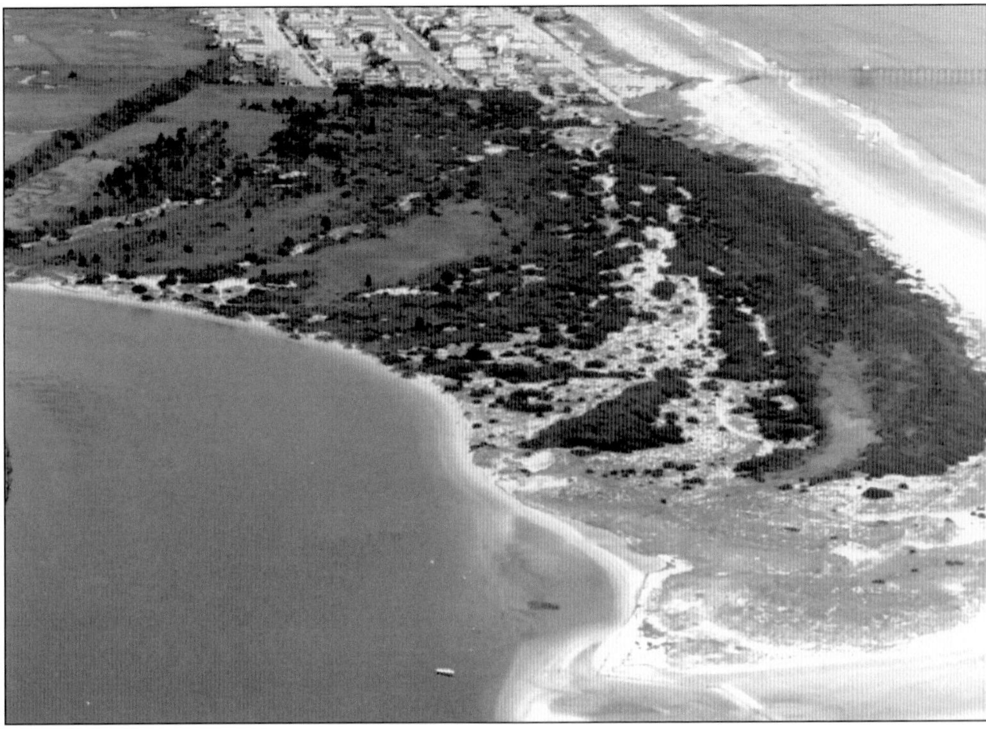

The Ocean Crest State Park at the southern tip of Ocean City was established in 1963 to help protect and preserve one of the last undeveloped tracts of land along the state's oceanfront. Green Acres bond money was used to acquire the land for the park. In 1980, the park was renamed Corson's Inlet State Park.

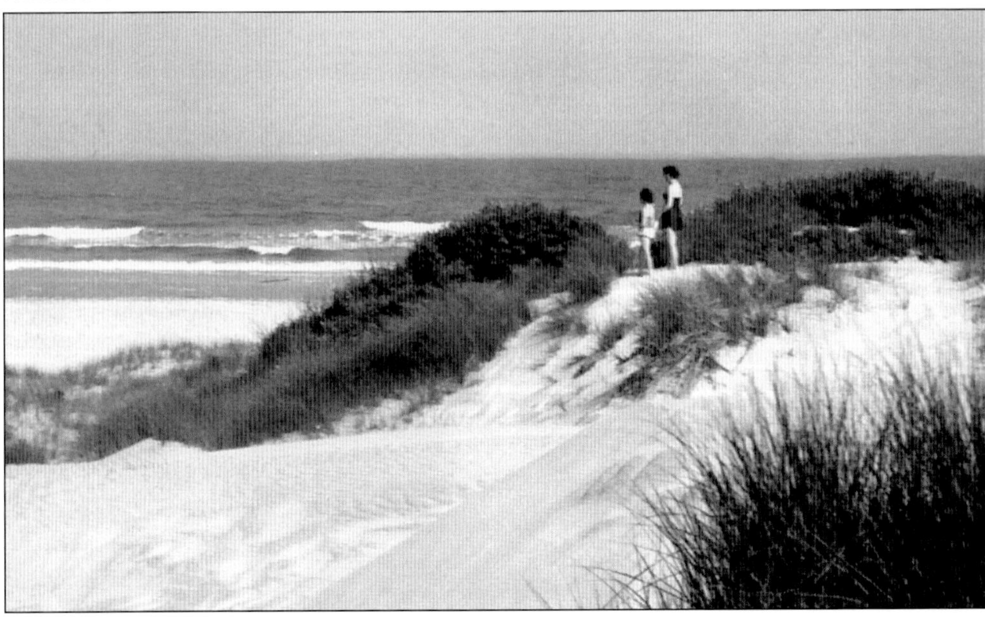

The state park at the southern end of Ocean City is rich in wildlife diversity with primary and secondary sand dune systems, shoreline over wash, marine estuaries, and upland areas in which hundreds of wildlife species live and breed.

Five

Condos Go Up, Hotels Go Down 1970–1974

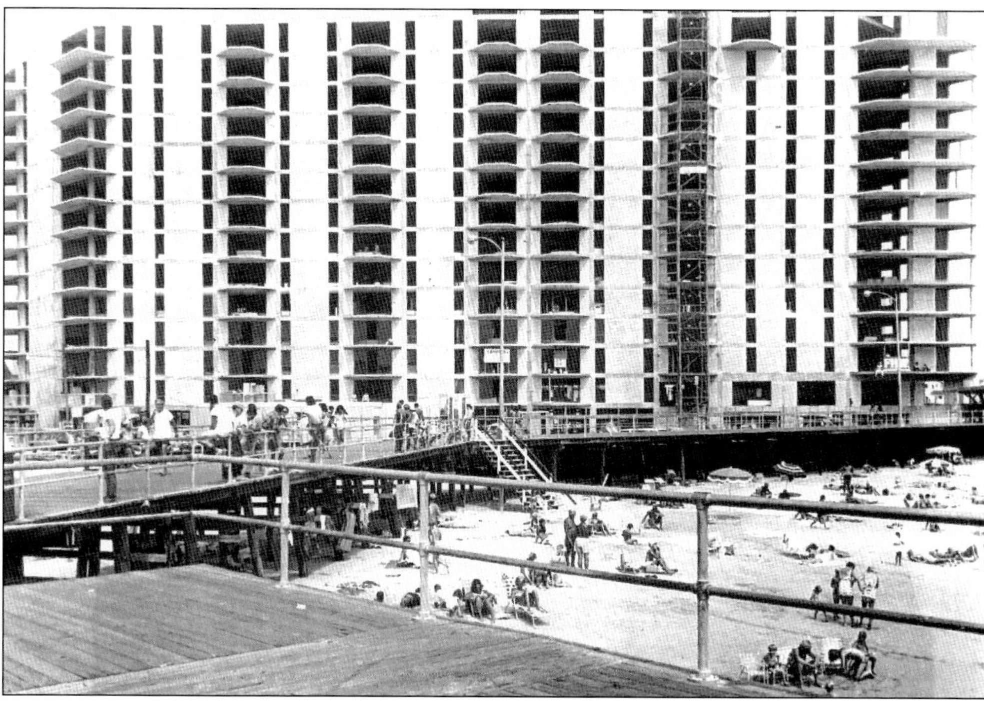

During the summer of 1972, the lifeguards were in an excellent position to watch the building of the city's first high-rise condominium, the Gardens Plaza, on the boardwalk at Third Street. The town's residents were afraid they were seeing the future of Ocean City: a high wall of concrete and glass. To prevent that, a municipal zoning ordinance was passed that prevented construction of buildings higher than 70 feet.

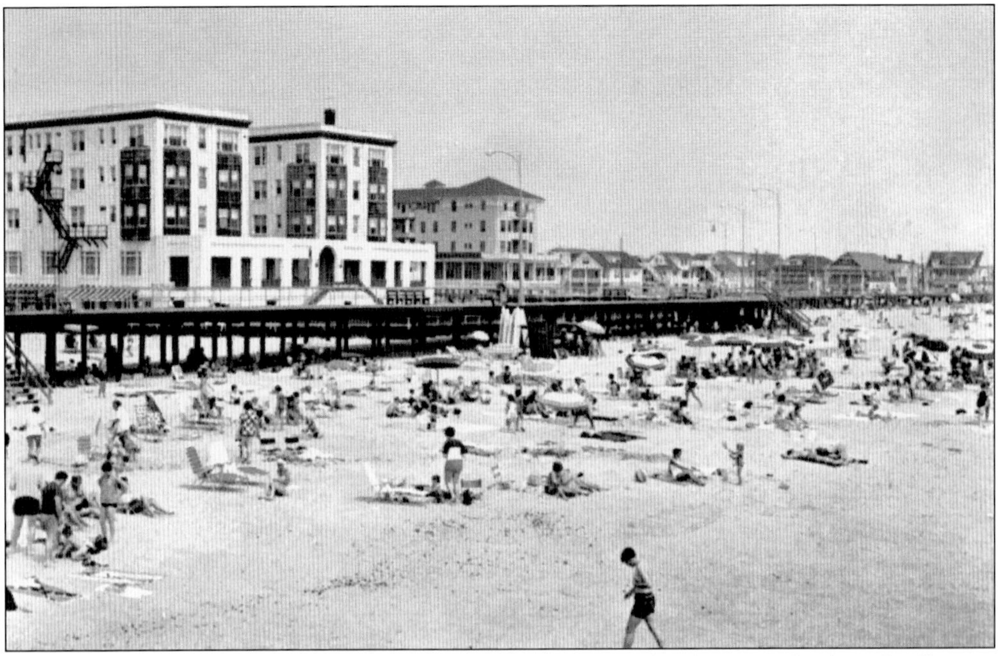

The Delaware Hotel (on the left), on Third Street to Park Place on the boardwalk, was demolished in 1971. Built in 1925, its advertisements boasted of having 175 rooms—all of them 100 percent fireproof. The Breakers Hotel (to the right with the slightly peaked roof), on the boardwalk at Delancey Place, opened in 1912. It was the first hotel built on the boardwalk. The Breakers had all the conveniences of the day, including an elevator, steam heat, and private baths. It was razed in 1970.

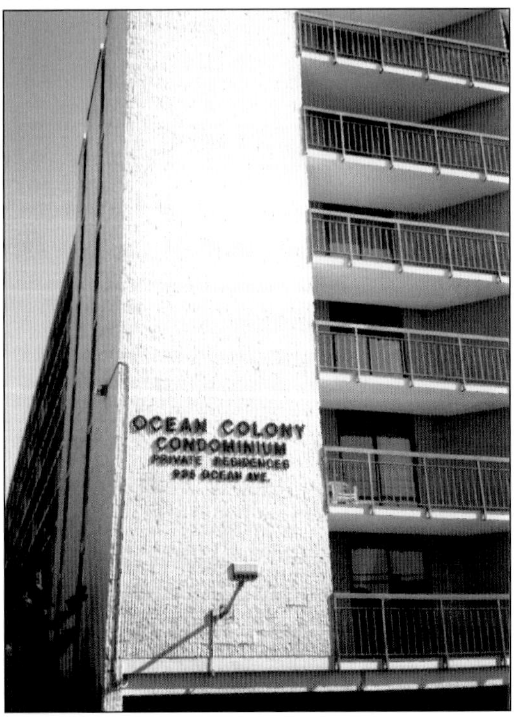

Ocean Colony Condominiums, located at 925 Ocean Avenue, was planned as a 27-story building. After the Gardens Plaza went up, however, and the municipal ordinance was changed to allow no buildings higher than 70 feet, it had to be scaled down. It was finally built with only seven stories.

This plaque was placed on the war memorial in the park between Fifth and Sixth Streets on Wesley Avenue on Veteran's Day, 1970. It was dedicated to all Ocean City men and women who served in the armed forces including Willie E. Granger, William R. Godfrey, John C. Martin, B. Michael Miley, Jon R. Morvay, Charles W. Sterling, and Robert A. Woodrow Jr., all of whom died in Vietnam.

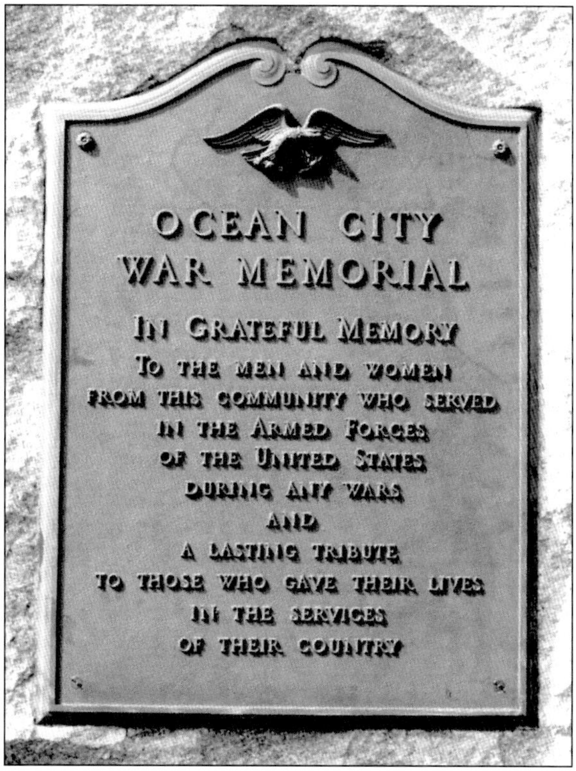

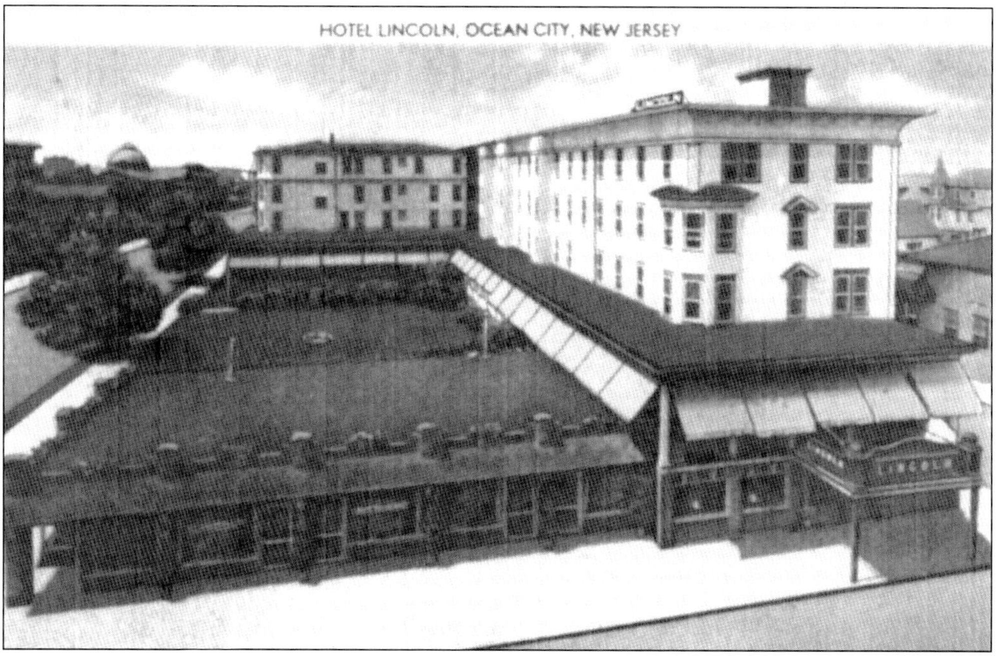

The Lincoln Hotel, at Ninth Street and Wesley Avenue, was originally two hotels, the Waverly, fronting Wesley Avenue, and the Hueling, facing Ninth Street. They were joined after World War I. The hotel had 150 rooms and, while once very elegant, it was described as a "crash pad for visiting young people" by the time it was demolished in November 1971.

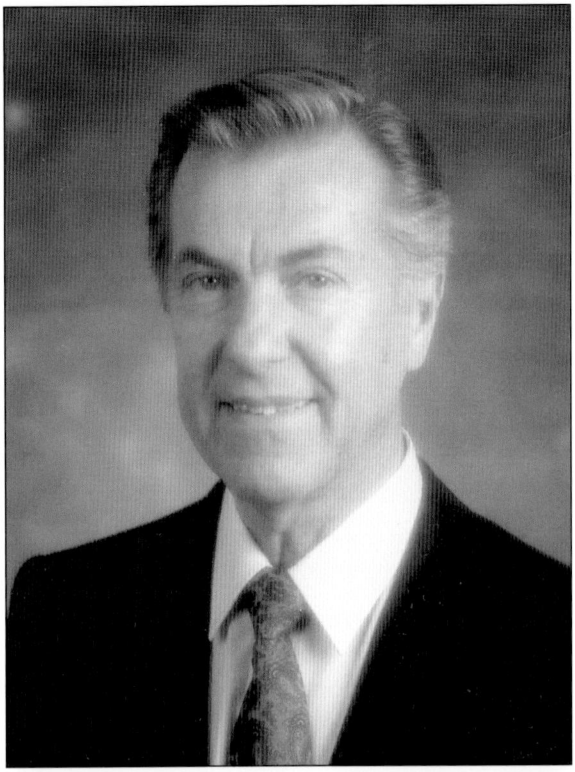

Roy Gillian, owner of Wonderland Pier, was an Ocean City commissioner before he was elected to the Cape May County Board of Chosen Freeholders on November 2, 1971. He defeated Democratic candidate William H. Woods for the freeholder position.

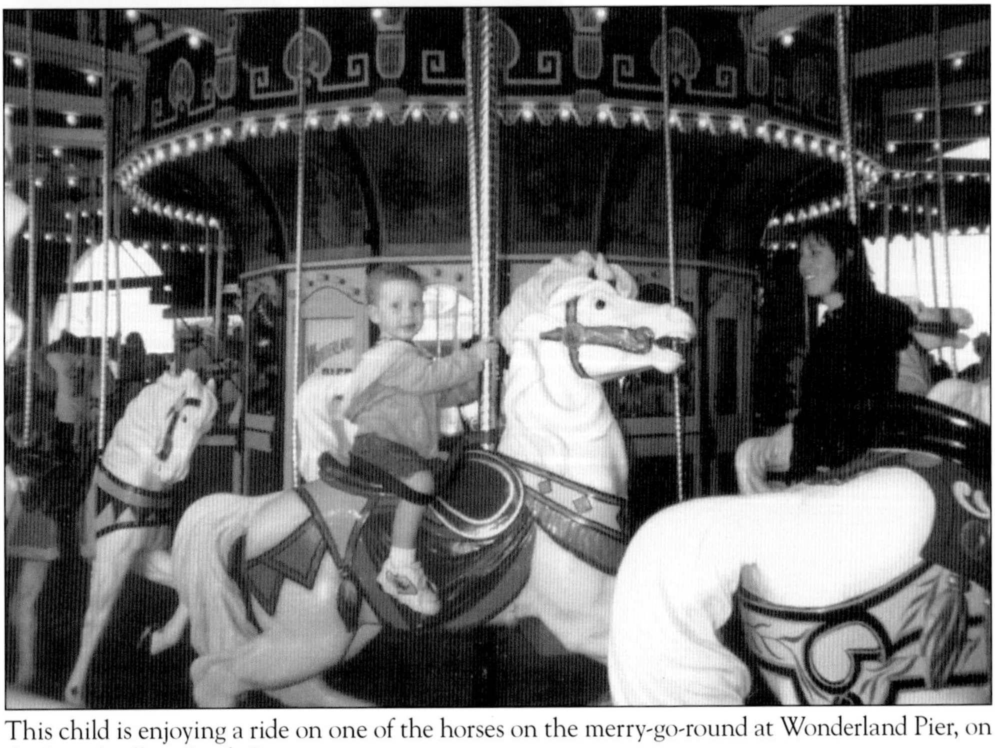

This child is enjoying a ride on one of the horses on the merry-go-round at Wonderland Pier, on the boardwalk at Sixth Street.

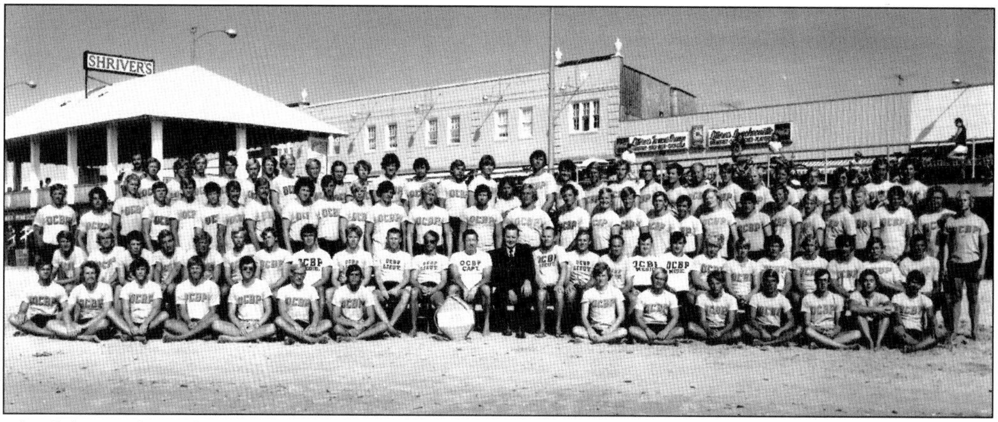

The lifeguards in this 1971 group photograph had much to celebrate—for the 11th year in a row, they won both the ocean and pool South Jersey beach patrol tournaments.

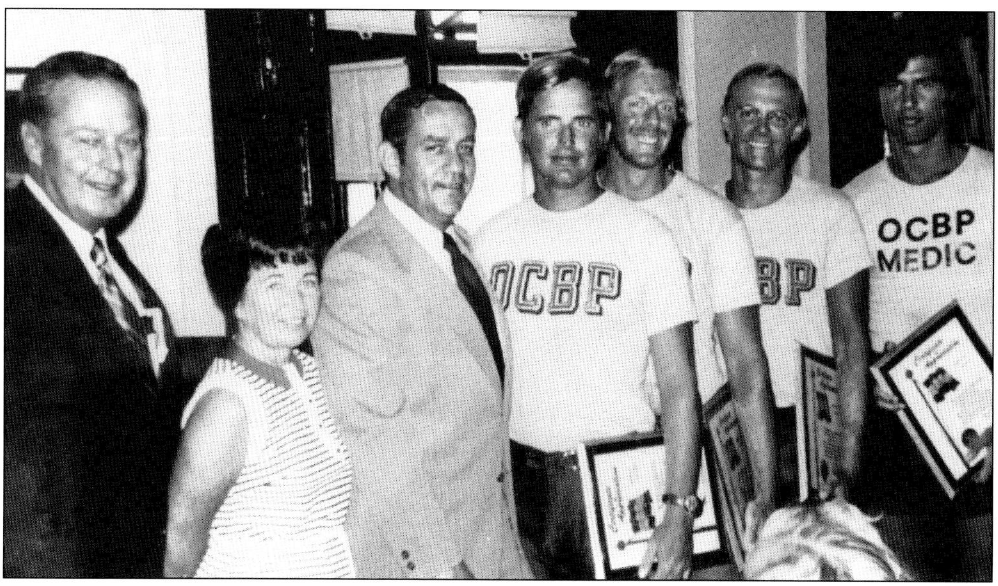

On July 21, 1972, Marilyn K. Moore, the first woman commissioner, Commissioner Luther L. Wallace III (left), and Mayor B. Thomas Waldman presented certificates of appreciation in recognition of exceptional rescues to four members of the Ocean City Beach Patrol. The lifeguards are, from left to right, Edward Roberts, Paul Painten, Jon Piper, and medic Robert Leoffler.

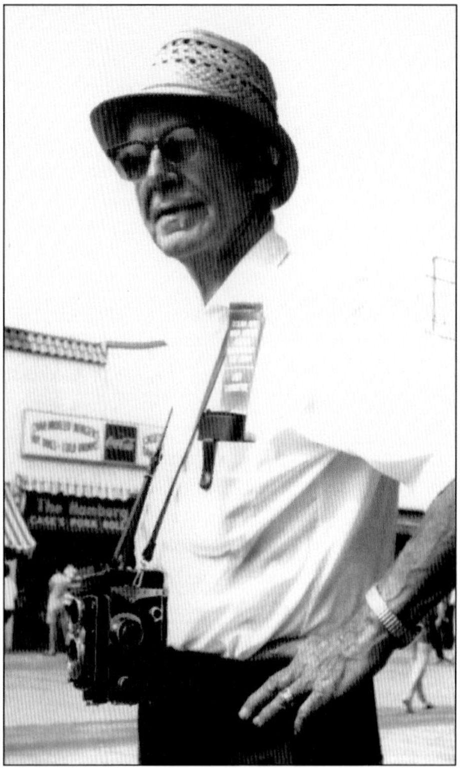

Al Senior, owner of Senior Studios at 838 Asbury Avenue, died on June 27, 1972. Before opening the store on Asbury Avenue, he had operated one on the boardwalk for 27 years. A fine photographer, he photographed most of the events and buildings in Ocean City for many years. Upon his death, his daughter and son-in-law, Doris and Bob Marts, took over the business.

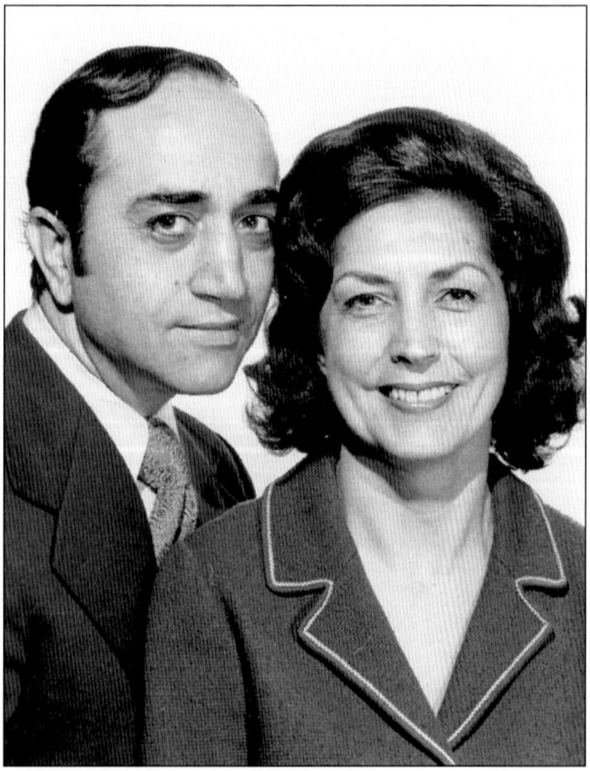

Ocean City native Angela Pulvino was the first woman elected as Cape May County clerk. Her husband, James N. Pulvino, was an art teacher at Ocean City High School for many years before being appointed assistant principal there in 1964.

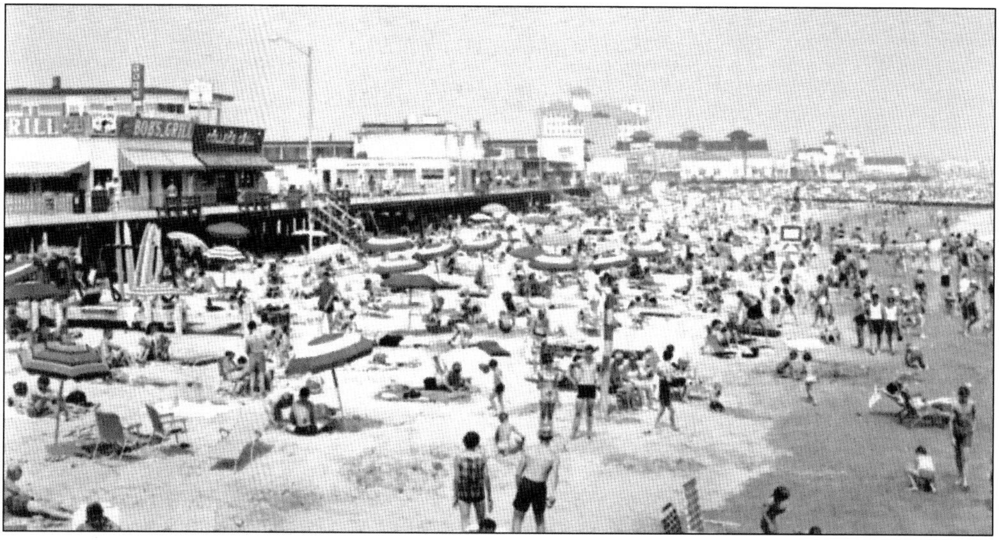

Bob's Grill on the boardwalk at Fourteenth Street, and the College Grill, next door, were popular eateries on the boardwalk for many years.

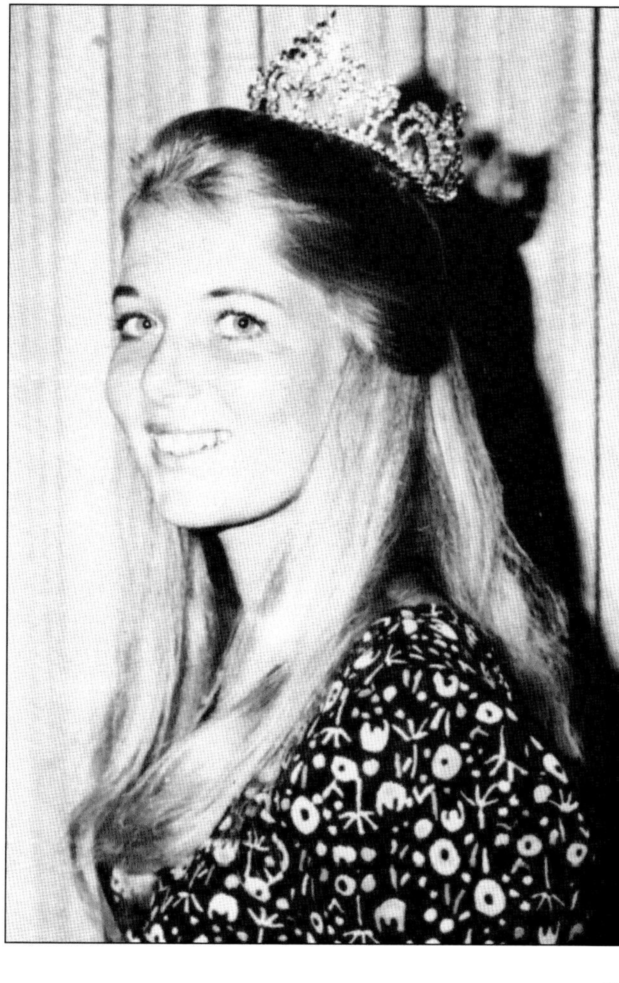

Miss Ocean City 1972, Deborah Mowbray, was the official city greeter for the year and represented Ocean City at various functions.

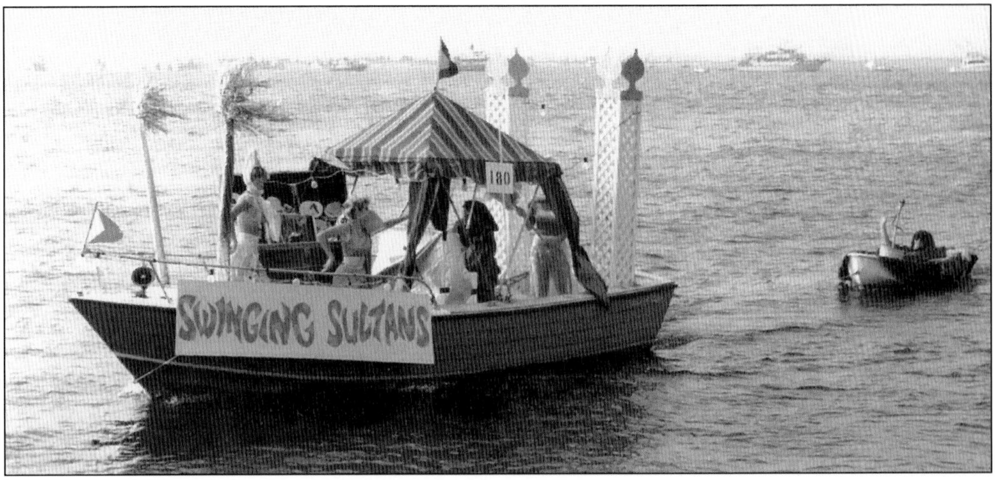

July 29 was the date for the 1972 Night in Venice boat parade, and the weather cooperated, thanks in part perhaps to Bill Kuster, the KYW-TV weatherman who was the guest of honor! The parade of decorated and lighted boats started at the Ocean City Yacht Club, on the bay at Battersea Road, and continued south in and out of the lagoons. A fireworks display set off in the marshes capped off the evening. This boat, decorated as "The Swinging Sultans," won a prize.

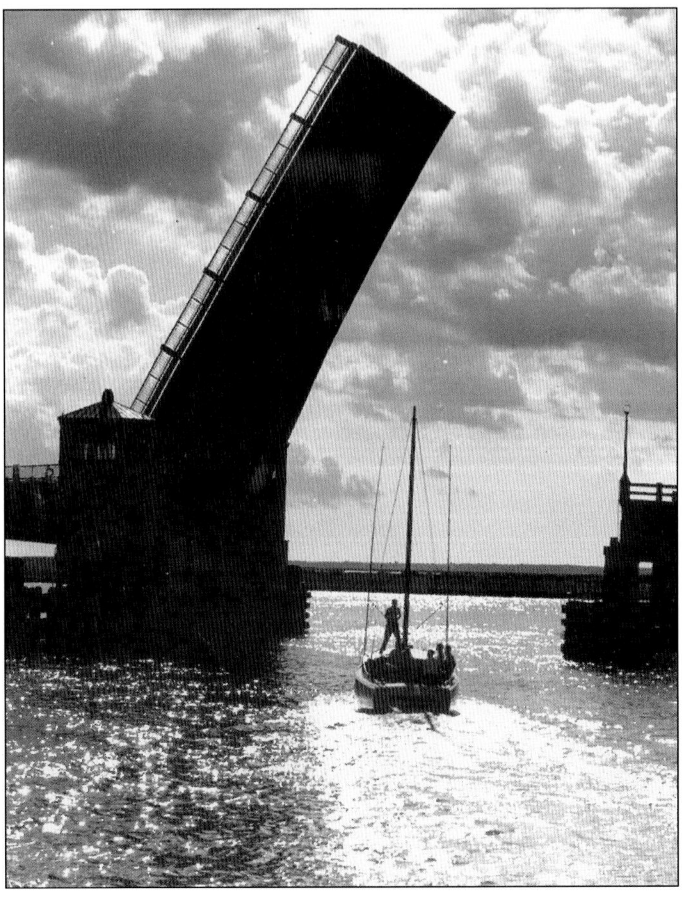

This scene of the Ninth Street bridge, open to allow a boat to pass through, is one that has been seen many times by people in cars stopped on the bridge. Four bridges, two of which are drawbridges, must be crossed on the causeway leading into Ocean City from Somers Point.

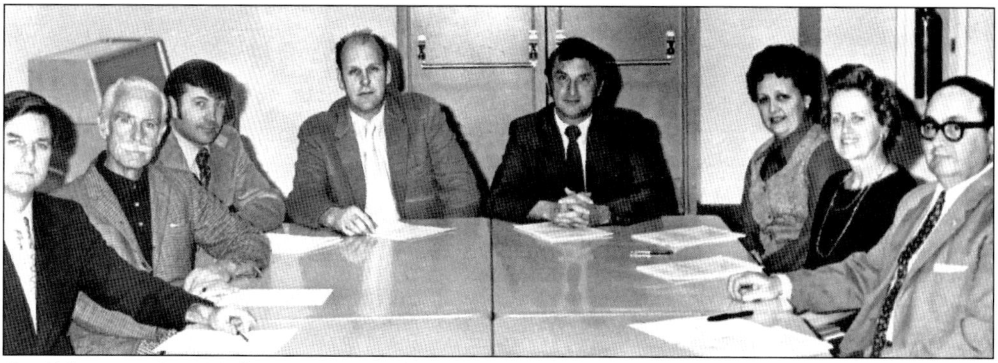

On February 13, 1973, history was made when, for the first time, voters were asked to elect four members of the school board and to vote on the school budget. The school board went from being a seven-member appointed board to a nine-member board, some elected and some appointed by the commissioners. In this photograph are, from left to right, Robert Lautenschlager (elected), Rodman Boone (elected), Robert Becotte (appointed), Frank Unger (appointed), president Herbert Adams (appointed), Margaret Sharp (elected), Anne Gerken (appointed), and David Blyler (elected). Vice president Robert Lowry (appointed) was absent from the picture.

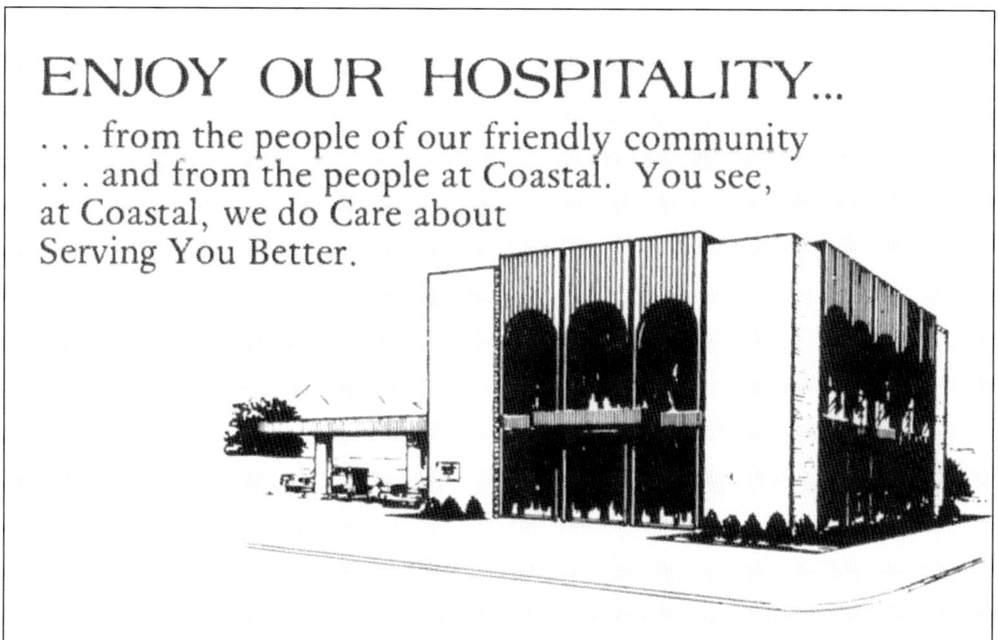

Coastal Bank, on the southwest corner of Ninth Street and Central Avenue, opened in 1971. It was the first new bank to open in Ocean City since the mid-1930s.

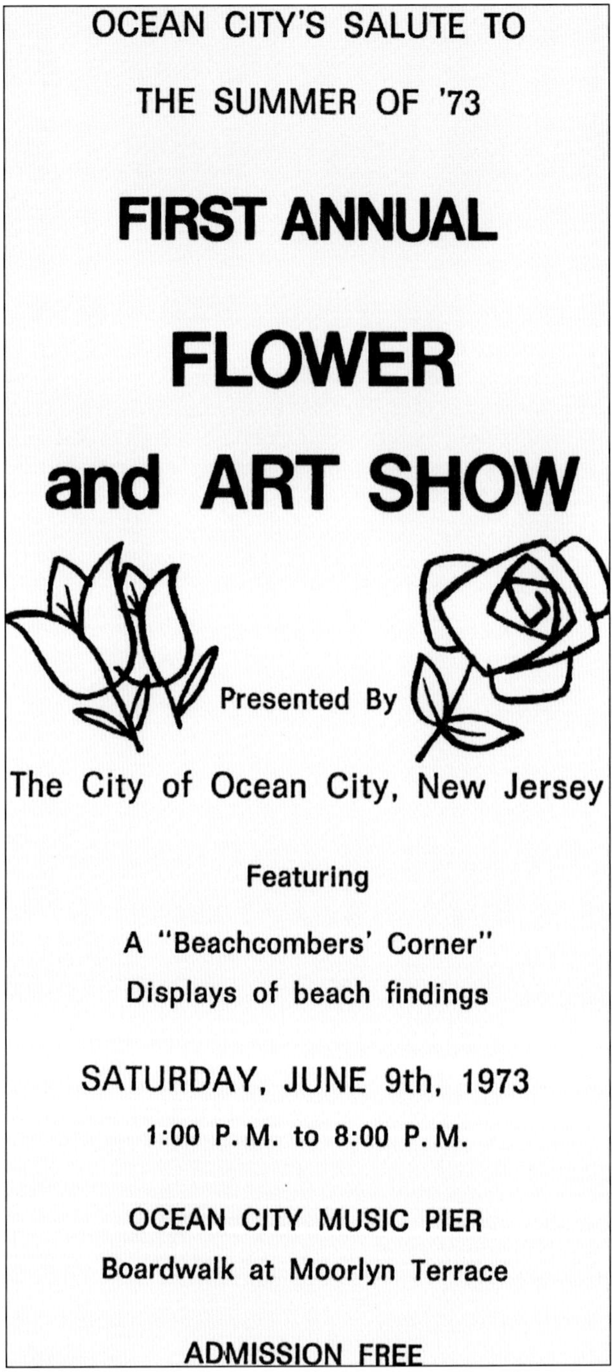

The First Annual Flower and Art Show took place on Saturday, June 9, 1973. The show was the idea of Ocean City's director of public relations, Mark Soifer, and local artist and owner of the boardwalk's Connoisseur Shop, Jim Penland, who recruited members of the Garden Club of Ocean City for the flower show committee. Besides exhibits of flowers and potted plants, there were displays of bonsai and of driftwood and shells. There were also special exhibits on conservation and education.

The Episcopal congregation was organized as a parish in 1894. Members purchased a lot on the northeast corner of Eleventh Street and Central Avenue and built this church, Holy Trinity. The building was not consecrated until it was entirely free of debt in 1907. In 1974, the congregation sold the building to members of the Central Baptist Church. The building was sold again in 1979, and razed in 1980.

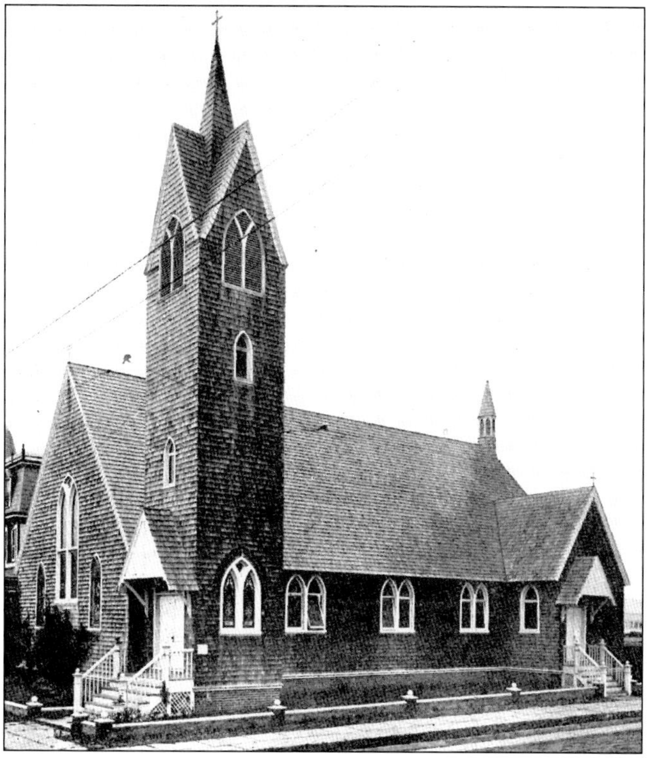

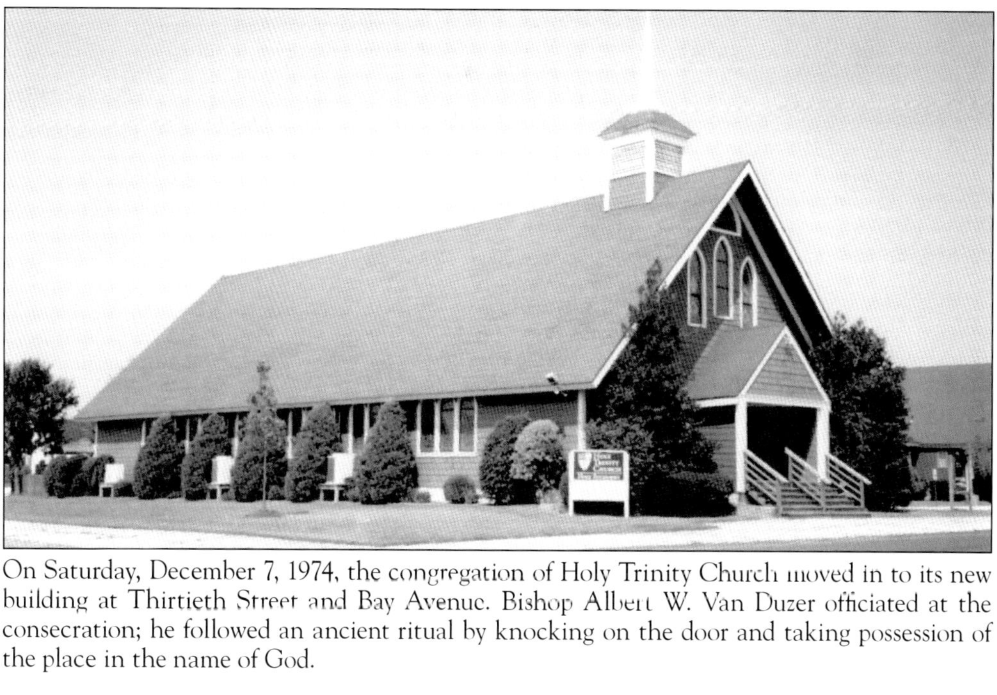

On Saturday, December 7, 1974, the congregation of Holy Trinity Church moved in to its new building at Thirtieth Street and Bay Avenue. Bishop Albert W. Van Duzer officiated at the consecration; he followed an ancient ritual by knocking on the door and taking possession of the place in the name of God.

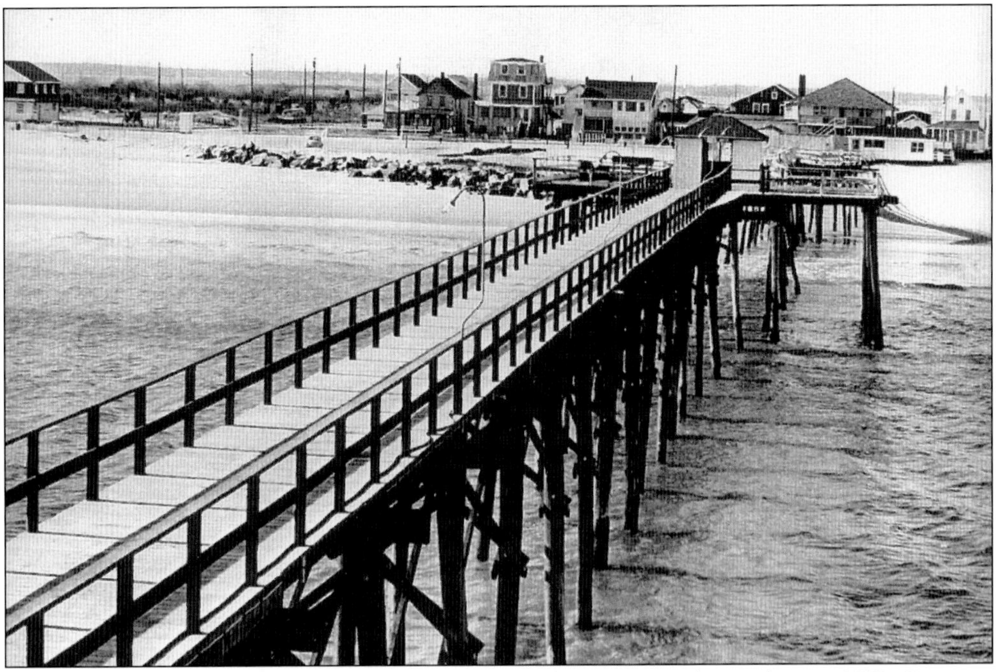

The public fishing pier at Fifty-ninth Street was a favorite spot for anglers in 1974. Open to the public throughout the year, it extended 1,000 feet into the Atlantic Ocean, making it the longest fishing pier in South Jersey.

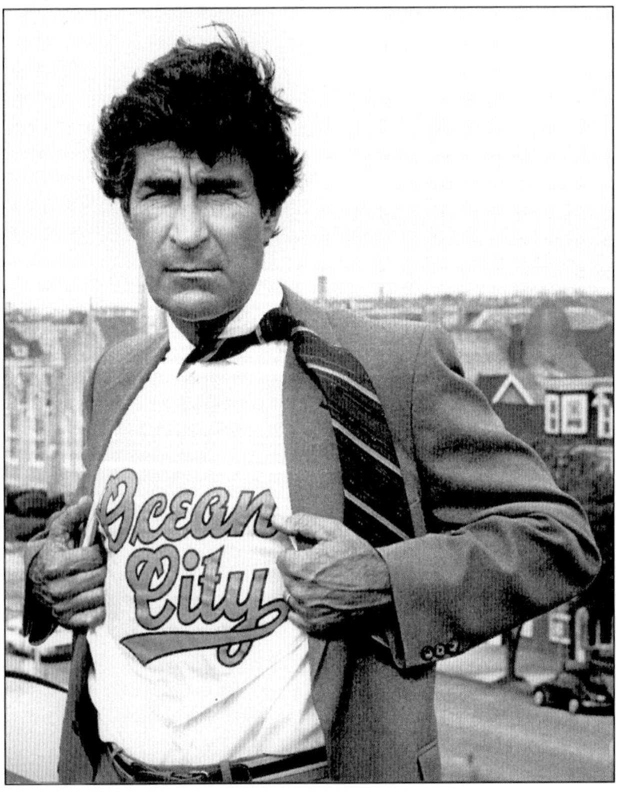

Mark Soifer, Ocean City's director of public relations, planned to be a journalist when he graduated from Temple University. Fortunately for Ocean City, when he was ready to look for a job, there was a newspaper strike in Philadelphia and he took a job in public relations instead. He began working on a freelance basis to promote the Ocean City Art Show and other events during the 1960s. In 1971, Mayor B. Thomas Waldman hired him full time. As public relations director, Mark Soifer has been credited with extending the tourist season and with inventing many weird and wonderful characters and events, all to promote Ocean City.

The road to happiness . . . .
is only a tankful away . . .
to Ocean City, New Jersey . . .

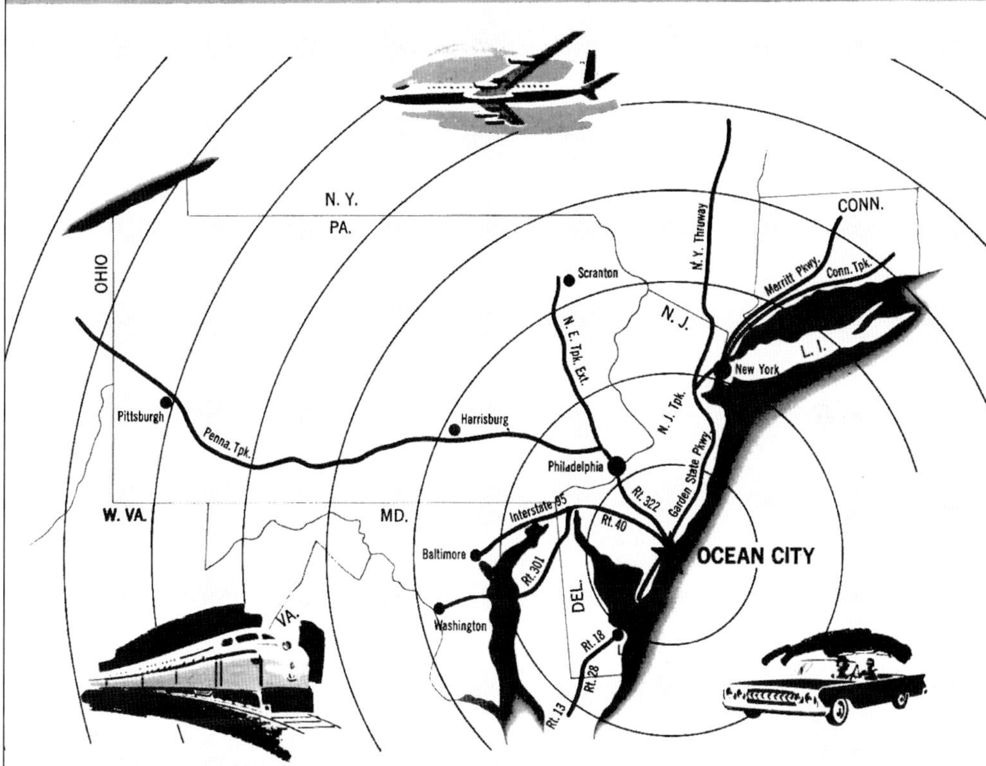

from West by car: Pennsylvania Turnpike or its Northeastern Extension to Schuylkill Expressway to Walt Whitman Bridge over Delaware River; follow New Jersey Freeway (N.J. 42) to junction with U.S. Route 322, or Atlantic City Expressway, to Garden State Parkway Southbound to Exit 30 to Ocean City, N.J.

from North by car: New York Thruway to Exit 14 A, Garden State Parkway connection, thru to Exit 30 to Ocean City; or Cross George Washington Bridge and follow U. S. 1 & 9 to New Jersey Turnpike to Exit 10, Garden State Parkway connection, South to Exit 30 for Ocean City.

from South by car: Follow U. S. 40 or Md.-Del. Highway Interstate 95 to U. S. 40; Cross Delaware Memorial Bridge, continue on U. S. 40 to junction N. J. County Road 563 to Garden State Parkway southbound to Exit 30 for Ocean City; or follow U. S. 13 to Laurel; take Delaware Route 28 and 18 to Lewes; ferry to Cape May; Garden State Parkway to Exit 25 to Ocean City.

by rail from All Points: At Philadelphia take Hi-Speed Line to Lindenwold; train leaves Lindenwold for Ocean City. Be sure your train is scheduled to arrive in Philadelphia in sufficient time to make connection.

by air from Anywhere: At Philadelphia or Newark, transfer to Allegheny Air Line Commuter Service; fly to Atlantic City; bus to Ocean City. Private planes land at Ocean City Airport.

Gasoline was in short supply in 1974, but Ocean City public relations director Mark Soifer reminded tourists "The road to happiness . . . is only a tankful away. . . . "

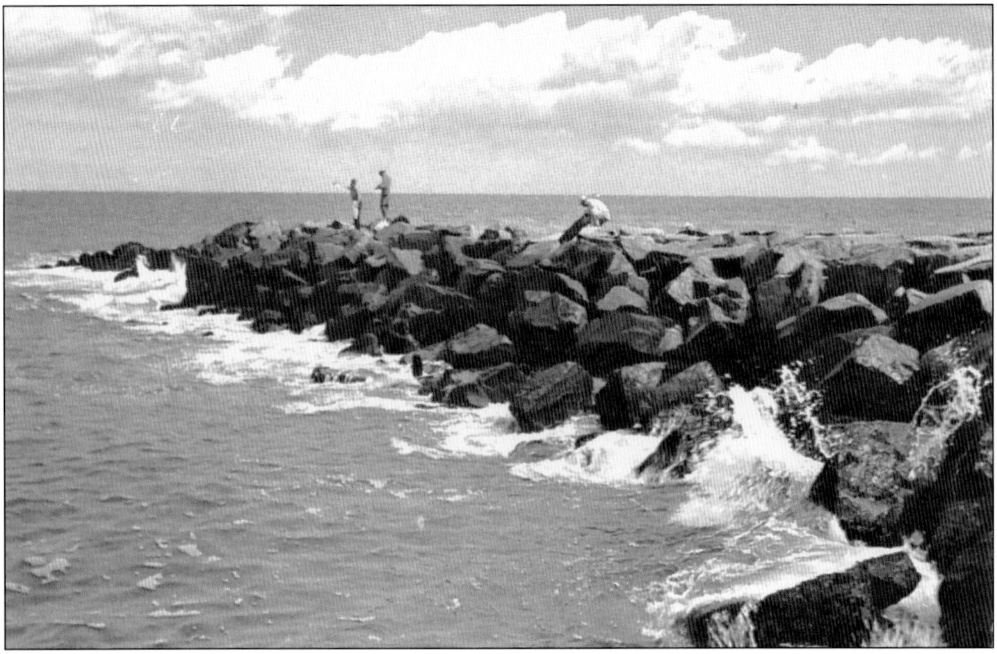

The Fifth Street jetty is used as a fishing pier. The top of this rock jetty was filled in with concrete to make it easier to walk on.

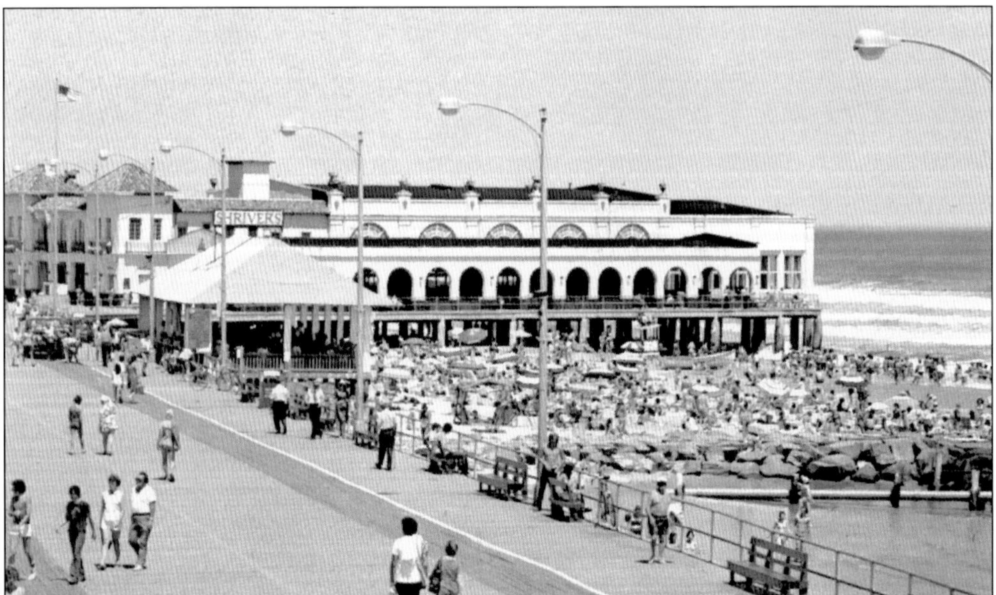

The Ocean City Music Pier, on the boardwalk at Moorlyn Terrace, is truly an Ocean City landmark. This picture shows the boardwalk and crowded beach just south of the Music Pier.

Six

Ocean City Celebrates 1975–1980

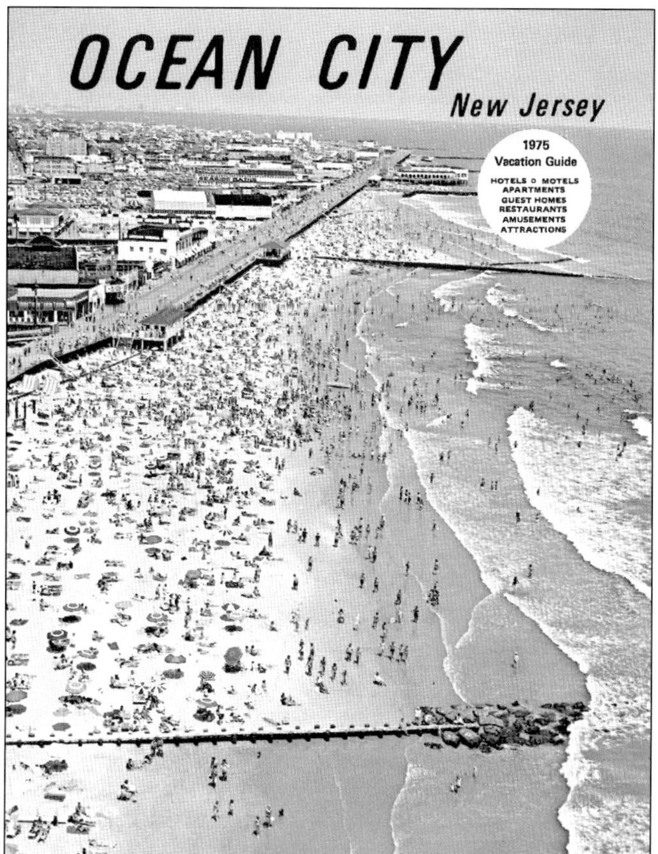

This photograph on the cover of the *1975 Vacation Guide* shows the wide beaches looking north from Thirteenth Street.

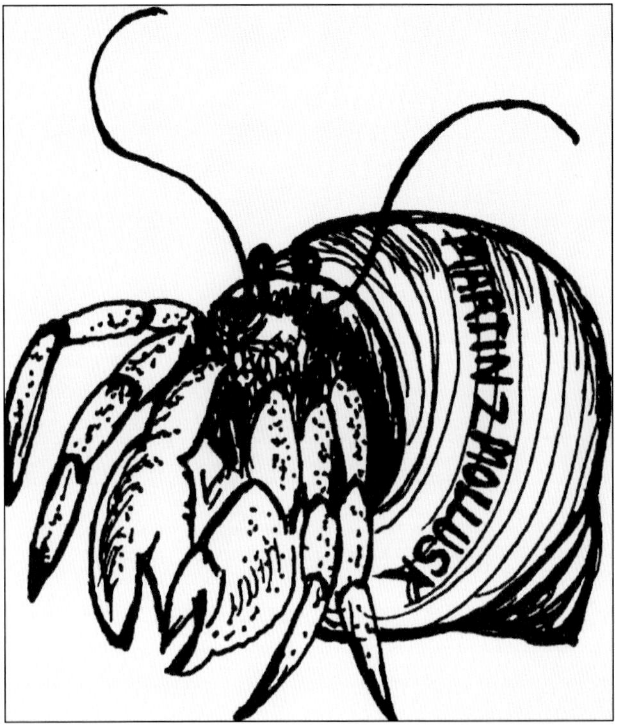

The story of Martin Z. Mollusk is told by Mark Soifer in *The Martin Z. Mollusk Story (Rhyme and Punishment)*: "The long awaited, feverishly anticipated life story of Ocean City's relatively famous Hermit Crab." Martin Z., as he is affectionately known, was invented by Mark Soifer. Martin Z.'s main job is to predict the beginning of summer. Each year on a Thursday in May he meets the Ocean City High School band and various minor celebrities on the Ninth Street beach near the Music Pier; if he sees his shadow, and he invariably does, summer will come one week early. Mary K. Simon made this illustration of Martin Z.

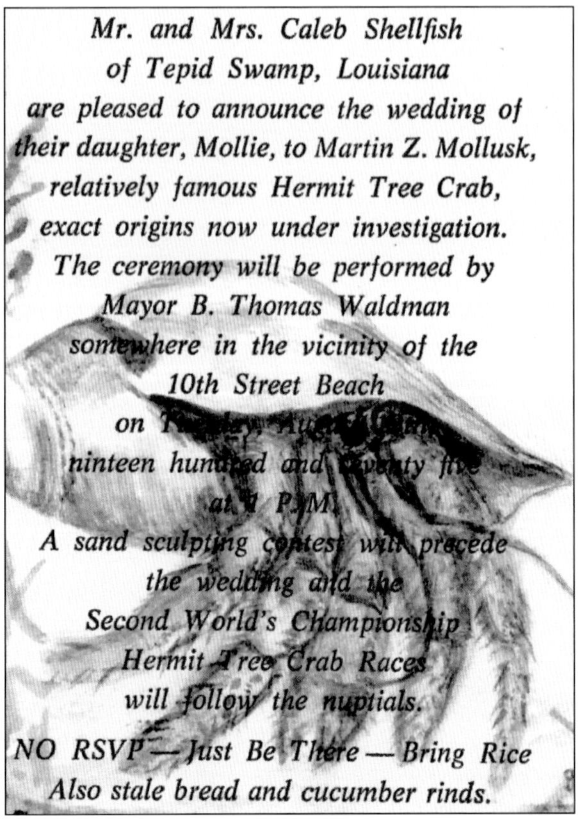

Mr. and Mrs. Caleb Shellfish
of Tepid Swamp, Louisiana
are pleased to announce the wedding of
their daughter, Mollie, to Martin Z. Mollusk,
relatively famous Hermit Tree Crab,
exact origins now under investigation.
The ceremony will be performed by
Mayor B. Thomas Waldman
somewhere in the vicinity of the
10th Street Beach
on Tuesday, August [illegible]
ninteen hundred and seventy five
at 7 P.M.
A sand sculpting contest will precede
the wedding and the
Second World's Championship
Hermit Tree Crab Races
will follow the nuptials.
NO RSVP—Just Be There—Bring Rice
Also stale bread and cucumber rinds.

The marriage of Martin Z. Mollusk to Molly Shellfish on August 19, 1975, was announced in the *New York Times*.

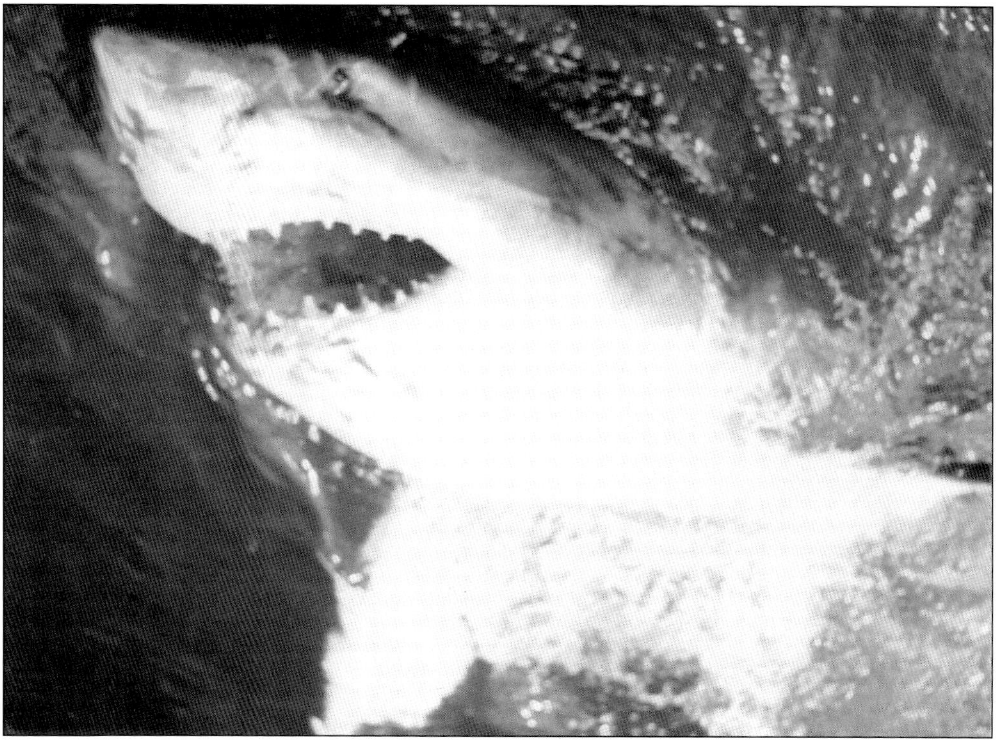

In June 1975, the movie *Jaws* was playing at the Village Theatre on Eighth Street and the boardwalk. Many bathers stayed close to shore after seeing the movie.

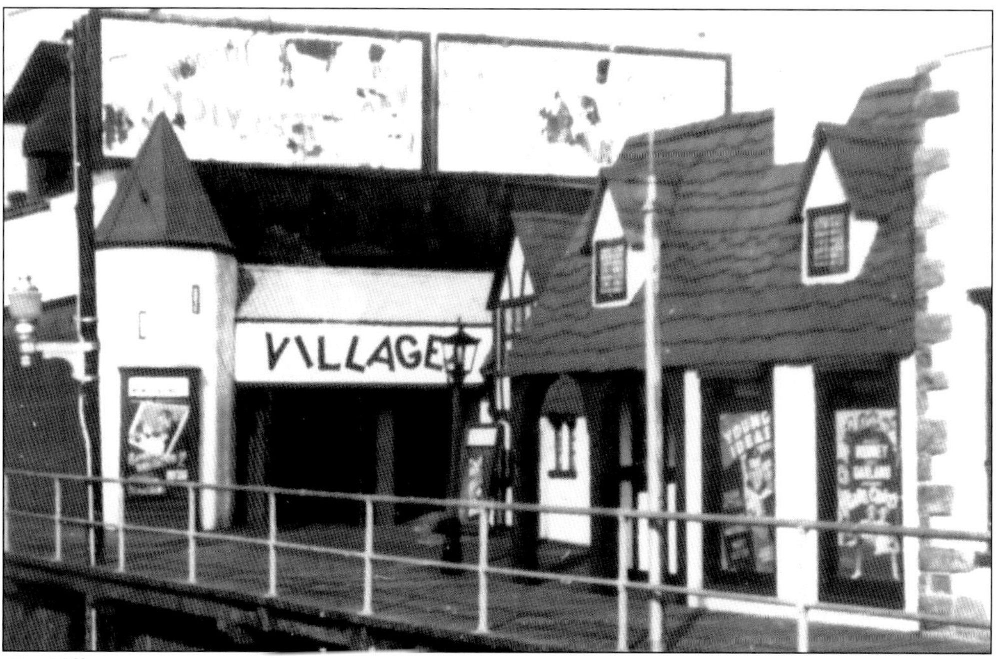

The Village Theatre at Eighth Street and the boardwalk was unique. The outside of the movie house was constructed to resemble an old-fashioned fishing village. The theater could seat 1,000 patrons.

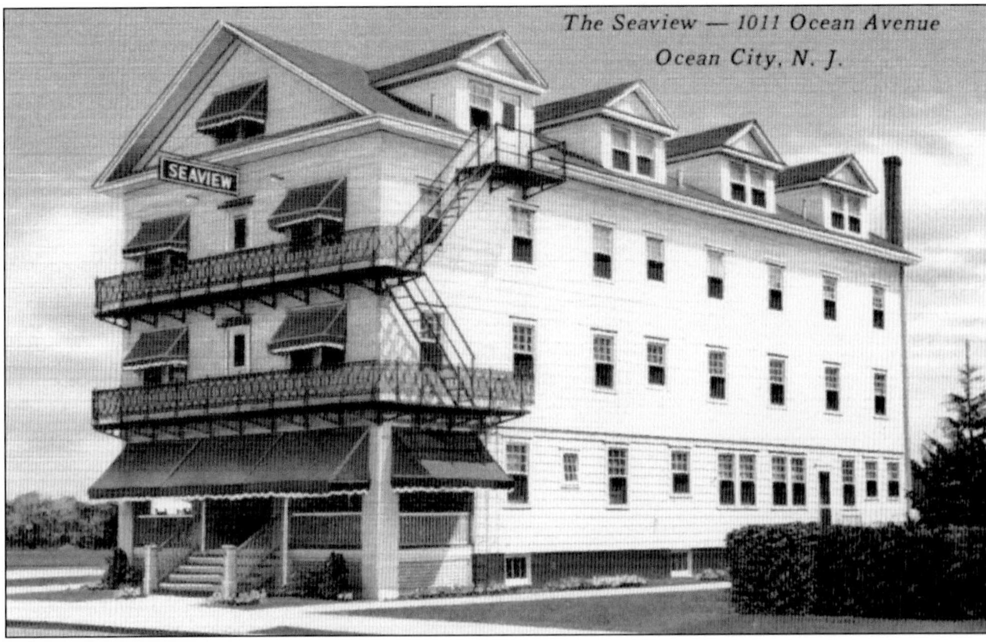

The Seaview, located at 1011 Ocean Avenue, offered "A pleasant, friendly atmosphere," and a modern community kitchen equipped with individual units. It was torn down in 1975.

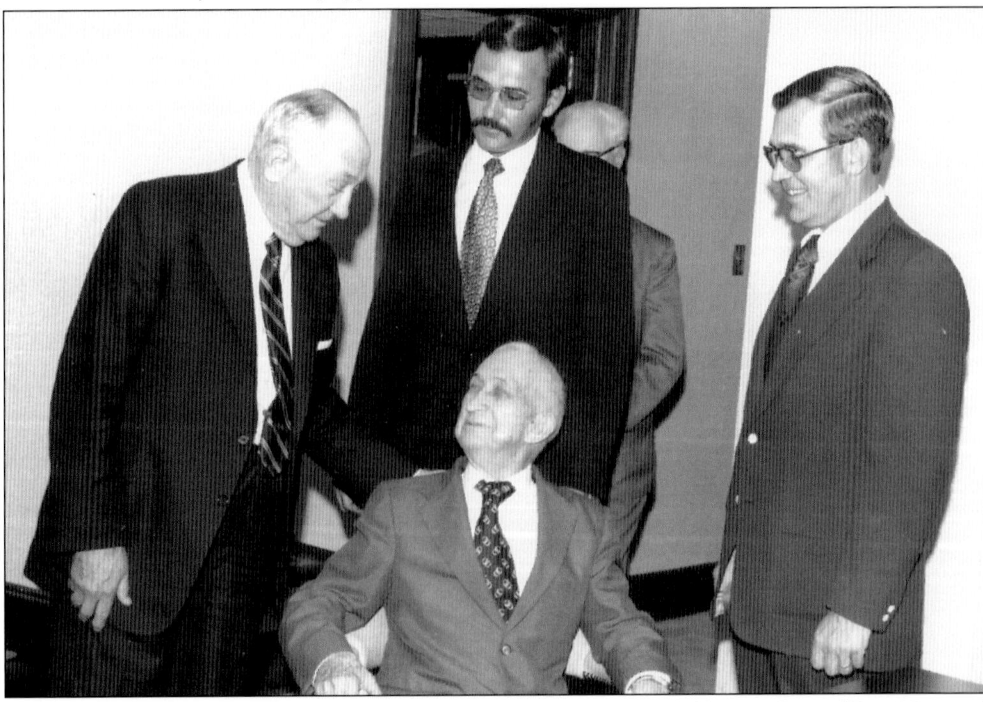

In this photograph taken on August 8, 1975, Elwood F. Kirkman (left), president of First National Bank of South Jersey, welcomes Howard S. Stainton (seated) to the new office of senior trust officer Gene Lindacher (right), while Arthur T. Ford III (center), Stainton's attorney, looks on. The trust office was located on the fifth floor of the First National Bank of South Jersey at 801 Asbury Avenue.

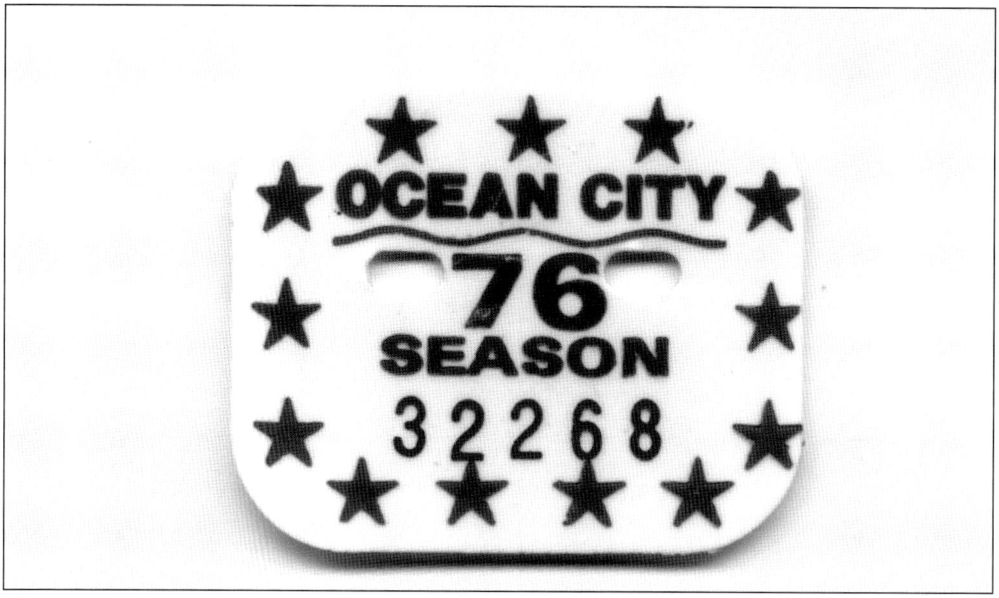

The year 1976 was the first year beach users were required to wear a beach tag. A seasonal tag was $3 if bought by the end of May; $5 after May 31. The weekly tags, good Saturday to Saturday, cost $1.50. The city had anticipated $440,000 from the sale of the tags, but at the end of the summer beach fee supervisor Clifford Phifer reported $761,240 had been collected.

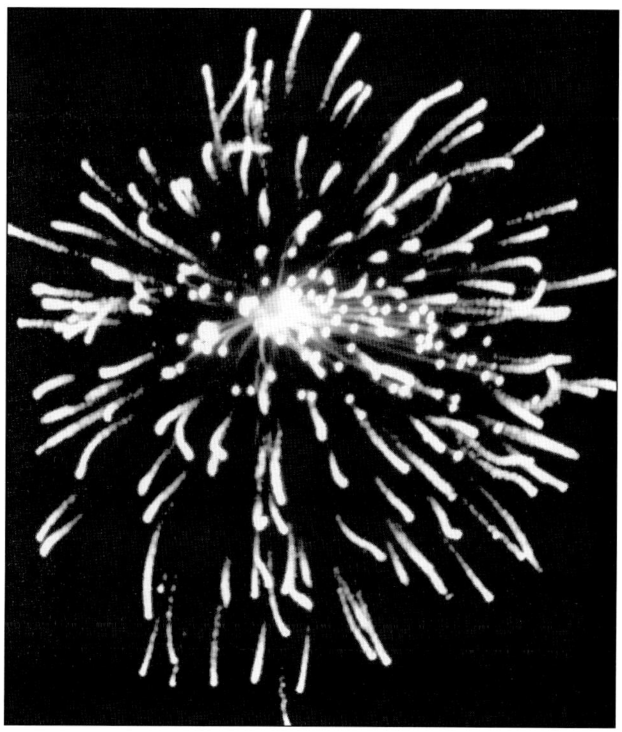

The Ocean City ordinance concerning what could or could not be done on Sunday was still in effect during the nation's bicentennial year. Amusement rides, movie theaters, and stores were closed on Sunday. This ordinance drew national attention when Ocean City officials decided to celebrate the Fourth of July on July 5 because the fourth fell on a Sunday.

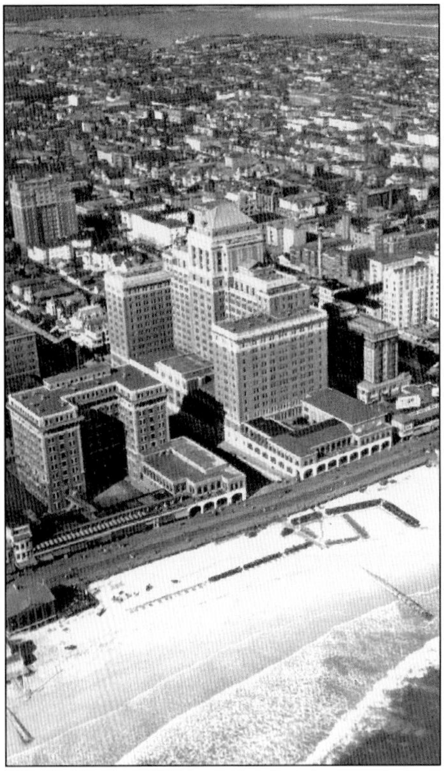

On November 2, 1976, Ocean City voters went to the polls in record numbers. The big surprise of the day was the local support for the state casino gambling constitutional amendment. A strong winner statewide, the question won in Ocean City, 3,595 to 2,968. Eighteen months later, Resorts International Casino opened in the renovated Chalfonte-Haddon Hall in Atlantic City.

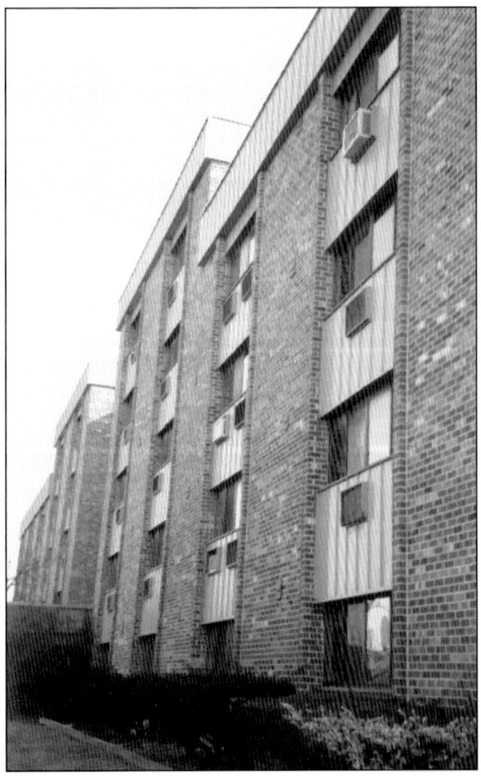

A new federally funded senior citizen housing building on West Avenue between Sixth and Seventh Streets opened in 1975. It contained 60 units, with the fifth floor central area set apart for recreational purposes.

Howard S. Stainton was 90 years old when he was featured on the cover of the 1975 *Weekly Guide of Ocean City*. A vital force in the economic development of Ocean City, he owned and operated the first department store in Cape May County and was a major developer in the resort. He was also a philanthropist; he contributed the property for the senior citizen housing building and when oil prices were very high, his Seashore Oil Company donated the oil needed to heat the Cape May County Rescue Squad and Marmora Volunteer Fire Department buildings.

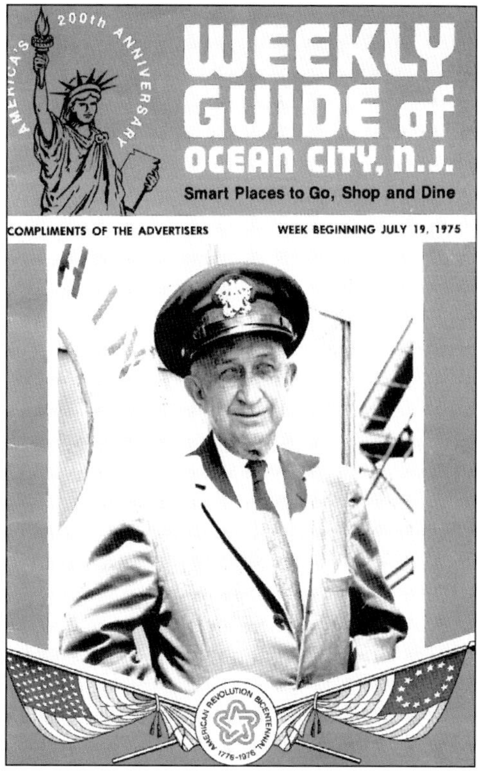

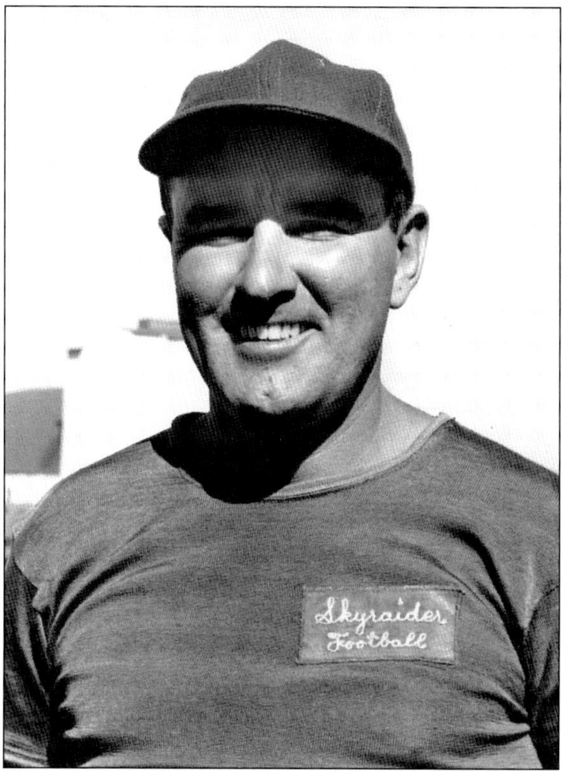

E. Fenton Carey, a long time teacher and coach at Ocean City High School, retired at the end of the 1976 school year. He coached football, basketball, track, baseball, and swimming. Throughout his career, he placed sportsmanship above winning and scholarship above athletics. When the high school yearbook was dedicated to him, the students wrote, "Coach Carey has molded the moral lives of countless boys now in all walks of life. As a man, he lives by the same moral creed he prescribes to his students."

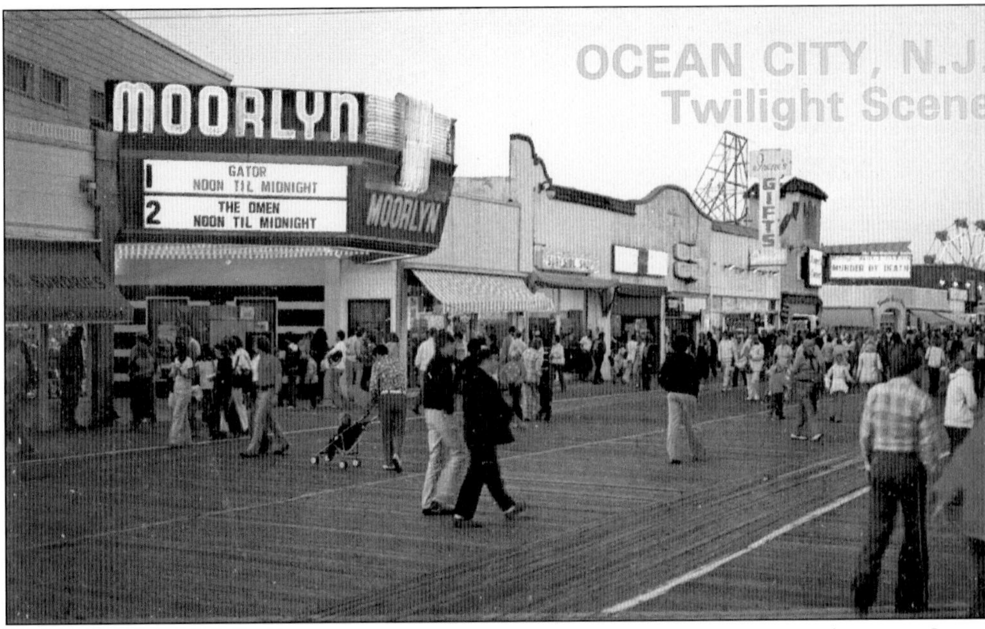

The Moorlyn Theatre on the boardwalk at Moorlyn Terrace was the first movie house in Ocean City to be remodeled into two separate theaters under one roof.

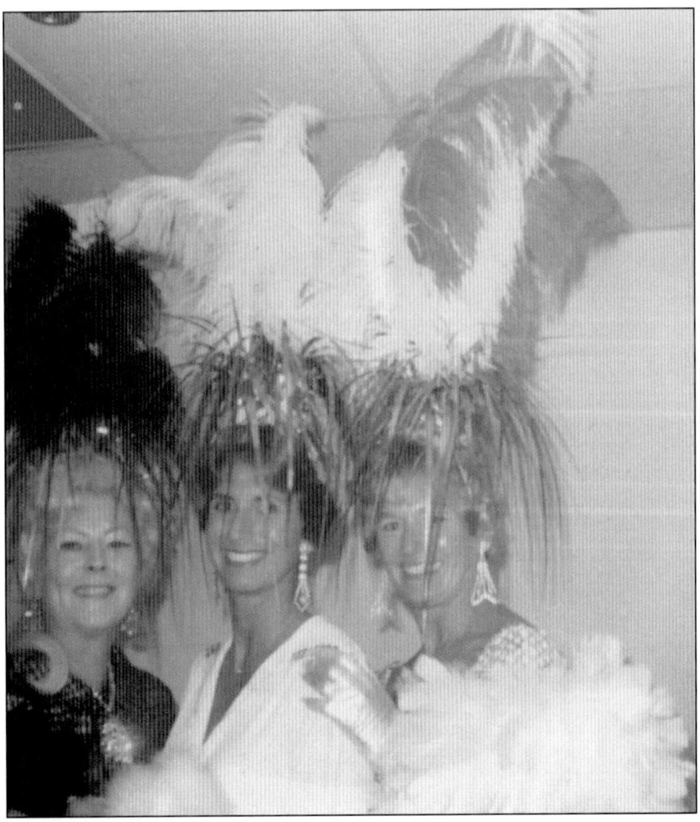

Colony Club women were very active in Ocean City. In this photograph taken on October 9, 1976, Colony Club members, from left to right, Marie French, Cathy Finnegan, and Dottie Raab appeared as show girls at the Colony Club Broadway Dinner Theatre.

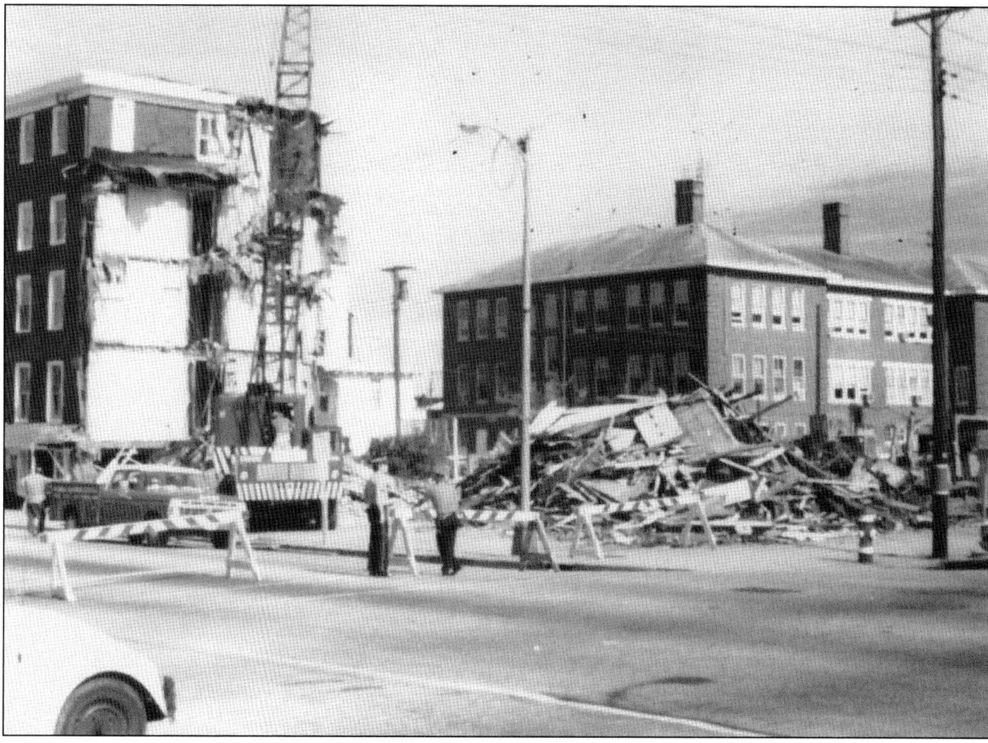

The Strand Hotel, on the northwest corner of Ninth Street and Wesley Avenue, was built in 1894. It advertised " Sanitary plumbing, electric lights, rates the lowest consistent with first-class service." It was razed in September 1977.

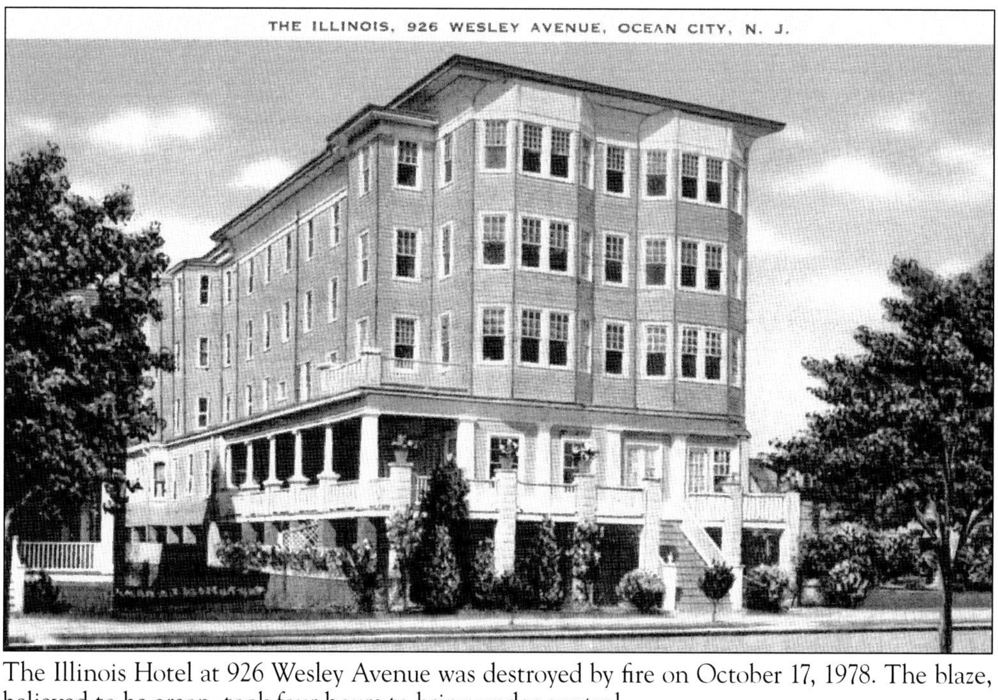

The Illinois Hotel at 926 Wesley Avenue was destroyed by fire on October 17, 1978. The blaze, believed to be arson, took four hours to bring under control.

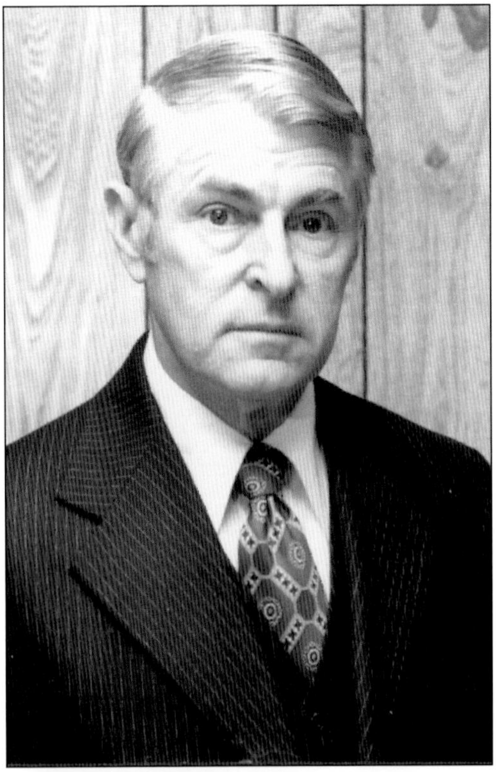

On March 1, 1977, Ocean City residents voted to change their form of government. Since 1911, the city had operated under the city commission form of government: three commissioners governed the city, sharing the administrative duties, with one of them chosen by the three to act as mayor. As 1978 began, Mayor B. Thomas Waldman and Commissioners Luther L. Wallace and Chester J. Wimberg were in charge, but the new mayor-council form of government would take over on July 1 after the May 9 municipal election. This photograph of Chester J. Wimberg was taken after the May 9, 1978, election in which he was the first person elected as mayor.

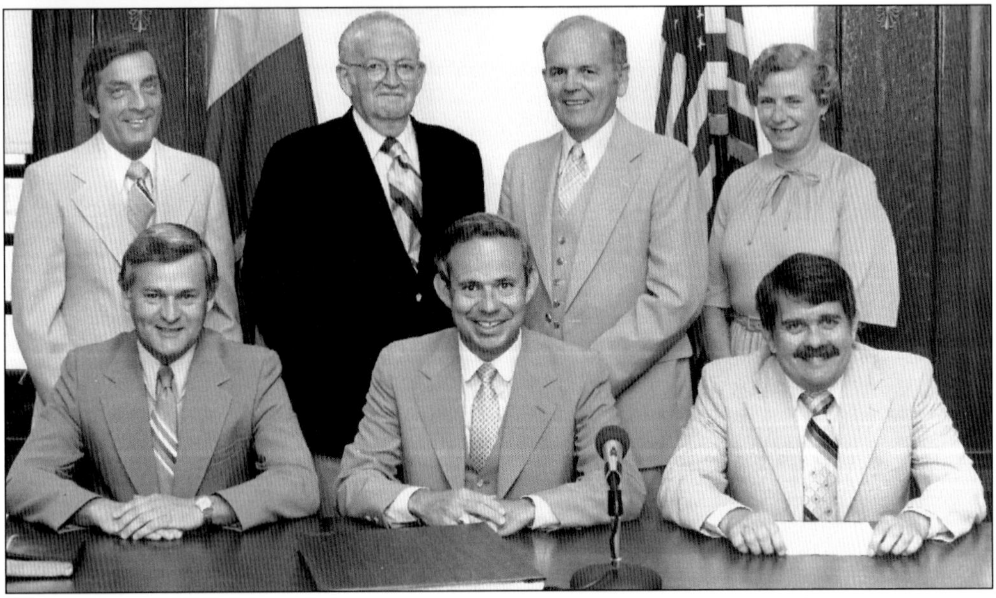

In the May 9, 1978, election, the first one under the new form of government, three were running for the position of mayor, eight were running for three council-at-large positions, and 11 were running for four ward-council positions. Shown are those who won the seven council seats. From left to right are (first row) Jack M. Jones, fourth ward; William H. Woods, first ward; and Henry S. Knight, council-at-large; (second row) Nickolas Trofa Jr., council-at-large; Herbert J. Brownlee Jr., council-at-large; William J. Meis, third ward; and Jeanne M. Clunn, second ward.

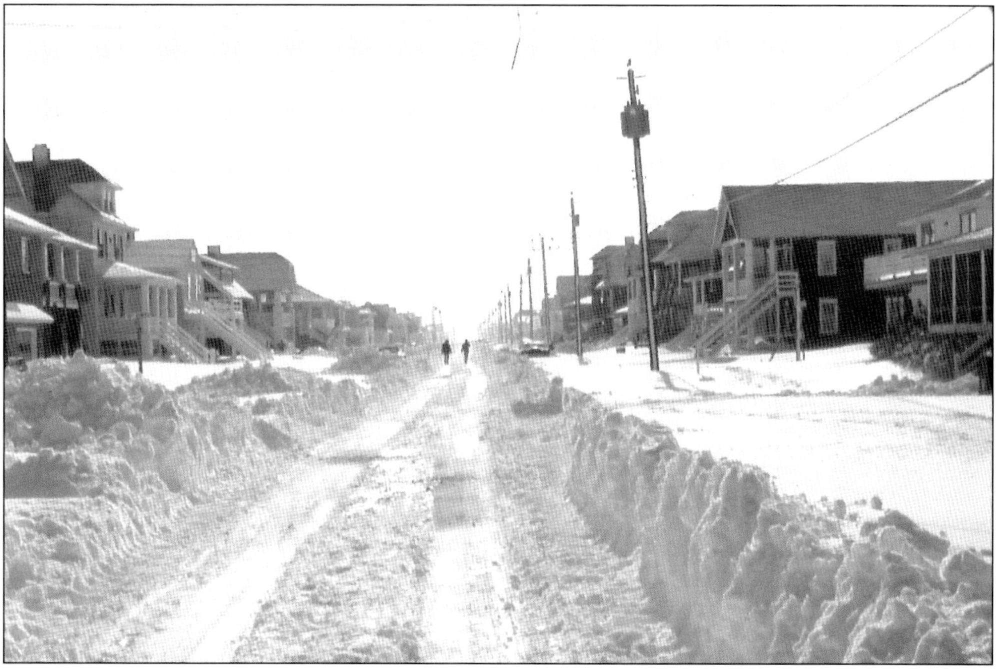

"Blizzard of '78 paralyzes city," was the headline in the Ocean City *Sentinel-Ledger* on February 9, 1978. A smaller headline reported it was the "Third biggest in history." The official total was 13 inches, but some snowdrifts measured 12 feet deep.

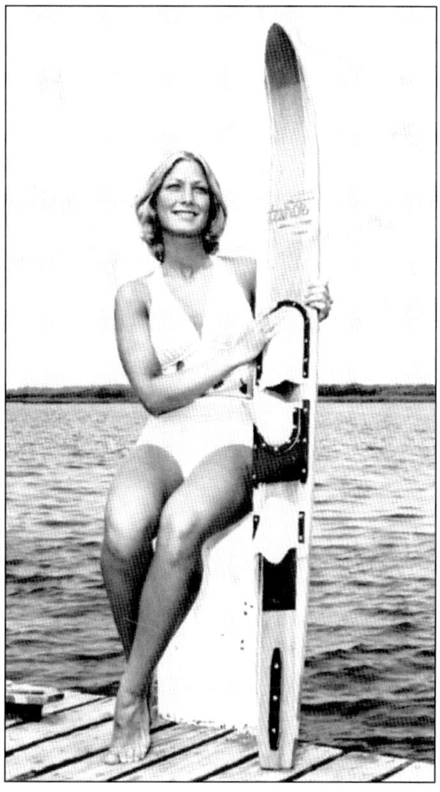

Laurie Berchtold, a 1975 graduate of Ocean City High School, was the first Ocean City woman crowned Miss New Jersey as part of the Miss America Pageant.

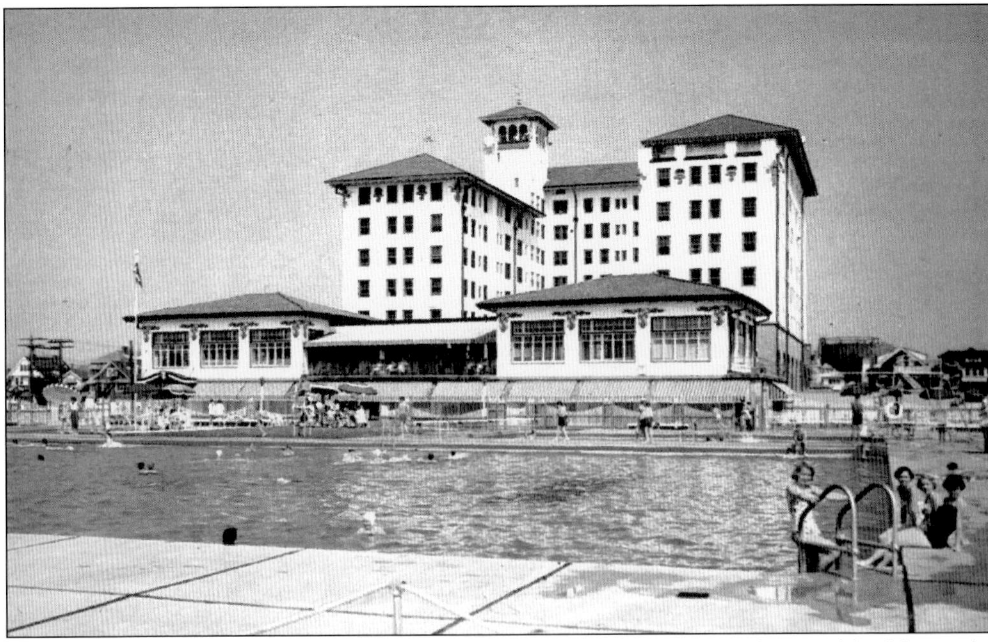

The largest of the Flanders Hotel pools closed on Labor Day, 1978. This pool had been the setting for some of the largest water shows in the country during the 1930s and 1940s.

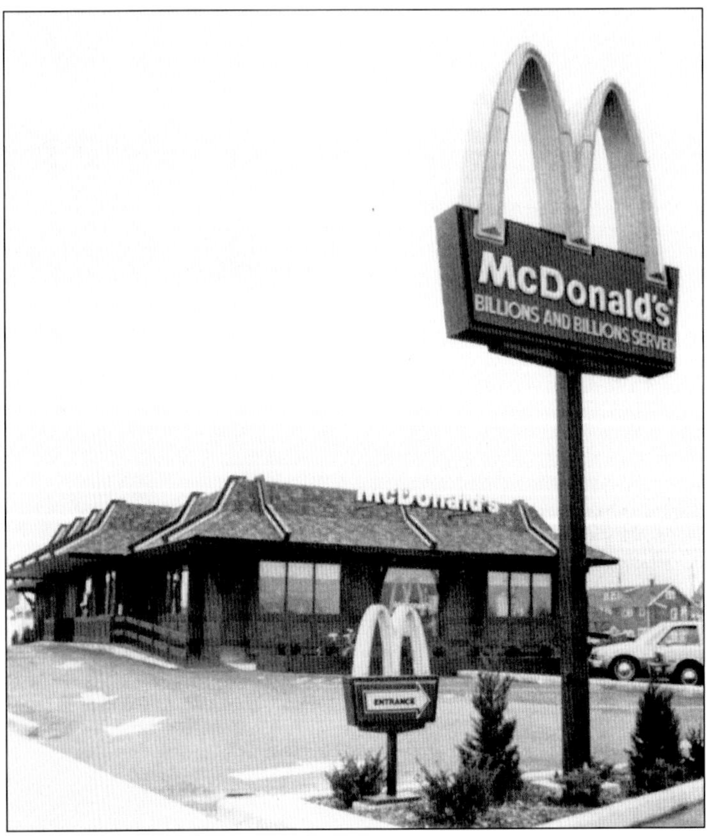

McDonald's opened on the corner of Ninth Street and West Avenue in 1978.

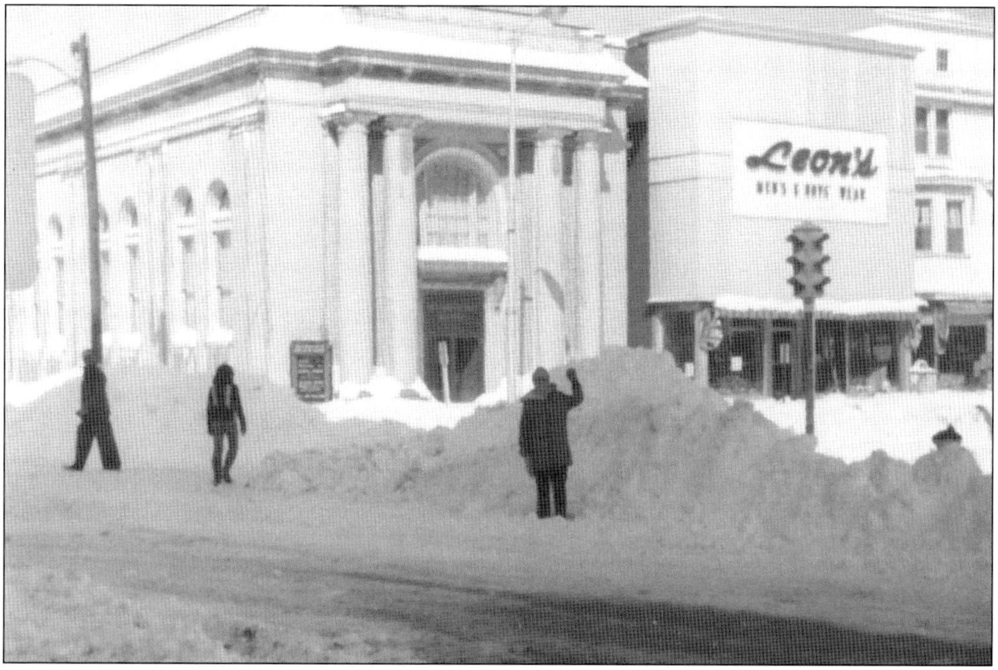

"Winter storm cripples the city," was the headline in the Ocean City *Sentinel-Ledger* on February 22, 1979. National Weather Service officials in Pomona said the two-day storm set a record for the largest amount of snow to fall in a 24-hour period. Seventeen inches of snow fell on Ocean City. This is a photograph of the corner of Eighth Street and Asbury Avenue after the snowfall.

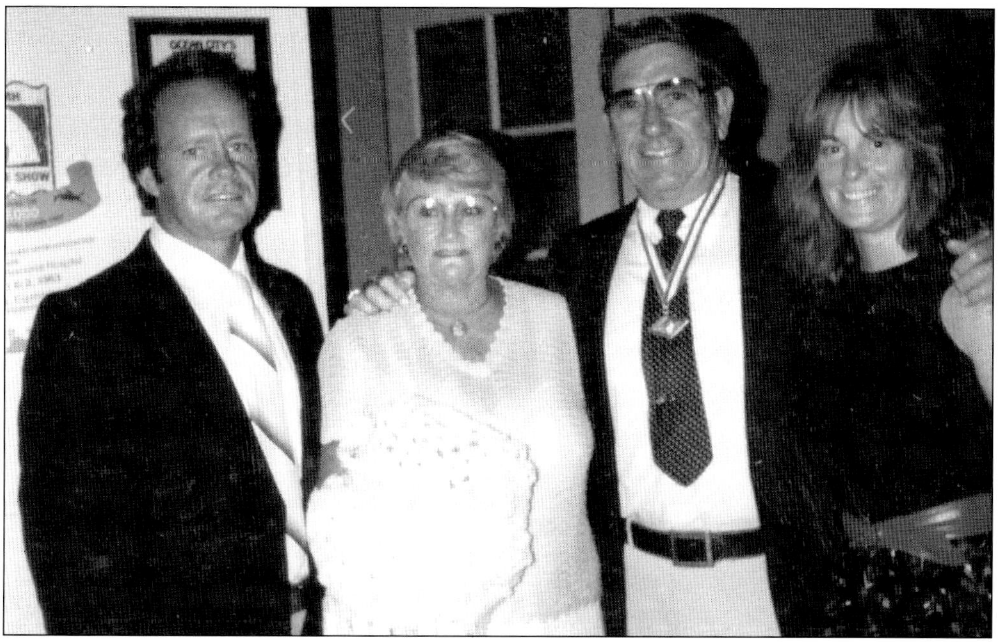

Shown from left to right are Fred Miller, Bettie Lafferty, George T. Lafferty, and Susan Miller at the 1980 Lifeguard Ball. Lafferty was the captain of the Ocean City Beach Patrol and Miller a member of the patrol.

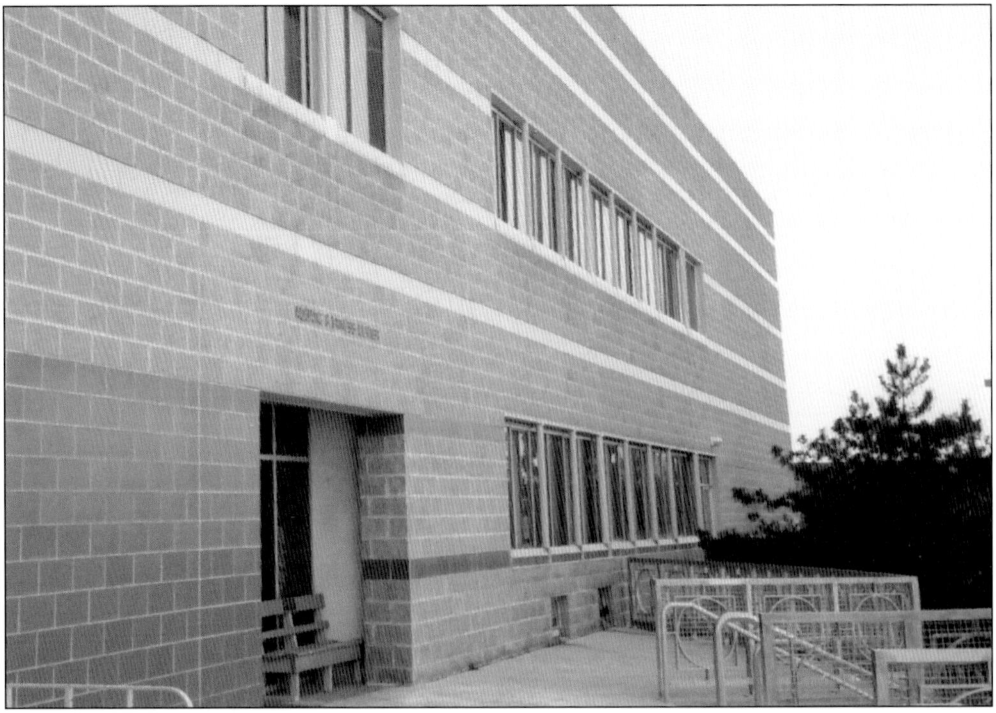

On Sunday, June 10, 1979, recreation commissioners Richard Kabat, Carolyn Murphy, and Thomas Heist cut the ceremonial ribbon to open the Ocean City Community Center.

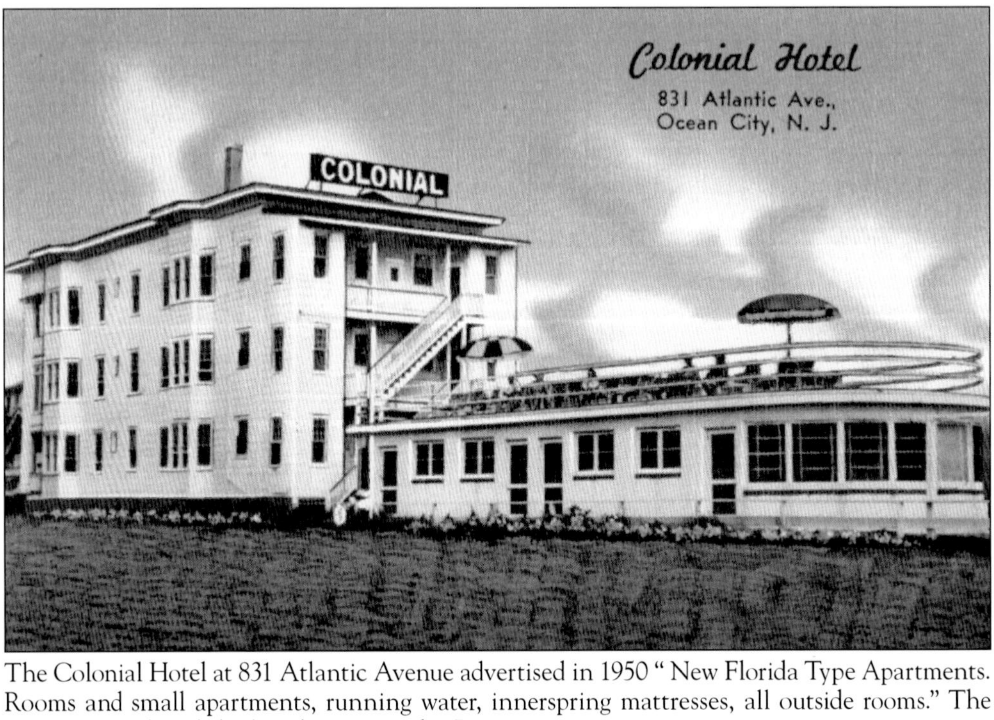

The Colonial Hotel at 831 Atlantic Avenue advertised in 1950 " New Florida Type Apartments. Rooms and small apartments, running water, innerspring mattresses, all outside rooms." The building was demolished in the spring of 1979.

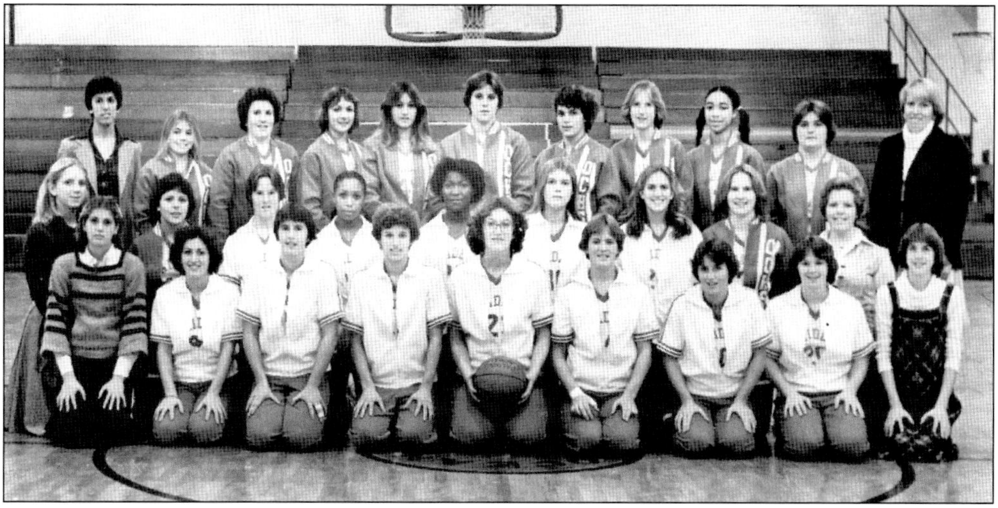

The Ocean City High School girls' basketball team, led by head coach Pat Dougherty and coach Sandra Corson, won its eighth straight Cape-Atlantic League title en route to winning its first South Jersey Group 3 championship.

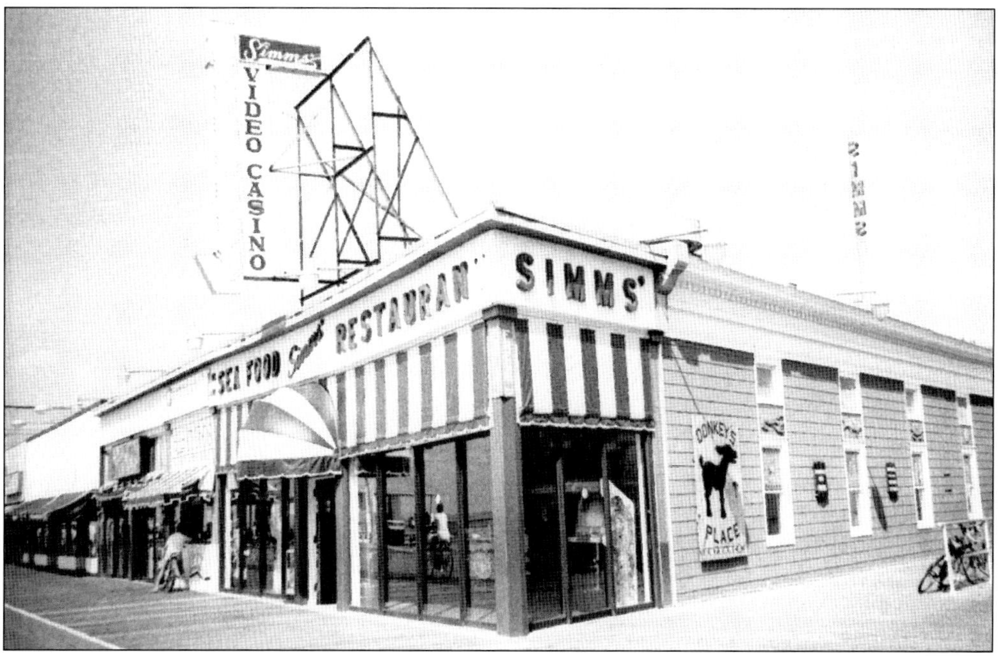

Residents were concerned following the installation of 26 coin-operated video arcade games at historic Simms' Restaurant at 822 Boardwalk. City council held a special meeting on June 17, 1980, to try to close a "loophole" in the arcade ordinance that allowed Simms' owner to move his arcade machines there from other locations.

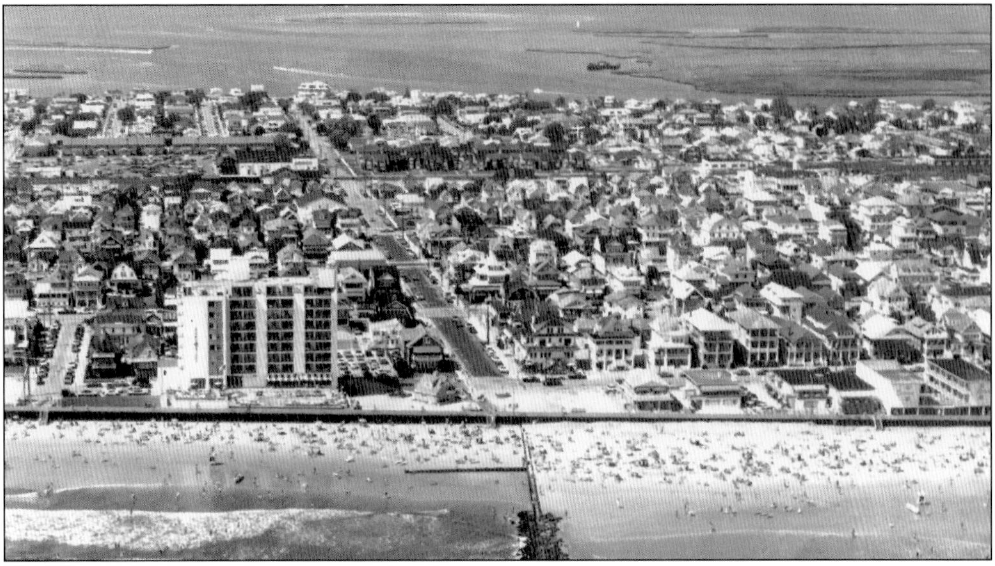

This is an aerial view looking toward the bay from the Fifteenth Street beach area.

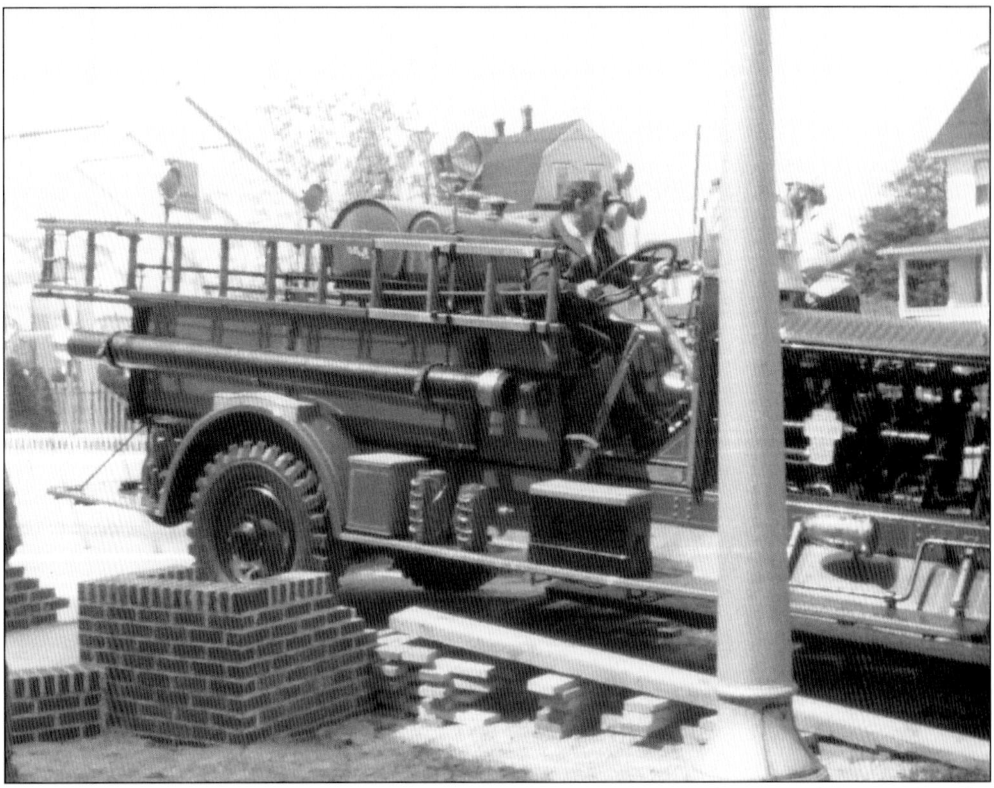

On April 29, 1980, this 1929 fire engine, an Ahrens-Fox pumper that served Ocean City for nearly 50 years, was put on permanent display in a glass showcase outside the Ocean City Historical Museum at 409 Wesley Avenue.

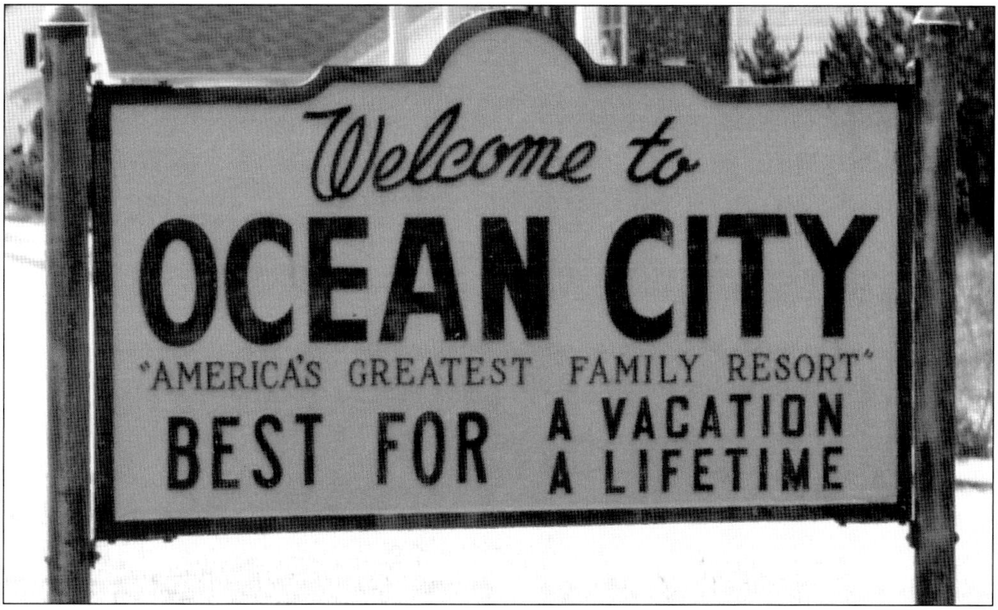

This sign greets visitors as they come over the Ocean City-Longport Bridge at the north end of the island. Ocean City has had the slogan "America's Greatest Family Resort" since 1920.

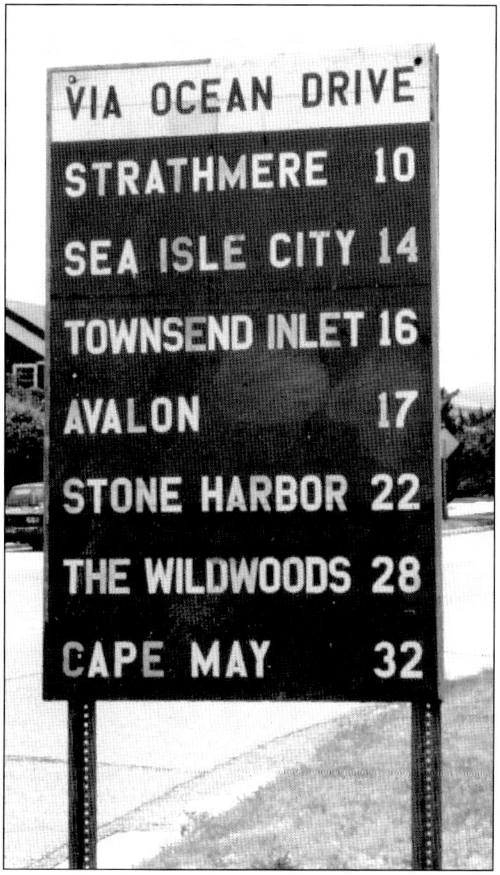

This sign is on Ocean City's Gardens Parkway near the north entrance into the city. Ocean Drive takes a scenic route through South Jersey's shore communities from Atlantic City to Cape May.

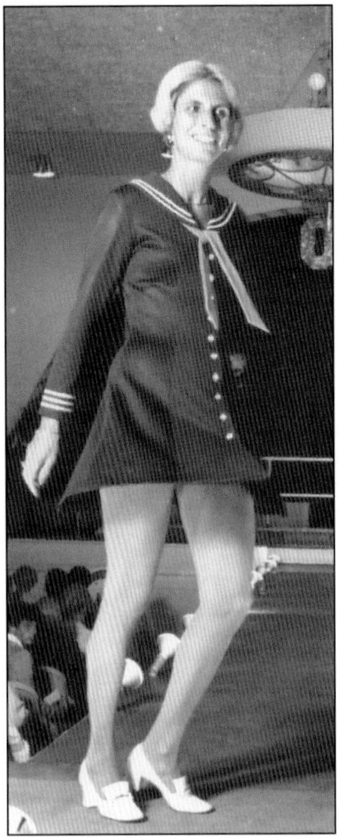

As part of Ocean City's 100th anniversary celebration in 1979, the Colony Club joined with the Ocean City Historical Museum to present "A Century of Fashion." In this photograph, Cathy Finnegan is modeling a 1971 sailor dress.

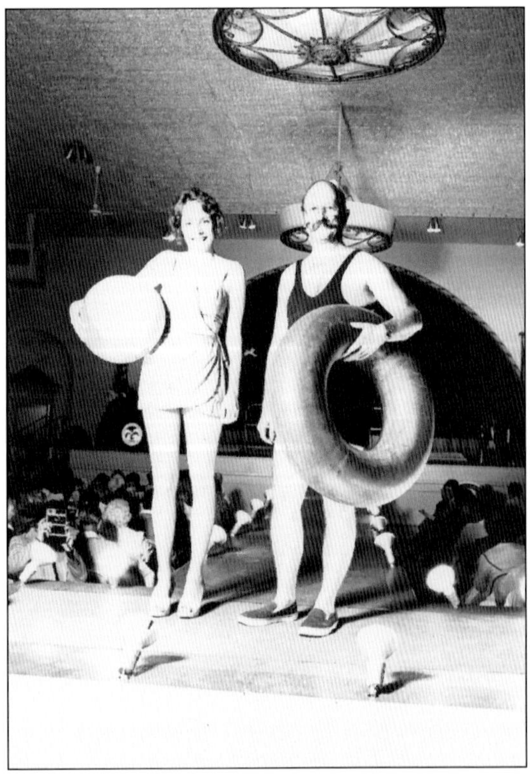

Terry Gallagher and Ed Wismer wear bathing suits from the Roaring Twenties for the anniversary fashion show, "A Century of Fashion."

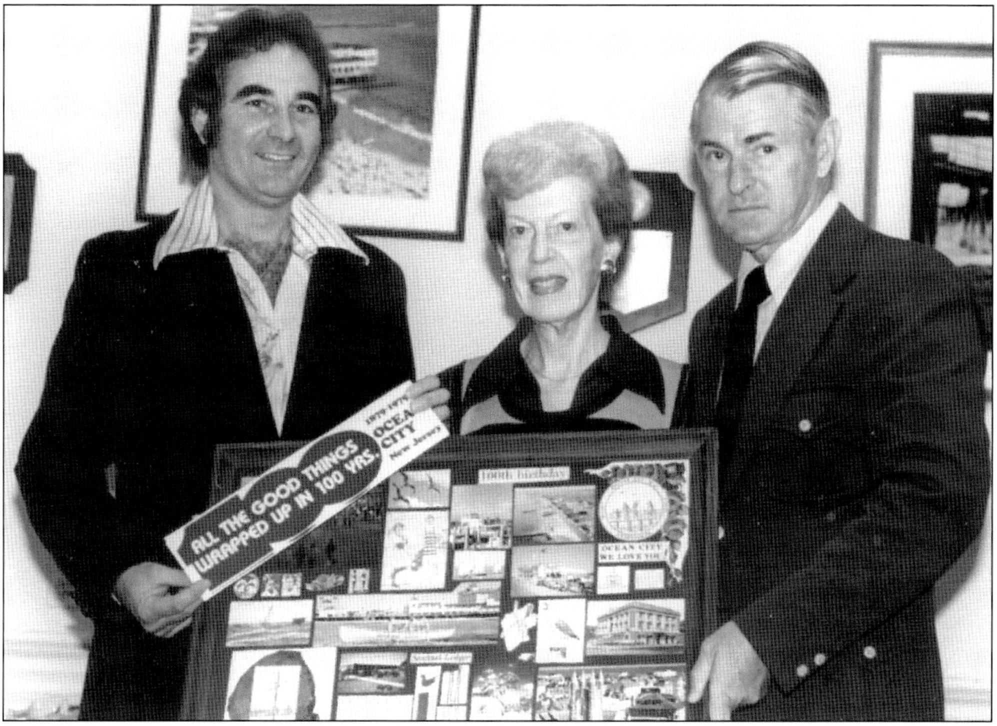

From left to right, Clint Campbell, Eleanor Whitaker, and Mayor Chester Wimberg show off some souvenirs and pictures celebrating 100 years of Ocean City's history put together for the yearlong centennial celebration.

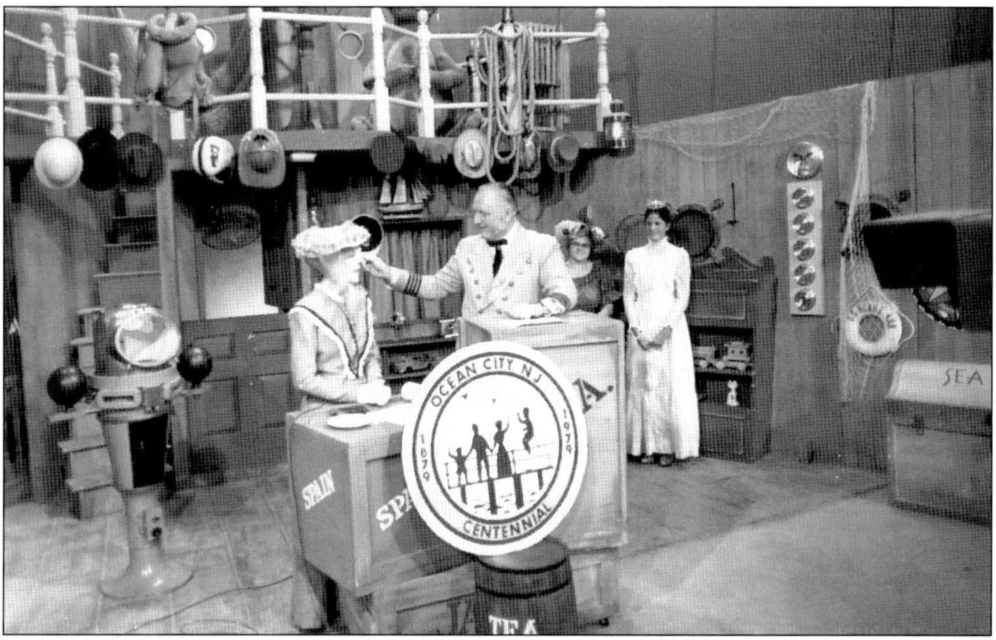

Children's television character Captain Noah participates in a skit during the 100th anniversary celebration. Rev. W. Carter Merbreier, who played Captain Noah, was born in Pleasantville, New Jersey, not far from Ocean City.

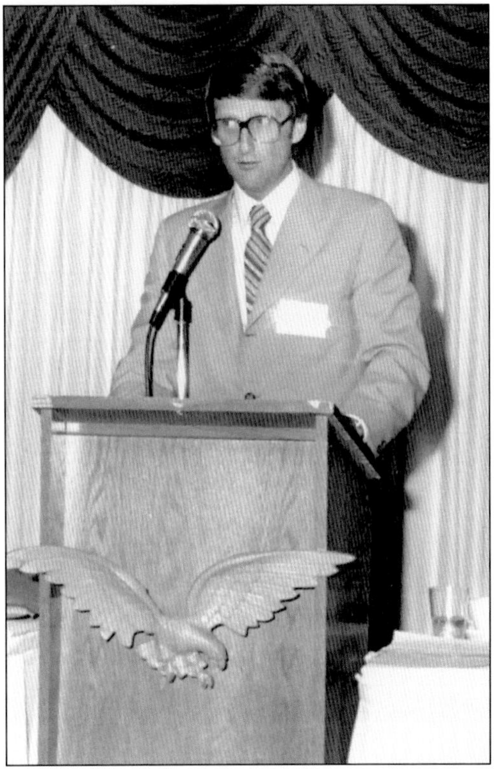

Ocean City resident and Cape May County prosecutor Donald R. Charles Jr. addresses a group of New Jersey county prosecutors in this photograph taken at a 1980 convention in Cape May, New Jersey. Gov. Brendon Byrne appointed Charles to the position in 1976.

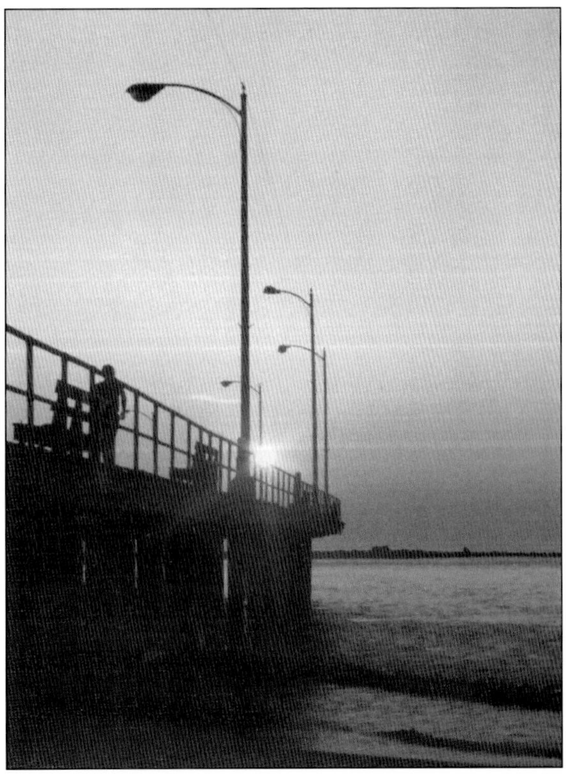

This view of a sunrise taken from the Fifth Street fishing jetty was a favorite of photographers. In 1980, this section of the boardwalk was moved closer to the shoreline.

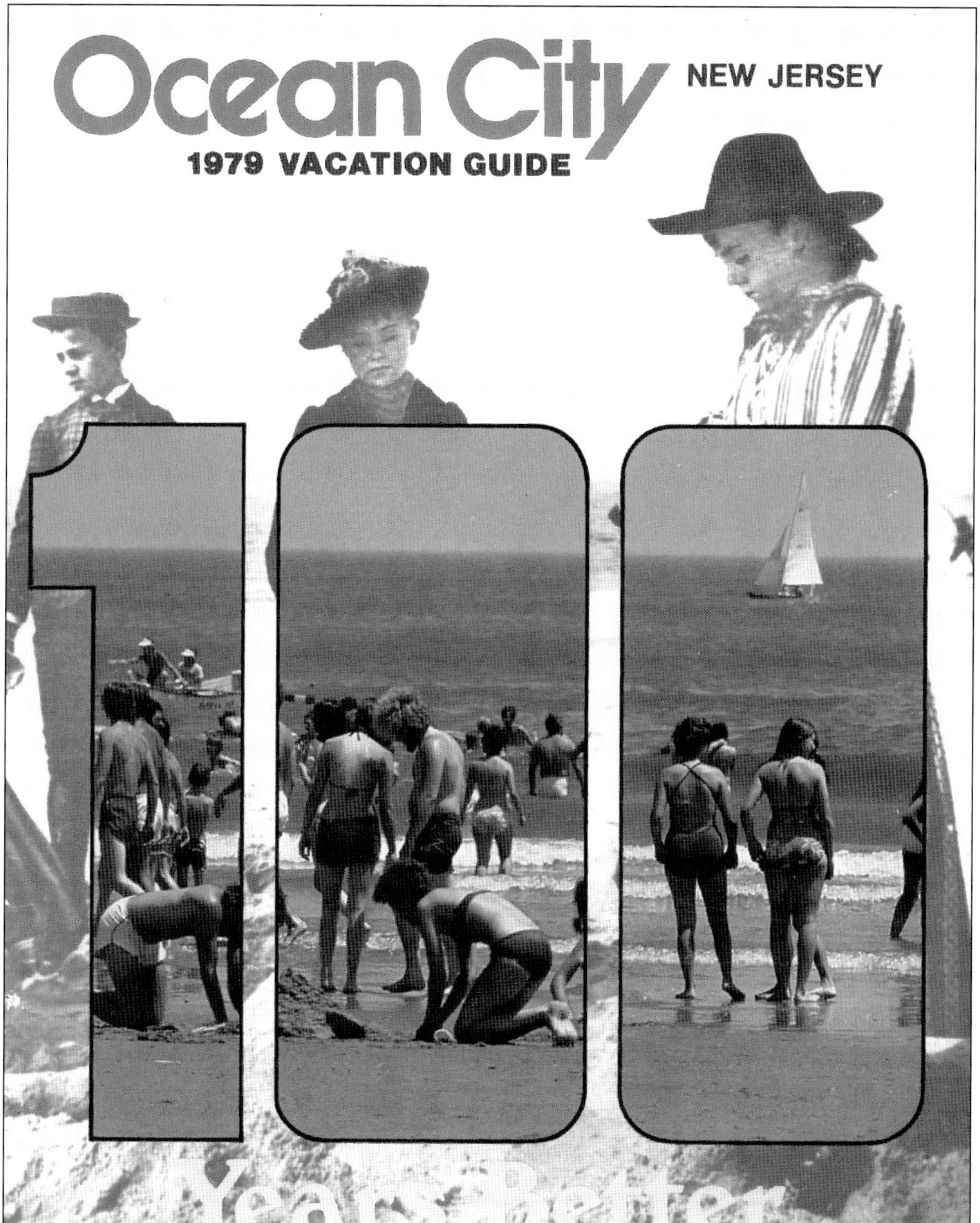

This is the cover of the *Ocean City Vacation Guide* celebrating Ocean City's 100th anniversary in 1979. This issue of the annual guide included a brief history of the resort.

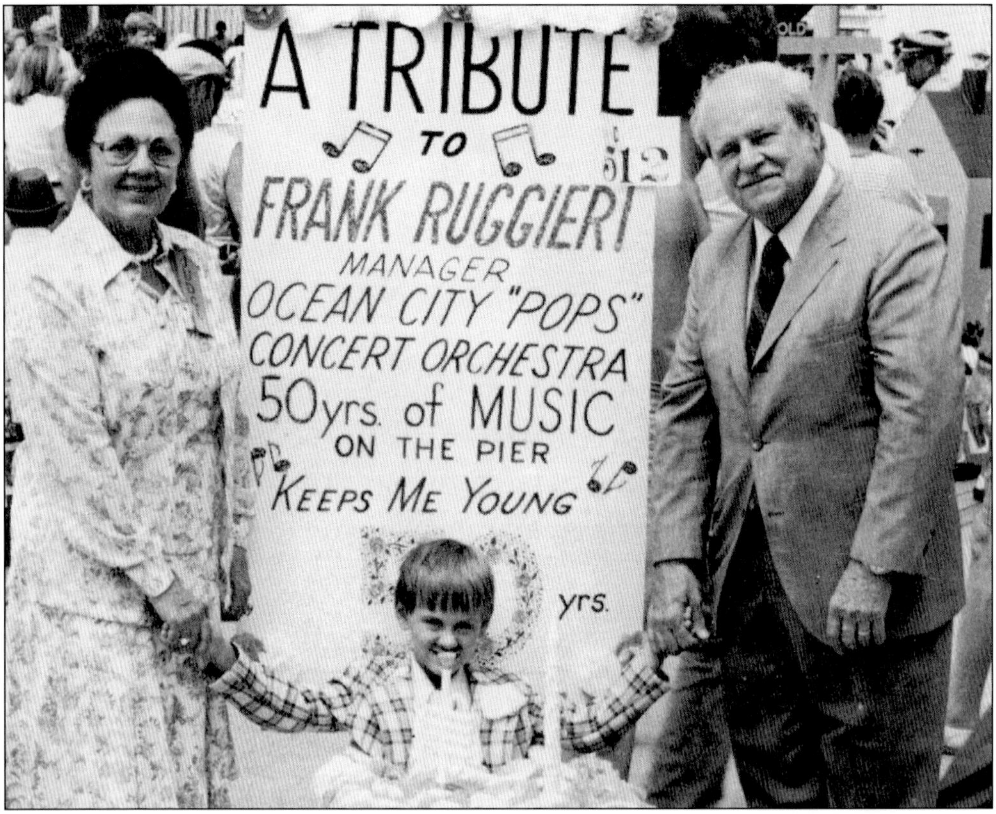

In 1979, Ocean City held a tribute to Frank Ruggieri, musical conductor and director of the Ocean City "Pops" Concert Orchestra. Ruggieri had been with the orchestra for 50 years; for many of those years he was bassoonist and business manager. During the middle of the 1978 concert season, he took over as conductor and director when John Warrington became ill.

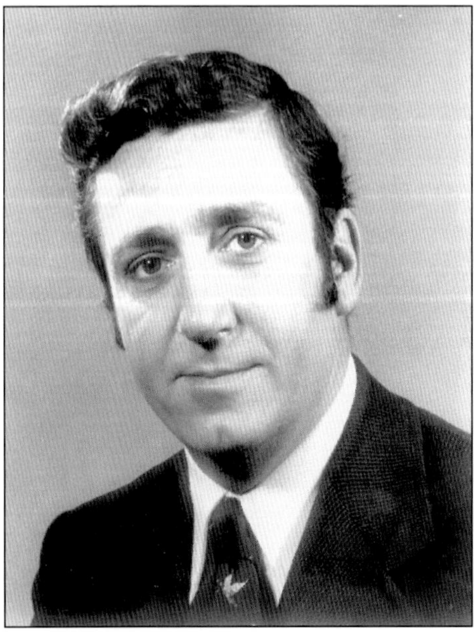

New Jersey congressman William J. Hughes has lived with his family in Ocean City's Gardens section for many years. In 1974, he defeated Republican incumbent Charles W. Sandman for the Second Congressional District seat. In 1980, the Ocean City Beach Patrol dedicated its yearbook to Hughes in appreciation of his efforts to protect the New Jersey coastline and its waterways and "for the recognition he has gained for the Ocean City Beach Patrol and the other beach patrols of South Jersey."

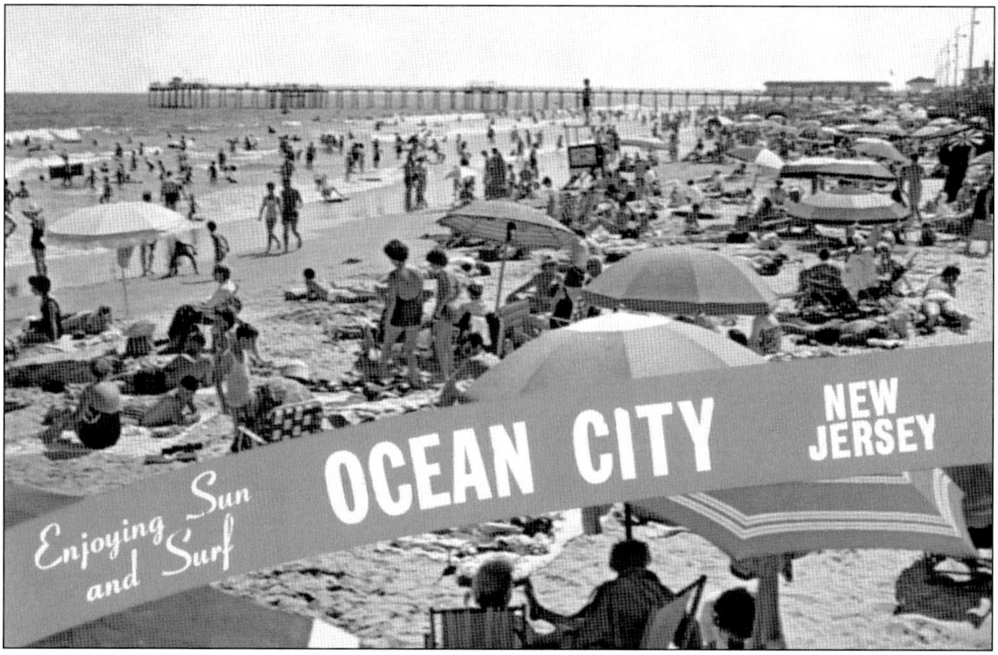

These two postcards are typical of the thousands that have been printed and mailed to family and friends from people fortunate enough to have lived in or visited Ocean City since 1879.

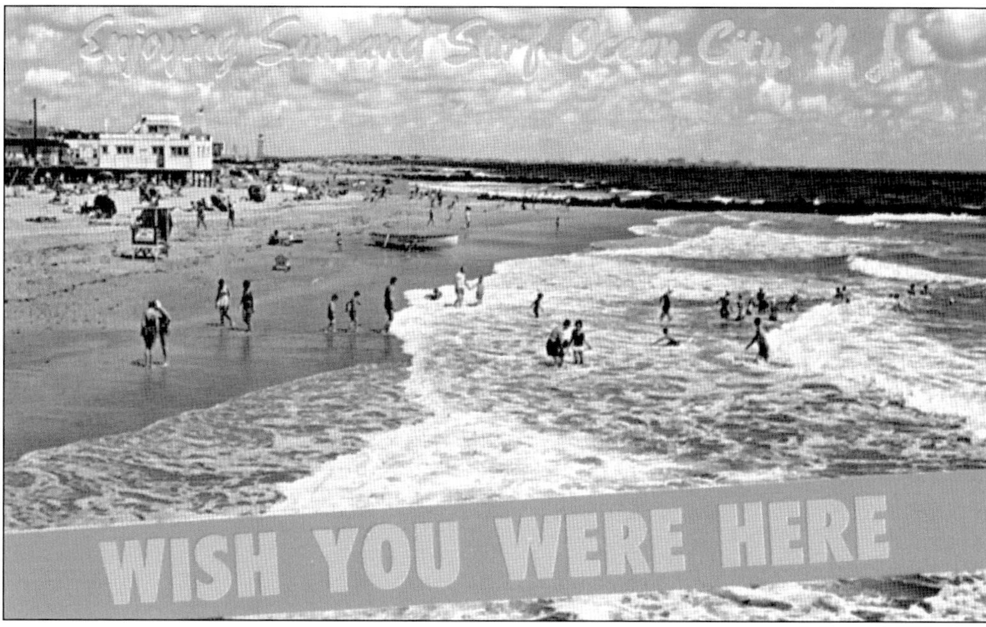

Consistent with our mission to preserve history on a local level, this book was printed in South Carolina on American-made paper and manufactured entirely in the United States. Products carrying the accredited Forest Stewardship Council (FSC) label are printed on 100 percent FSC-certified paper.

MADE IN THE USA